With best wishes.

Andrew Radzick.

1st July 2016.

BRACKNELL'S GREAT WAR FALLEN

I - BRACKNELL AND EASTHAMPSTEAD

By

Andrew Radgick

Grosvenor House
Publishing Limited

This book is published by
Grosvenor House Publishing Ltd
28-30 High Street, Guildford, Surrey, GU1 3EL.
www.grosvenorhousepublishing.co.uk

A CIP record for this book
is available from the British Library

ISBN 978-1-78148-684-9

CONTENTS

INTRODUCTION

In 2009, a new mass grave of bodies from World War One was found near Fromelles; 250 Australian and British soldiers are now buried in a new cemetery. This item on the national news prompted me to visit the Bracknell War Memorial, located beside the Royal British Legion in the town centre, to look at the names from the town recorded on it. There are none.

I then started on a journey of discovery, tracking down lists of names, initially in the town, but then right across the borough of Bracknell Forest. I visited churches and graveyards, I looked in Books of Remembrance, I gained entrance to schools, both current and closed, and found Rolls of Honour from clubs. Some names appear on more than one list; others discovered during my researches do not feature on any.

Who were these men and where did they come from? My research has discovered they come from all classes and ages, from farm labourers to young men educated at Eton College. Stanley Wade from Chavey Down was just sixteen; John Quick from Bracknell was more than thirty years older. A few are buried in the local cemeteries; many are listed on the huge memorials in France and Belgium, their bodies never recovered. Others are even further afield in the Balkans, the Near East, and India. It is estimated that 880,000 men from the United Kingdom lost their lives in the war to end all wars, plus a further 200,000 more from other countries in the British Empire and Commonwealth. Britain lost ten per cent of its male population between the ages of eighteen and forty (Germany lost 15% of its active males). While many died from injuries on the battlefield, others died from illness or in Prisoner of War camps. Practically every city, town and village across the country lost men. Some survived, only to die from their injuries soon after; others perished in the wave of Spanish Flu that swept across Europe in the aftermath of the conflict.

The advent of the internet has been invaluable in this project with so much information now readily available online. Birth registration, census returns, military records, cemetery information, newspapers, War Diaries and fellow researchers can all be accessed without leaving the house, while a Google search uncovers many other sources. Sometimes it is all too easy to get overwhelmed with facts, or get distracted and go off at a tangent to the main direction of research. So where does one start on a project like this?

From the initial idea of looking on Bracknell's War Memorial, I then found there were two lists in the town's churches, one inside Holy Trinity, partly hidden behind furniture and flags, and another in St Michael and Magdalene, Easthampstead. The latter has a cross inscribed with the names around its base in the churchyard, plus a marble tablet inside the church, detailing the units with which the men served, a vital clue in some instances, and a hindrance in others. But what about the churches that existed before the redevelopment of Bracknell? Only the Roll of Honour from the Congregational Chapel in Bracknell High Street, demolished in 1968, has survived; it is now located in St. Paul's United Reformed Church in Harmanswater. Binfield has two churches; the list on the triptych inside All Saints has a few additional names to the memorial in the grounds of St Mark's. Warfield and Winkfield Churches are obviously proud of their men, with the names prominently displayed and immaculately maintained. The latter again includes military details, and further names that have come to light since the original commemoration, have been added by a grateful parishioner. The interior of Cranbourne Church was gutted by a fire in 2006, but a replacement Roll of Honour, again with military details, has been erected to supplement the memorial and cross outside. The Roll of Honour at Crowthorne is uniquely situated inside the lych gate, on four panels. This is the longest list of names from any community within the borough, containing the names of more than one hundred men from the village who did not return. Some have only an initial with their surname, making it a challenge to find them, while others are more fully named and more easily identified. Sandhurst offers the most clues, listing rank as well as military unit against every name. But this is a reconstituted list, the original having been lost when the building housing it burnt down. A few errors have come to light during my research. I also looked at the lists in All Saint's, Ascot and St. Sebastians, Wokingham (on Nine Mile Ride), as although the churches are outside the borough, part of their parishes fall within our area.

As well as churches, some schools recorded those who had passed through their doors. Fifteen former pupils from Ranelagh School in Bracknell are listed; forty-six from Crowthorne Church of England School on Duke's Ride. Another Church School existed on Forest Road, just to the west of its junction with Binfield Road. Today, it is a private house with a tribute to the thirteen former pupils mounted in a recess in the side of the garage wall. This poignant list was probably erected just after hostilities ceased by those living in the immediate neighbourhood, before the authorities decided on the official memorials erected around the country. It is a rare survivor of many that were erected by streets, or small pockets of grateful people, up and down the country. Although located just over the border in Wokingham Borough, many of the names are those of Binfield men and has been included in this book. The private schools of Wellington College in Crowthorne, with several hundred former pupils, masters, staff and servants, Eagle House School between Sandhurst and Crowthorne, and Lambrook School in Winkfield Row, all poignantly display Rolls of Honour prominently. These latter three are not included in this publication.

Three other lists came to light from personal contacts during my research. I am indebted to Vera Bain, Chairman of Bracknell Bowling and Social Club, for allowing me to photograph the list there. It mentions all thirty-three former members who fought in the conflict, three of whom did not return. I would also like to thank local historian Ruth Timbrell who gave me a copy of her photograph from the now demolished Bracknell Working Men's Club, located in Stanley Road, just off Bracknell High Street. It contains the names of almost one hundred men who came back, as well as the twenty who did not. A casual conversation with a former member of staff at Binfield Club led me to the Roll of Honour in that building, listing practically all the men of the village who took part in the fighting.

When we talk of those who died in the First World War, we immediately think of the vast War Cemeteries and Memorials in Western Europe. For example, there are over fifty-four thousand names listed on the Menin Gate at Ypres, all men with no known grave. There are other huge memorials, among them Arras, Loos, Pozieres, Thiepval and Tyne Cot. There are nearly three thousand War Cemeteries in France alone. But battles were fought in the Balkans, and men from the borough are buried in Salonika, Skopje, Haidar Pasha (now a suburb of Istanbul), and on the island of Limnos in the Aegean. In the near east, the remains of our men are in Basra,

Beersheba, Jerusalem, Gaza, Tehran, and Kantara, on the east side of the Suez Canal. In India, we are represented in Madras and the Delhi War Cemetery, and listed on the Memorial there. Closer to home are the three massive Naval Memorials at Chatham, Portsmouth and Plymouth. Local men died in the Haslar Naval Hospital at Gosport and Netley Military Hospital at Southampton, and buried in the cemeteries alongside. Brookwood Military Cemetery near Woking contains also three of our natives.

While most never came home again, a few are buried in the local churchyards. There are three victims of the Great War in Larges Lane Cemetery, seven are remembered at Easthampstead, two in Binfield Cemetery. Warfield has two burials (although both were veterans and never served overseas in this conflict), five are in Cranbourne Churchyard (another is listed on a family grave), nine at Crowthorne, and a further two at Sandhurst. A few other names are listed on plaques erected inside the churches. The extension to the churchyard of Ascot (All Saint's) also lies within the borough, just off Priory Road in Chavey Down, and contains seven graves from World War I, while the churchyard at Wokingham St Sebastian's, on Nine Mile Ride, has the grave of a man listed at Easthampstead.

Probably the most useful website used in this research was www.ancestry.co.uk. It contains census returns, birth, marriage and death registrations, and military records.

Censuses were taken every ten years, starting in 1841. They generally only become available to the public after one hundred years, but the 1911 census was released early, and has been available for about five years at the time of writing. You hope to find every person listed in every census, but it does not always work out like that. Women married, people used nicknames, occasionally the enumerator only recorded initials rather than full names. A young lad, working away from home, may not be listed by either his parents or his employer, each assuming the other has done it. Ages or place of birth are either not known or falsified. Members of the forces on active service are not included, nor are many married women in the 1911 census who supported the suffragette movement. People moved in the three years between the 1911 census and the start of the war, so sometimes it can be difficult to find a name locally from just the census information, or find a link to a man living in a different part of the country.

Births are registered locally and then sent to central offices for recording and indexing; a few might get lost or not sent. An illegitimate child may be listed under the mother's maiden name or the father's (this may not be who the mother later marries). If a name has not been chosen, the child is just listed as male or female. In later life, another name may be used. For example, Jack Provins from Sandhurst was registered and appears in the first two censuses after his birth as Raymond. Christian names get reversed so Henry William becomes William Henry. Marriages failed but divorce was expensive and a social disgrace; the 'accepted' norm was for the couple to separate and be free to remarry after seven years - John Quick of Bracknell appears to have done this. An unmarried couple living together was also socially less acceptable; either the woman is listed as a 'housekeeper' in the census, or occasionally they are listed as married when no marriage has taken place. Although the population was becoming more mobile, the majority still lived and died in the same district. But with wounded soldiers being brought back for treatment, this may not be the case as deaths would frequently occur in hospitals far away from home. If a boy has added a year or more to get into the army, subtracting his age from the year of death will not necessarily give his year of birth.

The key to unlocking a man's military record is his service number. This may change if the men in units are renumbered, or if he is moved between regiments (or even between services – many young men dreamed of getting into the Royal Flying Corps, which became the Royal Air

Force in 1918). The first record to check is Soldiers Died in the Great War (SDGW). In 1921, His Majesty's Stationery Office published, on behalf of and by authority of the War Office, two lists of those who died during the Great War. One volume listed nearly 42,000 Officers, and another eighty volumes recorded the 'other ranks'. The latter record more information, often including place of birth and residence, as well as where the soldier attested. The man's service number, rank, regiment and battalion are included, date of death, location and type of casualty. Only men who are still in the army and who have served abroad are listed, so any who died during training, or had been discharged before their death, will not appear in these lists.

If a solider has served abroad, he will have a Medal Rolls Index Card (MIC). Regiment and service number changes will be listed, but not the dates when these occurred. All men who served overseas were eligible for the British War and Victory medals. Those who came under fire between the start of the conflict and 22nd November 1914 were eligible for the 1914 Star; those after this date but before end of 1915, were eligible for the 1914/5 Star. For these latter two awards, the date of eligibility (the date the man landed on foreign soil) is usually recorded, plus the theatre of war (France, Balkans, etc). Other medals, awarded for bravery, should also be listed. Often, but not always, the date of death is recorded, and for Officers, but rarely for other ranks, address of next of kin to whom medals are to be sent.

Originally there would have been a Service Record for every soldier who served, but around two thirds of soldiers' service records from the First World War were lost in a fire during the Second. But for those that do exist, it can open an intimate picture of the man and his life. The first page should be his attestation and records his stated age, trade, marital status, and date of signing up. A physical description follows on the next page, which duplicates some of the information from a medical inspection he would have had, as well as current address, and details of any marriage and children. There should also be a military summary of important dates, such as mobilisation, arrival overseas, spells in hospital, disciplinary matters, medals and decorations, etc. There may be letters and official documents between the Military Authorities and next of kin, even a list of a casualty's effects to be returned. Many other files, invaluable for WWI research, were lost in the fire, including information on Officers, the Royal Artillery, the Machine Gun Corps, the Royal Army Medical Corps, the Labour Corps, the Royal Air Force, honours and awards, casualty returns, prisoners of war, court martial proceedings, and daily orders covering postings, promotion, punishments and casualties.

More biographical information may turn up in the De Ruvigny Roll of Honour, also viewable online. Published in five volumes at the end of the conflict, this originally set out to list the details of every man killed, but as the war dragged on and losses grew, this became an unrealistic target. But there are still over 26,000 casualties listed, with varying amounts of information, the more detailed usually being for Officers, where the families had provided it.

The other genealogy site I have used in research is www.findmypast.co.uk. Again, censuses and birth, marriage and death registrations are available. The search mechanism differs from that of ancestry; sometimes an entry will show up on one site but not the other. But it also has entries for naval casualties which include date and place of birth, rank and last ship, cause of death, and name and address of relative notified. Even more information is available on men who served in the Royal Marine Light Infantry, which also includes the service history, plus a section of miscellaneous notes which may turn up some nuggets. Similar amounts of information are also listed in the Royal Marine Medal Rolls.

Scottish and Irish censuses (the latter for 1901 and 1911 only, earlier ones having being destroyed in the struggle for independence) are available at www.scotlandspeople.gov.uk and www.census.nationalarchives.ie respectively.

Full service records for naval personnel and officers in the Royal Air Force are available at The National Archives at Kew and downloadable from their website www.nationalarchives.gov.uk. The majority of Army Officer Service Records are also held. Also available are War Diaries for the vast majority of army regiments, although not all have been digitised yet. Some are also available online elsewhere, including the Royal Berkshire Regiment, in which many local men served, at www.thewardrobe.org.uk. More information on men from the flying services may also be found on www.flightglobal.com.

Over one million men and women of the Commonwealth forces, who died in the First World War, are listed on the Commonwealth War Graves Commission website at www.cwgc.org. Military details, stated age at death, next of kin and place of burial, or memorial where the casualty is listed, can be found, along with details on location and history of resting places. More men are being added to this list on a regular basis as new casualties come to light or omissions identified.

In the early part of the twentieth century, there were opportunities overseas in the Colonies for adventurous young men. Canada in particular was eager for new settlers, and some men from Bracknell and its surrounds crossed the Atlantic to forge a new life. When war broke out, new battalions were formed to fight for the mother country, and they joined up to fight with the Canadian Expeditionary Force. The attestation forms for most men from Canada, plus the circumstances of the death of many of them, are now online at www.collectionscanada.gc.ca. A few had gone even further afield, and fought under the Australian flag. Attestation and service records for men from Australia are available at www.naa.gov.au.

The Victoria Cross (V.C.) was the highest military honour to be awarded. Officers were also eligible for the Distinguished Service Order (D.S.O.) and the Military Cross (M.C.); for other ranks the equivalent awards were the Distinguished Conduct Medal (D.C.M) and Military Medal (M.M.). The London Gazette records citations for military decorations (except for the Military Medal), and also many promotions of Officers. These can be viewed at www.london-gazette.co.uk, but the search facility is a bit hit-and-miss. Some battalions also awarded a 'Green Ticket' to men who had been nominated for awards but failed to receive them. The War Diary of the 8th Battalion, Royal Berkshire Regiment makes several references to them being given.

Most of the photos of men in this book have come from the Reading Standard newspaper. Starting in February 1916, a monthly edition was published containing pictures of casualties, heroes, and brothers serving in the conflict. These are now available on a set of CDs. The picture of Allan Wiggett from Binfield, while being held as a Prisoner of War, was discovered in his Service Record at The National Archives. The remainder have mainly been discovered on the internet.

The Great War Forum at www.1914-1918.invisionzone.com is a great source of information, with many members willing to share their extensive information and experience on anything about the conflict, right down to the smallest detail. It is not unknown for a solider to be identified from an anonymous photo.

It must be remembered that all the information recorded at the time was either written by hand or occasionally produced on typewriters. Errors creep in, either accidentally or by men falsifying information. Some men served under an alias for a variety of reasons, and young lads added one or more years to their age to join up. Later transcription errors or 'typos' can also muddy the waters, leading the researcher down false trails or obscuring the truth. Sometimes you discover conflicting information and have to look elsewhere to verify the truth. Some records are lost or destroyed. As has been mentioned above, well over half of soldier's service records were lost in a fire. More information exists about officers than the ordinary rank and file. But what is the truth? Official War Diaries, written on a daily basis at the front, only record one side of the story, and were written to put our leaders in a good light. Of those charged with writing them, some are more efficient than others. One was obviously written by a frustrated author, containing huge amounts of detail on the conditions, the landscape, and the supposed feelings of the men, waiting to go 'over the top.' Some record the weather or others things of local interest. "We were successfully relieved by The Queen's at night, the relief taking 1 hour 55 minutes, again a record." "Leave rules came out, 1 Officer and 3 other ranks every fourteen days, which means at the end of eighteen months, every Officer will get home, and at the end of twelve years, every man." Others are less forthcoming with details. During the German Spring Offensive in 1918, when a desperate rearguard action was being fought, the War Diary entries can be particularly terse, just when we would wish for more information. For some, the details of their horses or even, in the case of the artillery, the guns, take precedence over the men. While the names of towns, villages and prominent landmarks appear in the diaries, some features of the landscape are referred to by the names used by troops on the ground or Amy staff (for example, Lone Pine, Brown Line, or Piccadilly Circus). Military maps used reference co-ordinates, meaningless to anyone without the map in front of them, and these have not been used in this publication.

Similarly, many regimental histories were written in the years immediately after the conflict when Britain was still patting itself on the back after victory. But it is also easy to misread things with the benefit of hindsight. Communications were poor; telephone lines were frequently disrupted, runners became casualties, signals were obscured by fog, smoke or gas. New technology was unreliable – the first tanks broke down or got stuck in the mud. Marching was often the way of moving from one part of the battlefield to another; flight was a still relatively recent innovation. We must take what we have and try to interpret it.

In the course of this project, the names of men have been discovered who died in the War and had a connection with the area, yet they are not commemorated on any local War Memorial. The passage of time means that it can never be known why a man was not included on one of the local memorials, but there are several possible reasons. Whilst a man may have been born in the area, surviving family members may have died, or moved away, by the time the memorials were being erected. Quite simply, there was no-one left to remember him. A single man, whose connection being perhaps having only briefly worked in the area. The family may not have come to live in the area until some time after the War, and the man may be commemorated on a memorial nearer his actual home. It may be that the family never saw the invitation to submit names, or thought that the man didn't qualify (for whatever reason), under whatever the criteria set by the organising committee for the particular memorial. Other families may have held out hope of their missing man returning, and the placing of his name on a list of those who perished would finally extinguish that hope. Advertisements appear in the Reading Mercury from 1919 onwards, aimed at returning Prisoners of War, asking for any information on men, still listed as missing. Or maybe the family simply didn't want him remembered in this way. Several of the memorials are inside a church. If the family felt the memorial was too closely connected with the Anglican Church, they may have chosen not to put his name forward. When reading the minutes of the Memorial Committee at Crowthorne, it becomes obvious the final position of the memorial, in the lych gate of St John's Church, was highly controversial, and many people did not want it placed there. On the other side of the same coin, the man's name might be excluded because the family was insufficiently connected with the church. In Crowthorne, a dialogue took place as to whether names would be included in the village or at St Sebastians on Nine Mile Ride, but more than one man finished up being listed at both! Occasionally, a name may appear on a memorial of a man who was not killed. One of the names at Wokingham had to be corrected; two men with similar names fought, with the wrong one being listed as killed. A name on the memorial at Pontardawe in South Wales was removed when the soldier returned from France four years after it was unveiled, having suffered from amnesia for the intervening period. William Hart, an Australian, was reported missing in August 1918 and presumed to have been killed. But he resurfaced two years later, using a different name, in the U.S. Army in Honolulu! No-one ever established how he came to be an American soldier.

Conversely, a name appears on a memorial, and no local man can be identified. Who was Herbert Cartwright who appears on a panel in Crowthorne lych gate? No-one with the surname appears in the 1911 census in the area. Only by investigating the eight men of that name who died in the conflict, can a reasonable guess be made. Or A. Cox? Arthur? Alfred? Bert Wood (Easthampstead) and Jack Franks (Bracknell Holy Trinity) would have been readily identifiable a century ago, but not now. Crowthorne has the added difficulty of Broadmoor Hospital. When conscription was introduced, a list of reserved occupations was also compiled, of work deemed vital for the war economy. "Attendants on lunatics", as the nurses at Broadmoor were then described, was one of these occupations, and men, attempting to avoid being called up, worked at the institution. This exemption lasted until June 1918; for this reason, there is no Roll of Honour in the chapel at Broadmoor.

Since 1908 the British Army had offered three forms of recruitment. A man could join the army as a professional soldier of the regular army, as a part-time member of the Territorial Force, or as a soldier of the Special Reserve. There was a long-running battle, with politicians and military men taking both sides, about whether Britain should have a system of national conscripted service. By 1914 this had not come about, and Britain's army was entirely voluntary.

A man wishing to join the army could do so providing he passed certain physical tests and was willing to enlist for a number of years. The recruit had to be taller than 5 feet 3 inches, and aged between 18 and 38 (although he could not be sent overseas until he was aged 19). He would join at the Regimental Depot or at one of the normal recruiting offices. The man had a choice over the regiment he was assigned to. He would typically join the army for a period of seven years full-time service with the colours, to be followed by another five on the National Reserve. When war was declared, there were 350,000 former soldiers on the National Reserve, ready to be called back to fill the establishment of their regiments.

The Territorial Force came into existence in 1908 as a result of the reorganisation of the former militia and other volunteer units. It provided an opportunity for men to join the army on a part-time basis. These units were recruited locally, and became more recognised and supported by the local community than the regulars. Men trained at weekends or in the evenings, and went away to a summer camp. Territorials were not obliged to serve overseas, but were enlisted on the basis that in the event of war, they could be called upon for full-time service. The physical criteria for joining the Territorials were the same as for the Regular army, but the lower age limit was 17. Not long after war was declared, all men in the Territorials were asked if they wished to serve overseas, but in some cases, it was assumed they did, and they had to 'opt out' rather than 'opt in'. If all your pals were going off to fight, would you want to stay behind, even if officially you were too young to go?

The Special Reserve was another form of part-time military service. Special Reservists enlisted for six years, had to accept the possibility of being called up in the event of a general mobilisation, and to undergo all the same conditions as men of the Army Reserve. This meant that it differed from the TF in that the men could be sent overseas.

On his appointment as Secretary of State for War shortly after the declaration of the war, Field-Marshal Lord Kitchener issued a call for volunteers to increase the size of the army. He did not believe that the Territorial Force was an appropriate structure for doing this. The poster of the moustachioed Lord Kitchener, pointing his finger at the reader, with the slogan "Your Country Needs You", is probably the most famous in history, although recent research has claimed the poster was an urban myth, and was never used. The men would only have to enlist 'for the duration of the war,' but legally, they were joining the regular army. There was no recruiting office in Bracknell, the nearest being in Wokingham and Ascot. Most local men attested at the former, although many went to Reading, many from Sandhurst went to Camberley, and a handful from the north of the borough signed up in Windsor or Maidenhead. Others, for whatever the reason, went further afield, to London, Sussex, and even, in the case of Harry Willis from Binfield, to Yorkshire. The wartime volunteers had a choice over the regiment and unit they joined. They had to meet the same physical criteria as the regulars, but men who had previously served in the army would now be accepted up to the age of 45. There are many recorded instances of underage, and indeed overage, men being accepted into the service. It was not necessary to produce evidence of age, or even of one's name, in order to enlist, and Recruitment Officers were paid for each man they enlisted. If a youngster, keen to join, was known by the local recruiting officer, he could go elsewhere and join with no questions asked. If a boy was too short or insufficiently developed, surely a few months of army training and food would bring him up to the mark.

Although death was part of everyday life, war was not. Most children, especially in large families, had lost a sibling at a young age, and old relatives were 'laid out' in the front room of the home before the funeral took place. Battles, on the other hand, took place far away overseas, and before the advent of photographs, were depicted by paintings or idealised drawings in newspapers, showing heroic men in scarlet uniforms performing heroic deeds. For the youth of the time, soldiers were heroes. The British Army had been practically invincible (the Boer War was a sharp reality check), and boys were brought up on a list of stories and books, extolling the fighting man, his bravery and courage. In school, pictures of great military heroes adorned the walls, and famous days in the military calendar, such as the Battle of Waterloo, were commemorated. Between five and ten per cent of children born in 1900 were given names associated, in one way or another, with the Boer War. The British Empire covered a quarter of the globe, and a posting in the armed forces gave youths a chance to travel that was simply not available to the ordinary youngster. India, South Africa, Hong Kong, and the West Indies were all far-away exotic places, out of reach of all but the top end of society. The media gave one-sided, glamorous reports of conflicts, where the British were always superior, always victorious, and always had right on their side. The chance of going to France, of putting the evil Bosche in his rightful place, and of being home again by Christmas, proved too much of an opportunity to be missed by many teenagers of the time. But while soldiers were heroes to the youth, the adult population had a different view of the Army. The fighting force was full of dodgy characters, men on the edge of society, those escaping a life of drudgery or the arm of the law, and where it was possible to desert one night, by climbing over the depot wall, and re-enlist in the next county the following morning with a different name in a different regiment.

The public response to Kitchener's appeal was rapid, and at times overwhelming, but soon died down to average only 100,000 men per month. While many were inspired to enlist by the news, drum-beating and pressure to conform, some joined up for all manner of reasons, including a natural desire to quit a humdrum or arduous job, take a chance of seeing another country, or to escape family or troubles. Many travelled considerable distances to attend a depot or recruiting office for a particular unit. They would be attracted to a Regiment or Corps by its reputation, the fact that it was the local one, or where they had relatives or pals. Members of the Territorial Force were used for home duties in the early stages, and Boy Scouts were used to safeguard railways, telegraphs and reservoirs, or act as despatch riders.

War was declared on 4th August 1914, and the first contact between Germany and British troops occurred on the 23rd of the same month. The British were totally outnumbered; the Germans had two and a half times as many men, and twice as many guns. The numbers volunteering did not remain constant. Even the initial perceived rush to join did not happen. The queues at recruiting offices in the early days mainly consisted of recalled Reservists. It was only the news of major setbacks to the British Army, or of enemy atrocities, that caused a surge in numbers. The retreat from Mons in August 1914, January 1915 (after Christmas), German attacks on Ypres and their use of poison gas, the sinking of the passenger ship 'Lusitania', and the Zeppelin bombing raids led to another increase in the spring of 1915, while the execution of the nurse Edith Cavell and other bad news increased the number of volunteers in the autumn. While some 300,000 enlisted in the first month of the war, the number rose by 50% in September.

But by spring 1915, it had become clear that voluntary recruitment was not going to provide the numbers of men required. The Government passed the National Registration Act on 15th July 1915 as a step towards stimulating recruitment, and to discover how many men between the ages of 15 and 65 were engaged in each trade. The results of this census became available to the authorities by mid-September 1915.

On 11th October 1915, Lord Derby, who had played a major part in raising volunteers, was appointed Director-General of Recruiting. He brought forward a scheme five days later, always called the Derby Scheme, for raising the numbers. It was half-way to conscription. Disappointed at the results of the Derby Scheme, the Government introduced the Military Service Act on 27th January 1916. All voluntary enlistment was stopped. All British males were now deemed to have enlisted, that is, they were conscripted, if they were aged between 18 and 41, resided in Great Britain (excluding Ireland), and were unmarried or a widower on 2nd November 1915. Conscripted men were no longer given a choice of which service, regiment or unit they joined. This act was extended to married men on 25th May 1916. Some occupations were considered necessary to the running of the country or the War effort, and men in these jobs were exempt for being called up (these were known as Starred Occupations). This list was regularly updated, with some 'necessary' occupations being dropped; attendants at Broadmoor were exempt until June 1918, although several of them ignored the protection, and joined up anyway. There was also an appeals mechanism for men who objected to serving, whether for health, family or moral grounds, but with many appealing, the system became overburdened and slow, postponing the conscription of many who were only trying to avoid being called up. The tribunal in Bracknell in November 1917 found a coal branch inspector, a grocer's manager, and a pharmacist exempt, but only until another re-evaluation the following year.

From September 1916, men called up were first assigned to a unit of the Training Reserve. It had been found that the traditional regimental means of training was not keeping up with the flood of men coming through, and the TR was established as a means of doing so. A further extension of the Act on 10th April 1918, followed a serious political crisis concerning the provision of manpower, which along with a large extension of the British section of the Western Front, was cited as a prime cause of the defeat of the Fifth Army in March 1918. This act reduced the minimum age of recruitment to 18. The introduction of conscription made it very much more difficult for a recruit to falsify his age and name. Conscription ceased on 11th November 1918 and all conscripts were discharged, if they had not already been so, on 31st March 1920.

As casualties mounted, parents of under-age boys, serving at the front, became alarmed, and clamoured for their return. Training could be as short as fourteen weeks before men were sent to the fighting, ill-prepared for what awaited them. It has been estimated that as many as 15% of the volunteers were under-age, although not all of them reached the front; a few lasted barely four days' training before being discharged, and one fifth less than a month. But at a conservative estimate, over 250,000 enlisted. For those who reached the front, many were ill-equipped physically, mentally and emotionally to cope with what they encountered, and the extreme cold of the winter weather. Stanley Spencer from Chavey Down died aged just sixteen; Harold McEune from Crowthorne enlisted at the same age. In Parliament, the parents of these youngsters had a champion, Sir Arthur Markham, a Liberal MP from Nottinghamshire. A wealthy industrialist from Mansfield, employing 25,000 men in mining and the iron and steel industry, he concentrated his efforts on his constituents' welfare and interests. Many of his workers heeded the call to enlist, and after talking to some of them, he was quick to ask why they were called upon before the Government were in a position to equip them. The question of under-age soldiers soon came to his attention, and a perceived indifference of the issue from the War Office drove him on. The introduction of the Derby Scheme and registration cards all but eliminated the problem at home, although some boys managed to still beat the system (including a 14-year old who reached the front line by assuming the place of an older brother who had deserted while home on leave). But that still left the thousands of under-age boys serving in the front line overseas. Instructions were issued to commanders, but with 'get-out' clauses, and reluctance on the part of some, many boys that should have been sent back were not. If the young man was a well-trained, efficient soldier who was fighting well, and who wanted to continue to serve his country, why should he be released? Newspapers were also sending mixed messages, one minute decrying the use of boys for fighting; highlighting the heroics of a young teenager the next. Holding camps were set up at the French Channel ports for young soldiers removed from the line, who could be rapidly recalled if necessary due to excessive 'wastage' on the front line. The authorities were slow to realise what to do with these young men; the Army was geared up to ship men to the front, or the injured to England; they had no plans for young men there on a more permanent basis. It was left to a few volunteers to arrange distractions for those who were typically young tearaways, and for whom the Army had imposed the first meaning and discipline on their lives. Education, sports, and entertainment were organised, with mixed results; an old Officer who spent over an hour talking about the correct way to salute was not as well received as an undersized young lad, talking about his experiences in the trenches in limited, but colourful, language. Other problems were faced by those sent back to England. Men who had been invalided out of the Army were awarded a Silver War Badge which could be worn in public places, indicating their unfitness for service. But for under-age boys, especially those of large stature, there was no such 'mark', and many were seen as shirkers, who should have been fighting, but had somehow evaded the call. Army life and improved food had made them taller and heavier than the average. Women in particular, would give a white feather to those they thought should have been away, fighting for the country.

In the second half of March 1918, the Germans launched a massive offensive in a last-ditch attempt to win the war. The United Sates had proclaimed a strict policy of neutrality at the beginning of the conflict, although she was an important supplier to Britain and the Allies. Even the loss of 128 American passengers on the 'Lusitania', sunk by a German submarine in May 1915, was not enough to drag America into the fighting, although their call for attacks on passenger vessels to cease was heeded. But in January 1917, the Germans resumed unrestricted submarine warfare. They also invited Mexico to join the fighting, in return offering them money and help to regain territories lost to the United States seventy years earlier. Britain intercepted the telegram, and reluctantly, America entered the war, bringing another four million troops to the side of the Allies.

From 1914, Germany and her allies had been fighting on two fronts; facing the French and British in the west, and Russia in the east. The Russian Revolution of October 1917, and Russia's subsequent peace treaty with Germany, allowed the Central European powers to move all their resources to the Western Front. These factors, combined with economic troubles at home, brought about by Britain's naval blockade of the North Sea, preventing food and materials reaching Germany, and mismanagement at home, gave Germany the momentum for a big push to win the war. Britain's troops were also in need of a rest and training after offensives at Ypres and Cambrai in 1917, as well as the diversion of some troops to Italy. The British line now stretched over 120 miles, much longer than it had been the previous year; Britain's resources were being stretched thinly. The German push gained 25 miles in places, against a line that had been almost stable for two or three years. Over 90,000 British and Empire troops were taken Prisoner of War in six weeks.

Following the 'war to end all wars', a flu pandemic spread across the world, taken back by soldiers returning to their homes. Men, who had survived the conflict, died in their own beds from an unseen enemy. The official cut-off date for war casualties was 31st August 1921, so those who died from the disease are officially registered as having died as a result of the war. Those who died on 1st September 1921 are not. How many later deaths were due to physical and mental injuries, sustained during the fighting, will probably never be known.

The Bracknell area is not unique in its list of casualties, but every man who gave his life defending the country is unique. The fallen are not just names on a list; they are real people, sons, husbands, fathers. Each one has a story; this book tells their stories.

BRACKNELL

HOLY TRINITY CHURCH

The Roll of Honour inside Holy Trinity Church consists of 57 names, listed on five wooden panels, in the south chapel. It was dedicated on 20th March 1921.

GEORGE E. ALMOND

George Edward Almond was born 1st June 1886 in Watford, Hertfordshire, where his father ran a grocery business, and was also a preacher in the local church. The business must have prospered as, despite having six children, the family were able to employ a servant by 1901, and ten years later, his father had retired and moved to Kent. George had left school by then, and come to Bracknell, boarding at Oak Villas, Station Road, and worked in the Stanley Road Stores as an ironmonger and grocer. In 1912, he married Ethel Pitman in Richmond, and they lived in their own home in Station Road, Bracknell, where they had two children, Audrey born in 1913, and Charles four years later. A month after his son was born, George was called up, and posted to Grove Park in Greenwich, a workhouse commandeered by the Army Service Corps as a Motor Transport Depot, where he trained as a driver. His Service Record states he was a little over 5'7" tall and "fit for service in the field at home and abroad," despite having slight varicose veins in his left leg. From here, he transferred to the 971st Mechanical Transport Company at Bulford Camp on Salisbury Plain. On 8th July 1917, the Company set sail from Portsmouth, arriving at Basra (in modern-day Iraq) at the end of the following month, where the British and their allies were fighting the Turks. After six months of general driving duties, he was allotted to the Expeditionary Force Canteens as a driver, and continued to work with them for a further six months. The last entry on his Service Record is dated 28th September 1918 with the words "died of smallpox." Illness was rife among troops serving in the Middle East, and more died from malaria, dysentery or, in this case smallpox, than lost their lives in the fighting. He is buried in Basra War Cemetery.

The late Pte. L. H. BAKER, 2nd Batt. Yorks Regiment, Stanley Road, Bracknell.—Killed in action.

LUKE H. BAKER

Luke Henry Baker was born in Bullbrook in 1885, and baptised 15th March the same year, one of four children. His father, William, was a carpenter from Windlesham. After leaving school, Luke worked for a time as a commercial clerk before joining the 2nd Battalion, Yorkshire Regiment in 1906, attesting at Aldershot, and the 1911 census finds him in the British Barracks at Khartoum in the Sudan. At the outbreak of war, the 2nd Battalion were in Guernsey. They returned to the mainland at the end of August, and spent a few weeks in preparation before crossing from

Southampton to Zeebrugge, arriving on 6th October. The Battle of Ypres started on the 19th and continued for over a month, before bringing the advancing German army to a standstill. All units suffered grievous losses. On the 30th, the War Dairy records the battalion occupied trenches on the right of the position of the assailant. "The Germans were seen running in front of our trenches behind a hedge and appeared to be concentrating on the right. 2/Lieut. H. G. Brookebank, who was commanding a Platoon on the extreme right of the Battalion, reported (at about 1pm) that a large force of Germans, approximately five hundred had occupied trenches in front of him. He opened fire on them and caused a great deal of damage. It was impossible to reinforce him at the time. A message was received at 3:30pm ordering the Battalion to retire. The message had been delayed two hours on account of the Orderly having great difficulty in getting through the woods owing to constant strafing and shrapnel. The Battalion were placed in a very awkward position owing to the delay, and also our Commanding Officer Lieutenant Colonel C. A. C. King having been killed. As our Second in Command had also been killed (Captain E. L Gruern), the command of the Battalion were taken over by Captain B. L. Spence Blundell, who had to make up his mind immediately whether to rush the retrenchment in daylight in heavy fire or to risk the chance of being able to hold out until dusk. He decided on the former and withdrew his left Company first, leaving the Platoon on the right to hold back the enemy beforementioned till last. The result of this move was that he was able to withdraw his whole Battalion with the loss of only ten men. The casualties were heavy before retrenchment took place owing to some very accurate sniping." Luke Baker was one those killed, his body was never recovered and his name is listed on the Ypres (Menin Gate) Memorial.

GILBERT BARBER

Gilbert Barber was born in 1878 in Wooburn, near Bourne End, Buckinghamshire, where his father was the municipal rate collector. He was one of six children, with a seventh dying in infancy. In 1898, Gilbert passed the exam to work in the Post Office and moved to Bracknell, initially living as a boarder in Broad Lane with the family of a work colleague, but moved into the High Street after marring Mary Tranter in 1908. He volunteered for service, attesting at Wokingham in 1915, and joined the Royal Engineers, arriving in France a year to the day after the war had started, as part of 1st Division, Signal Company. Signallers were often close to the frontline troops, providing signals communications back to Company and Battalion Headquarters. Wired telephones were used where possible, but this involved laying landlines, a hazardous job due to enemy shelling, and the lines were frequently broken. At the start of the war, flags were also used for signalling, but this practice was little used as the war years progressed. Where it was not possible to lay landlines, many forms of visual signalling were used, making use of light, either from sunlight during the day or lamps at night. Messages were sent in Morse Code, one man operating the signalling device and one man, using a telescope where distances were great, to read the message sent back. Signallers were also used in forward positions to assist the artillery and provide information on their enemy targets. Often isolated, the signaller became very vulnerable to enemy shelling and attack. At the beginning of September 1918, after a period of rest in Monchy-Cayeux, Gilbert's unit moved to a position near Arras, where they remained for seven days. At 9pm on the first evening, an hour's barrage knocked out the line between the Corps and Arras, but it was restored within half an hour. One bomb explosion killed or injured an officer, seven other ranks, and 22 horses. The War Diary contains few other details but summarises September: "During the month, there was continual fighting and movement for 1 Division, and Signal Company had little leisure throughout the period. Communication, despite many difficulties, was successfully maintained by all sections of *the* Company under all conditions. Successful maintenance of cable lines during battle ascribed to *their* being laid always well away from roads and across country, valleys being avoided and lines kept on high ground. Work of *the* linesmen was excellent, and they responded stoutly to all calls on their strength." Casualties during the period were heavy, mainly due to bombing and gas shelling; five men were killed and a further 32 wounded. Gilbert was one the later, dying from his injuries on 9th September in 8th Casualty Clearing Station, and is buried in the nearby Duisans British Cemetary, Etrun.

The late Pte. E. BLAY, Park Road, Bracknell.—Killed in action.

ERNEST BLAY

Ernest Blay was born 17th September 1890, and baptised 2nd July 1892 along with his elder sister Eva. He was the youngest of eight children born to John Blay, a labourer, and his wife Sarah, both from Bray. Work was obviously insecure as the children were variously born at Warfield, White Waltham, Binfield and Easthampstead, and the family took in lodgers as well. Ernest's mother died in 1906, and his father two and a half years later. By now, Ernest was working as a labourer for a corn merchant, living at lodgings in the London Road, along with two of his brothers. He did not rush to sign up as so many young men did, being conscripted into the 2nd Battalion, Royal Berkshire Regiment, attesting at Wokingham in 1916, and would have been mobilised in February. By now he was a married man with responsibilities, having wed Emily Bull in 1912, and two daughters (a third was born the year after his death). The War Diary records three drafts arriving in May, so he was probably present on the first day of the Battle of the Somme on 1st July, and remained on the Somme front during the winter of 1916. After spending a few days in billets at Meaulte at the beginning of November, the battalion returned to the front line on the 9th, where it remained for just over 48 hours, a position it repeated on the $14/15^{th}$ after a couple of days in Brigade Reserve. Casualties were heavy on the four days in the front trenches, with some fifteen men killed and seventy-five wounded from a heavy bombardment of gas-shells. Ernest was one of the casualties on the 10th, his body not being recovered; he is listed on the Thiepval Memorial.

BERTIE BOULT

Bertie Boult was born at Maiden's Green in 1881 and baptised in Winkfield Church on 23rd April. He was one of six surviving children born to carpenter Albert Boult and his wife Kate. After leaving school, he worked as a gardener, before joining the 2nd Battalion, Royal Berkshire Regiment, attesting on 25th June 1898 at Reading, and was in Meerut, India at the time of the 1911 census. Although Bertie spent his life growing up in Winkfield, his parents moved to Broad Lane (which would explain why his name appears in Holy Trinity Church, and, not St Mary's, Winkfield). Sometimes it is easy to forget names on memorials are put forward by surviving family members who may have moved away from where the fallen soldier lived. Bertie's battalion were still in India when war broke out, only arriving back in England on 22nd October 1914, but the first contingent arrived in France just two weeks later, with Bertie following a month after. The battalion were involved in actions at Neuve Chapelle in 1915, the

Somme Front, Ovillers, Vermelles the following year, Passchendaele in 1917, and faced the German advance during the spring of 1918. Having survived the Battle of the Aisne, which saw heavy casualties, there was a reorganisation of the remnants of the 8th Brigade into one composite battalion, plus a second including many newly-arrived reinforcements. Both these new battalions went into the front line in the Bois de Eclisse on 8th June, a position they were to hold for three days. Although there is no mention of casualties in the War Diary for these three days, Bertie, by now a Sergeant, lost his life on the 11th, possibly when the battalion were being relieved, always a time when the risks were higher. His body was never recovered, and his name is listed on the Soissons Memorial.

SAMUEL BOWYER

Samuel Bowyer was born towards the end of 1885, the tenth of eleven children. The family lived in Priestwood Cottages in Binfield Road where his father, Henry, worked as a bricklayer. Samuel worked as an errand boy after leaving school, but by the outbreak of war, was working at Fromow Nursery, Windlesham, who specialised in rhododendrons, trees and shrubs, especially from America, and roses (the company was wound up in 1972, and the site is now occupied by retirement homes in Fromow Gardens). He immediately volunteered for service, attesting at Camberley, and joined the 6th Battalion, Royal West Surrey Regiment. The battalion saw action at Albert and Pozieres in 1916, and at Arras and Cambrai the following year. On 3rd April 1918, the battalion were in billets at Henincourt, and carried out Lewis gun and musketry instruction on this day and the next, during which the village was shelled intermittently, but with no casualties. On the following day, the village was heavily shelled, and the battalion moved into open ground to the east of Millencourt, with orders to occupy the Corps Line if the necessity arose. At 4:30pm, the battalion were ordered into support of the 36th Infantry Brigade in front of Albert, which was completed by 7pm. However, casualties were heavy with three men killed and a further thirty wounded, Samuel being one of them, dying soon afterwards. He is buried in Hedauville Communal Cemetery Extension which had only been open for a couple of weeks. He is also listed on Windlesham War Memorial.

The late GEORGE BRANT, Martin's Lane, Bracknell—Killed in action.

GEORGE E. BRANT

George Edward Brant was born in 1876 near West End, Warfield, and baptised in St Michael's Church, Warfield, on 5th November. He was one of the ten children of labourer John Brant and his wife Caroline. By the age of fifteen, George had left school and was working as cow boy at Moss End Farm. He continued to work in general labouring jobs, and married Louisa Gould in 1910. They then lived in Chavey Down with their two children, John, born in 1911, and Rose, born the following year. George volunteered early in the conflict, attesting at Camberley, and joined the 2nd Battalion, Royal West Surrey Regiment. The battalion had been in South Africa when war broke out, returning to England in mid September, and proceeding to France less than three weeks later. George was with a draft of new recruits that arrived in France on 4th January 1915. The War Diary reports the new men joining the billeted battalion a week later. After spending three evenings employed as working parties in the trenches at La Toulette, which were badly flooded after a wet spell of weather, the battalion suffered casualties on the 16th when the Germans dropped five or six shells in the vicinity of the billets, one of which burst over the farm in which 'D' Company was billeted, killing one man and wounding four. The one man was George Brant; he had been in France for just sixteen days.

SILAS W. BROWN

Silas William Brown was born in Lowestoft, Suffolk at the beginning of 1881. He was one of seven surviving children, with another five dying in infancy. His father worked as a carpenter and joiner, while Silas's four sisters would later set up their own millinery business in the town's High Street. By 1901, Silas may have moved to London to work as a stableman, living in lodgings in Clapham, using his middle name (no other entry in the census for him can be found). In 1908, he married Gertrude Marshall back in Suffolk, and they moved to Berkshire, initially to Reading where a daughter was born, and then to Bracknell. The young family lived in Albert Road, close to the town centre, where Silas worked as a grocery manager. Initially conscripted into the Royal Berkshire Regiment, attesting at Wokingham, he was later transferred to the 8th Battalion, Gloucestershire Regiment. On 20th September 1917, the battalion participated in an offensive at Klein Zilbeke in Belgium, part of the Battle of Passchendaele. Zero hour was 5:40am, and the first objective reached with comparative ease and the line consolidated. During the advance to the final objective, strong posts and snipers had to be dealt with, before it was eventually reached at 7am the next morning. Enemy artillery barrage on the original front and support lines was very heavy, and there were heavy casualties; Silas was one of 160 killed, missing or wounded, and is buried in Oxford Road Cemetery, to the northeast of Ypres.

ALBERT BUTLER

Albert Butler was born towards the end of 1884 and baptised in Holy Trinity Church on 30th November the following year. The family were living at Chavey Down at the time, but soon moved into Bracknell High Street. Here he grew up with his five surviving brothers and sisters, three others having died in infancy. Albert's father, who worked as a carpenter, died soon after the move, forcing his mother to take in washing and lodgers to make ends meet. Albert worked as a baker after leaving school, but went to Reading in February 1900, and joined the Royal West Surrey Regiment. He was just fifteen years old, but claimed to be three years older, passed the medical inspection, and was accepted. He was 5'4" tall, weighed eight and a half stone, with hazel eyes, dark brown hair, and a fresh complexion, a mole in his right armpit, and a scar on the back of his neck. However, in October, his real age was discovered, and he was discharged. Albert stayed in Reading and found work, again as a baker, although he had added a couple of years to his age in the census of the following year. He then disappears from the records completely, only resurfacing to attest at Brentford, Middlesex, when he was conscripted in 1916. Initially serving in the Royal Fusiliers, he was later transferred to the 19th Battalion, Manchester Regiment. On 15th December 1917, the battalion were carrying out work and patrols in and around the front line, just to the east of Ypres. This included erecting and strengthening wire along whole Brigade front, improving the trenches and posts in shell holes, and bringing up material for the Royal Engineers. Three patrols went out after dark, but none of them into contact with the enemy. Although no casualties are recorded in the War Diary, there would have been a constant danger in the front line, and two men from the battalion were killed during the day. Albert was one of them, and is buried in Hooge Crater Cemetery.

The late Pte. F. BUTLER, Stanley Road, Bracknell.—Killed in action.

FREDERICK BUTLER

Frederick William Butler was Albert's brother, being born two years earlier in 1882, although he was not baptised until the last day of June four years later. He attested in Reading on 20th April 1898, and joined the 3rd Battalion, Royal Berkshire Regiment, a training battalion. He was 5'6" tall and weighed less than eight stone, with dark brown eyes, black hair, a dark complexion, and had a scar left side of his head; he had also added a year to his age to enlist. He is absent from the 1901 census, serving in the Boer War in South Africa, although the battalion were not involved in any major operations, and transferred to the Royal West Surrey Regiment on his return. After completing his army service, he moved to Adlingbourne near Chichester, Sussex, working as a nurseryman's labourer. On the outbreak of war, he was recalled to the Royal West Surrey Regiment, arriving in France with the 1st Battalion, in early September 1914, by which time the battalion had been there for about five weeks. The War Diary notes that reinforcements were received on both the 5th and 8th of September; Frederick was probably in the latter. The first serious confrontation with the enemy occurred on the 14th near Paissy, when 150 casualties were incurred, and they were forced to retreat. On 26th, they repulsed an attack, but most of the day's casualties were caused by the British Artillery firing 'short'. Two days later, Sir Douglas Haig, Commander of the 1st Army Corps, rode over to congratulate the infantry. On 20th October, the battalion marched off at 5:50am through Silvestre, Stenvoorde, l'Aberle, and Poperinghe, and went into billets in scattered farms just west of Elverdinghe, where the companies found their own protection. The following day, they moved out on to the main road at 2:45am, and marched through Elverdinghe, Boesinghe and Langemarck, before deploying on the north-east of the latter village. The objective was to make good a line of road running north-west/south-east through Poelcappelle Station. The Regimental History records: "As the firing line advanced, they came under heavy fire from enemy trenches as well as some frontal fire. At about 1pm, the South Wales Borderers made an attack on the right flank of the battalion which was unsuccessful and they fell back, exposing the right flank of 'B' Company. Captain Hunter therefore found it necessary to drop back the right of his Company. Through a miscarriage of orders, the remainder of 'B' Company also fell back, forcing 'A' and 'D' Companies to withdraw as well, and considerable losses were suffered during this retirement. A fresh line was occupied and entrenched where the supporting company were located, and no further opposition was met with before being relieved by the Welch Regiment at 7pm, and retired to bivouac in a field 400 yards south-west of Langemarck." Three officers were wounded during this action, thirteen N.C.O.s and men killed, 68 wounded and a further six were missing. Frederick was one of those missing, and his name is recorded on the Ypres (Menin Gate) Memorial.

ARTHUR CHAPLIN

Frederick Arthur Chaplin was born 15th March 1896 at Swinley, Ascot, and baptised in Holy Trinity on 24th May the same year. His father worked at the brickworks in Swinley Road where he drove one of the stationery engines (the brickworks were on the opposite side of the road from the current sawmills). Arthur was one of nine children, two of whom died young. In the 1901 census, as well as the family there were four labourers from the brickworks, listed as lodgers, all living under the same roof. Arthur had left school by the age of fifteen and was working as a baker's assistant, by which time the family had moved to Chavey Down. He had already joined the 1/4th Battalion, Royal Berkshire Regiment, a Territorial Battalion, but did not go to France until 1916. It is difficult to try and piece together Arthur's war experience as it is not known precisely when he arrived in France. In the second half of 1916, the battalion were involved in the fighting at Pozieres, Thiepval and Albert. The winter was particularly trying, with the chilly and wet weather giving way to bitterly cold conditions. There was little, if any, shelter in either the Reserve or Support Lines, while there was at least twelve inches of liquid mud in the bottom of the front trenches. No hot rations could be brought up, and the "Tommy's Cookers" available to each section, were useless without shelter from the rain and mud. There was more sickness than at any other time in the war. The War Diary makes reference to inspections of the men's feet, and specifically mentions "all feet were washed and powdered, and dry socks put on" on 17th February. March gave way to "fine days, cold nights", and there was heavy snow on the 4th. There is much reference to work on improving the trenches, with a thaw making conditions worse. Arthur succumbed to the conditions in the 14th Corps Main Dressing Station, which was situated just behind the front lines, on 18th March 1917, and is buried in the nearby Bray Military Cemetery. The Germans had just started to withdraw after the long offensive on the Somme and the War Diary records "weather – a lovely day. Played a football match against the ASC (*Army Service Corps*) and we won 4-2." In the midst of war, there was still time for the national game.

The late Pte. F. COATER, Royal West Surrey Regt., Bracknell.—Killed in action.

FRANK COATES

Francis Henry James Coates was born in 1888 at Cheddar in Somerset, one of five children. His father, also born in Cheddar, worked as a carpenter and joiner, sometimes working away from home, while Frank's mother was a Winkfield girl. It is not clear exactly when the family moved back to the area, but by 1911, Frank's parents and younger brother were living in Stanley Road, Bracknell. Frank worked as a domestic gardener after leaving school, and married Jemima Ephgrave in Edmonton, North London, on 11th December 1909, with the first of three daughters being born five months later, and a son finally completing the family. In 1911, they were living at Long Cross, Surrey, but later moved to Welwyn, Hertfordshire, Chobham and then Fulham. Frank volunteered for service, attesting on 6th April 1915 in Guildford, and joined the 1st Battalion, Royal West Surrey Regiment. He was part of a draft that went to France at the end of September, joining the battalion on 3rd October at Bethune, and had his first taste of the front line a week later. A bombing attack, three days later, left twelve men dead, and almost fifty wounded. They then settled into a routine of turns in and out of the front line, working on trenches, and general fatigues, interspersed with rests, over the winter months. There were two accidents during bombing practices early in the new year, while a successful raid on a German trench was made in late March. In early May, the Germans exploded a mine nearby, but a quick reaction by the Surreys prevented the enemy from occupying the crater. On a lighter side, there was a concert to attend and a boxing tournament during the same month. The Germans exploded another mine on 22nd June; the British retaliated with one of their one the following day. The battalion left Bethune, at short notice, on 8th July, and moved to the Somme to support the massive attack that had started a week earlier, and were in action at High Wood a week later, suffering almost three hundred casualties. They were in action for about a week, and then started training again. There were Brigade sports on 17th August, with the Surreys coming second overall. On 23rd August, Frank's battalion were in trenches west of Delville Wood, where they were shelled continuously throughout the day and night. Operation Orders were issued for an assault on the new German position the following day. The morning passed more quietly with Zero not until 5:45pm, with the assaulting companies launching their attack just over an hour later. There was a preliminary artillery bombardment of two hours, and a final barrage of intense fire thirty minutes before the assault was launched, the barrage lifting as the front troops drew up to it. The objective was reported as taken and the work of consolidation in progress at 8:30pm, and reinforcements were asked for. However, messages were received from the front line to say that the battalion had suffered very heavy officer casualties, mostly due to shell fire prior to the assault. Nineteen other ranks were killed in the assault, including Frank, and a further 76 wounded. His body was never recovered and his name is listed on the Thiepval Memorial.

The late Pte. S. R. COATER, Worcester Regt., Bracknell.—Killed in action.

STANLEY COATES

Stanley Reginald Coates was Frank's younger brother, born at Cheddar in 1895. After leaving school, he worked as a grocer's assistant in one of Bracknell's shops. Stanley was conscripted, attesting at Wokingham on 17th January 1916 (there was no place in Bracknell for this, the nearest being Wokingham and Ascot), by which time the family had moved from Stanley Road just round the corner into Rochdale Road. He was quite a large lad for the period, being almost six feet tall and nearly ten stones in weight. He remained in the UK until 5th July, then sailed from Southampton, reaching Rouen the following day and joined his unit, the 1/7th Battalion, Worcestershire Regiment, on the 20th. The rest of the summer and autumn was filled with the long campaign on the Somme. Stanley had missed the infamous action on July 1st, but may have been in the front line on the 27th, when his battalion relieved the 1/4th Gloucestershire after the Battle of Pozieres Ridge. He would have seen action at Ovillers in August, but no other major action, although his battalion took its turn in the front trenches. They also took no part in the attack against the Butte de Warlenncourt on November 5th which marked the end of the heavy fighting on the front of the Fourth Army. It was realised that the ground was impassable, and there was little chance of any further attack being able to gain ground sufficient to achieve any strategic advantage. Attacks ceased, and energy was devoted to maintaining the position gained. The slow advance had carried the British front line forward across some three miles of ground. That ground was so shattered and soaked with rain that enormous efforts and huge carrying parties were necessary to supply the troops in the front line with the necessary munitions and food. From November 6th to 22nd, the two Territorial Battalions, the 1/7th and 1/8th, remained in the battle area, either labouring on new defences, struggling up and down the greasy slopes as carrying parties, or holding front-line or support trenches near the Butte de Warlenncourt. The weather was abominable and all ranks suffered severely. Stanley was one of the casualties, being killed on 13th November 1916, and is buried in Flatiron Copse Cemetery, Mametz. Stanley's parents had had five children; the other three had already died, and now both their surviving sons were lost, just four months apart, in France. The poignant entries on the form that Stanley's father returned to the authorities to claim his son's personal effects tell their own story – brothers of the solider, "none left"; sisters of the soldier, "none left".

Both Francis and Stanley are listed, along with their siblings, on a gravestone at Sunningdale Baptist church.

GORDON COURT

Albert Gordon Court was born in Windsor in 1894, but by 1900 the family had moved to Bay Road, Bullbrook, where a younger brother was born (a third child died in infancy). Albert's father worked as a cheesemaker, probably in one of the grocery shops in Bracknell High Street, and after leaving school, Albert went to work in a shop as well, making clothes for a tailor. He volunteered for service in November 1914, travelling to London to attest, and joined the 9th Battalion, London Regiment, one of the battalions of the New Army, formed at the start of the war. Gordon was in their ranks when they landed in France in May 1915. The battalion were involved in the Battle of Loos at the end of September, but a break from fighting occurred on 9th December, when his battalion were given the unusual task of assisting in a round-up of spies and other "uncertain characters" in the streets of Bethune. They took part in the Battle of the Somme in July 1916 and at Pozieres the following month, the Arras Offensive and Operations in Cambrai in 1917, as well as the German Offensive and the Allied breakthrough in 1918. The battalion were in reserve at Rongy on 22nd October, when they were shelled overnight by the enemy, causing twenty casualties. There are no further reports of injuries before 5th November, the date on which Gordon died of wounds. He is buried in Cambrai East Military Cemetery, which was used by two nearby Casualty Clearing Stations.

The late Corpl. A. DAVIS, Station Road, Bracknell.—Killed in action.

ALFRED DAVIS

Alfred Frederick William Davis was born in the area round the Royal Berks Hospital, Reading, in 1895, but the family had moved to Station Road, Bracknell by 1901. With three elder sisters, Alfred was the eldest boy in the family, and a younger sister and a brother were born subsequently to complete the family. His father worked as a stonemason, originally coming from Compton, near Goring. By the time Alfred had left school to work in a corn store, his father was already there as the storekeeper and able to keep an eye on his son. Alfred joined the 2/4th Battalion, Royal Berkshire Regiment, a Territorial Battalion set up two months after the war started, attesting at Reading. This battalion was for Home Service, consisting of men who had not agreed to serve overseas, although later in the war this was changed, and all Territorial soldiers were eligible to serve on foreign soil. He must have shown some leadership potential as he was promoted to a Corporal during his time with the battalion. It is not known when Alfred joined the battalion, but training had started at Maidenhead in November 1914 with almost one thousand recruits. The first war duty they performed was providing guards for a Prisoner of War camp at The Philberds, a large house located between Holyport and the M4. The thirteen captured men there were among the first to arrive from France, and the camp later became one of the Officers' Prisoner-of-War Camps. The adjutant became suspicious when the inmates all suddenly took a keen interest in gardening, and a few weeks later, a well-constructed escape tunnel was discovered, almost ready for use. In February 1915, the battalion moved to Northampton to continue training, and two months later to Chelmsford, where their work involved digging trenches at Epping for the defence of London, and sentry duty around the roads of Essex. At the beginning of March the following year, they moved again to Salisbury Plain, and the Division was inspected by the King at Bulford on 5th May before setting off for France, landing at Le Havre towards the end of the month. The Berkshires were involved in the attack at Fromelles on 19th July 1916. This was designed as a subsidiary attack to the much larger offensive taking place further south on the Somme, but it was an unmitigated disaster with very heavy casualties and no significant gain; the Division was not used again, other than for holding trench lines until 1917, when it was involved in operations on the Ancre, the Battle of Langemarck, and at Cambrai late in the year, when massed tanks were used for the first time in the conflict. At the beginning of 1918, the Berkshires spent time doing specialist training, despite the ground being covered by several inches of snow. On 6th January, they were due to move into the villages of Curchy and Etalon, but found French troops there were suffering from dysentery. The French left the following day, but the Berkshires were only there for two days, before marching on to Ugny, arriving in another snow storm. Two days later, they proceeded to Beauvois in rain, although this did clear the snow underfoot. On the 14th, the battalion moved into the front line facing Pontruet, and there were several minor skirmishes over the next few days until they were relieved four days later. They were in Maissemy two days later, when the enemy fired three shells into the village, one of which fell into a party of men, killing three and wounding eighteen others. The names of all those injured are listed in the War Diary, among them being Alfred, with the comment that he subsequently died of the wounds received. He is buried in Marteville Communal Cemetery, Attilly.

Pte. CHRIS. G. ELWICK, 1/4th Royal Berks Regt., Chavey Down, Cracknell.—Missing since August 14th, 1916.

CHRISTOPHER ELWICK

Christopher George Elwick was born towards the end of 1892 in Reading, but within six years, the family had moved to Church Road, Chavey Down. He was the eldest of three children, another dying in infancy. Originally a stable hand, his father had progressed to a domestic coachman by the time the 1911 census was taken. Christopher had left school and was working as a domestic gardener, possibly at Warfield Park or Lily Hill Park, both of which were nearby. Christopher's mother was also looking after two small children, probably for a small fee to supplement the family's income. He was already a member of the $1/4^{th}$ Battalion, Royal Berkshire Regiment, a Territorial Battalion, when war broke out, having attested at Wokingham. They had started their annual training at Marlow two days earlier, but immediately brought back to Reading. All the men were invited to volunteer for overseas service, with the majority heeding the call, but Christopher chose, for whatever reason, to stay in England until 1916. The Berkshires were not involved in the Battle of the Somme on 1st July, but received orders for an attack two days later, but this was cancelled at short notice, much to the disappointment of the men. They were not involved in an attack again until the 23rd, when about one third of them were wounded. There was a two week respite, while a new draft arrived and were incorporated, but "the knowledge of the rifle by these newcomers was imperfect, and of the bomb, nil." At this time, the average length of service for the new arrivals before death or serious injury was no more than three months. On August 9th, the battalion marched for three days over crowded roads to reach Bouzincourt, and after a night bivouacking near the village, went into support the next day. At 9:30pm, the 4th Oxford Light Infantry reported the Germans were trying to bomb them out of the front trench. Two platoons took bombs up to the front line, with more waiting in the communication trench. As the Oxfords were not in a position to make a counter-attack, it fell to Christopher's battalion instead, and they were ordered to make the move at 4:45am, after a short barrage from the artillery. However, although the Berkshires were ready, the Oxfords were not in position, and the start was put back half an hour. Day was now breaking and somehow, two of the Berkshire Companies got ahead of the game and set off five minutes too soon. The Regimental History recorded: "As they tried to cross the two hundred and fifty yards of open ground, the Germans, profiting from the absence of shell fire, stood up in their trenches aiming deliberately and accurately at the advancing lines." Fifty-nine men from the ranks were killed or missing, Christopher being one of the latter; his name is inscribed on the Thiepval Memorial.

Stanley Ewins

Stanley Herbert Ewins was born 17th February 1896 and baptised on the 26th of the following month in Holy Trinity. He was the youngest of five children, two more dying in infancy. The family lived in Bracknell High Street where his father worked as a carpenter but later, as he approached sixty years of age, switched to a hire carman (a driver of a horse-drawn vehicle for transporting goods, the forerunner of a delivery driver). After leaving school, Stanley worked as a telegraph messenger, before becoming a postman in 1912. He volunteered for service and joined the 1/1st Berkshire Yeomanry, attesting in Reading in Aril 1915 (the Yeomanry was the mounted arm of the Territorial Force, a part-time version of the cavalry). They sailed, first to Egypt in April 1915, and then on to Gallipoli in August, but Stanley was not with them, only joining them at Mudros on 6th November. The Yeomanry returned to Egypt the following month, and campaigned during the spring of 1916 in the Western Desert, joining the British advance on Jerusalem the following year. After two unsuccessful battles in March and April to evict the Turkish Army from Gaza, the British forces were reorganised under their new commander General Allenby, and the third Battle of Gaza was a notable success, culminating in the capture of Jerusalem in December 1917. During this campaign the Berkshire Yeomanry were involved in two successful cavalry charges against the Turks. Towards the end of November that year, they were fighting in the Judaean Hills. On the 19th, they marched to Beit ur et Tahta, and bivouacked the night in seasonal torrential rain; soldiers only had a waterproof sheet, heavy baggage having been left behind. Next day, they continued towards Beitunia, coming under heavy machine gun fire from the village, which they then attacked. About 200 Turks, ensconced behind boulders, held them up, and they were forced to spend another night on a ridge, facing the enemy, in more heavy rain. "We were so cold that it was impossible to fire any longer," wrote one soldier. The fighting continued on the 21st, but with no progress possible, and the Turks counter-attacking, driving other units back, the regiment evacuated the ridge in the early evening and descended to Fokha, arriving at 4am next morning. Here they remained for several days, although the horses were taken back to Ramleh. A bombing raid by seven enemy planes on the 27th injured nine men and 25 horses, and damaged saddlery and equipment. Meanwhile Fokha was shelled, as was an outpost at Abu Zeitoun, which was also attacked by about six hundred Turks, supported by artillery. For four hours, the Berkshires held out against repeated advances. Despite reinforcements, by nightfall, just one officer and twenty-six men of the Berkshire Yeomanry were left. Both Stanley Ewins and Richard Legg from Bracknell were killed that day; both are buried in the Jerusalem War Cemetery, two graves apart.

GEORGE FISH

The late Pte. GEORGE FISH, London Road, Bracknell.—Killed in action.

George Daniel Fish was born in 1885 and baptised 14th August the same year in Easthampstead Church. He was one of seven surviving children, three siblings having died in infancy. Initially the family lived in Priestwood, but after the death of his father, a labourer, in 1899, they moved to New Road, Bullbrook, where his two elder brothers supported the family, also working as labourers. George married Ellen Gray in 1907, and they set up home on the London Road and had four children in seven years. By this time, he was working as a grocer, and joined the 2nd Battalion, Royal Berkshire Regiment under the Derby Scheme, attesting in Reading. As a married man aged about thirty, he would have been mobilised at the end of May 1916, and joined the battalion during September. On 16th October 1916, the Berkshires arrived at Doullens, and six days later were in the support trenches for an attack on the 23rd. This was due for 9:30am, but postponed by five hours. As the leading troops advanced, the Berkshires moved up into the newly vacated trenches, but suffered heavy casualties from German artillery fire while doing so. During the course of the afternoon, all four companies were added to the attack, but it failed to reach its objectives, and all the attackers were withdrawn back to their starting points. Another attack was ordered for 3:50am the following morning, with the Berkshires on the right, but this too failed, owing to heavy machine gun fire, and the battalion were ordered back to its original position, where it remained until the night of the 27th, when it moved into Brigade Reserve trenches further back. Five officers and fifty other ranks were killed or died of wounds as a result of this action. George is officially recorded as having been killed in action on the 25th October 1916, and is buried in Combles Community Cemetery Extension.

HENRY FLETCHER

The late Pte. HARRY FLETCHER, Mount Pleasant, Bracknell.—Died.

Harry Fletcher (he never appears in the records as Henry) was born in 1883 and baptised on 14th October at Easthampstead Church, the second of four children. The family moved to Nonington in Kent, midway between Canterbury and Dover, where Harry's father worked as a gardener. But by 1901, the family were back in Bracknell, living in Broad Lane, but without their mother who had died the previous year. Young Harry was now a domestic gardener, but his father worked as a builder's labourer. Harry married Maud Jackson in 1907, and they lived in Mount Pleasant, beside the railway line, with Harry's father; a son was born to the young couple in 1914. Harry joined the 7th Battalion, Royal Berkshire Regiment under the Derby Scheme, attesting at Reading. The battalion had been in France for a couple of months at the end of 1915, before moving to Salonika, now Thessalonika, in Greece, where Harry would join them in the autumn of 1916. Although the names of battles are not as familiar as those of the Western Front, the fighting was just as fierce. The battalion were involved in the capture of Bairakli and Kumli (May 1917) and Homonodos (October 1917), as well as the Battle of Tumbitza Farm (November/December 1917). At some time in 1918 (the records state either January or November), Harry was taken ill, and died in one of the many hospitals that had been set up in Salonika. He is buried in Salonika (Lembet Road) Military Cemetery.

Malaria was always a threat in the area, and by November, the Spanish flu was also affecting many of the men.

JACK FRANKS

Ernest James Franks, known as Jack, was born in 1896 in the Kensington area of London. Both he and his elder brother were illegitimate, but his mother married George Franks the following year, and both boys took their stepfather's surname. George died within two years, and the boys' mother remarried in 1903, her new husband being Walter Tatford. Walter was also illegitimate, but his mother was to be the wife of an attendant at Broadmoor, making Jack a relation by marriage to a local family, although it is not known why he appears on the Roll of Honour at Holy Trinity rather than at Crowthorne. Jack had joined the Special Reserve, a form of part-time soldiering, in some ways similar to the Territorial Force. Men would enlist into the Special Reserve for six years, and had to accept the possibility of being called up in the event of a general mobilisation. Jack served in the 26th Battalion, London Regiment, which was formed in July 1915, around the time of his 19th birthday, making him eligible for service overseas. It is possible his experience in the Special Reserve was useful in training groups of new recruits when the new battalion was being formed. After nearly ten months of training, they crossed the Channel in early May 1916, and took part in two later stages of the Battle of the Somme in the autumn of the same year. At the beginning of June 1917, the battalion were in a camp near Poperinghe, providing working parties. On the 5th, two companies went into the front and reserve lines, and the artillery of both sides was active all day. Parties went out at night and discovered the enemy wire was cut, providing no obstacles. The other two companies moved into the second line. The artillery continued all the next day, in preparation for an attack from Observatory Wood to St Yves on the 7th, the first day of the Battle of Messines. The battalion should have been in position just after 1am, but were delayed due to considerable traffic in the communication trench, and were almost an hour and a half late. The author of the War Diary at this time may have been a frustrated author, as there follows a list of the training done leading up to the attack, the anticipation, and the supposed thoughts of the men while they waited. "Although a bit tired, the men were in splendid spirits," he wrote. Just before 3am, the enemy saw the battalions in front, assembling in No Man's Land, and sent up the 'stand to' signal ("a rocket bursting in golden red stars"), and their artillery opened a barrage, "but *it was* weak and caused no trouble." Twenty minutes later, the British artillery opened up, and the line moved forward. Five seconds later, the St Eloi mine "went up with a large blaze and a rocking of the ground." The enemy barrage came down in No Man's Land after four minutes, but it only caught the rear of the advance, and caused little damage. The 32nd Battalion, Royal Fusiliers, took the enemy first and reserve trenches in a little over half an hour, and continued to Dammstrasse, the first objective, a heavily-fortified sunken road, which the artillery had already subjected to a heavy barrage. This too was taken without much resistance, the enemy sheltering in strong concrete dug-outs, and between three and four hundred Prisoners of War were taken. A line was dug a hundred yards in front of Dammstrasse and consolidated behind a barrage. The 3rd Battalion now came through and captured Black Line on schedule. At 3:30pm, the 20th Division came up, continued the advance, and captured all its objectives by 5pm. Meanwhile, large numbers of prisoners were steaming back. The attack had been a textbook success, but had cost the battalion almost two hundred casualties. Jack was one of 25 men killed, and is buried in Voormezeele Enclosure No. 3.

The late Lce.-Corpl. E. GAMBRIEL, K.S.L.I., 3, Hampshire Cottages, London Road, Bracknell.—Died of wounds.

Ernest Gambriel

Ernest Charles Gambriel was born 12th August 1893 and baptised in Holy Trinity on 15th October. He was the second eldest in a family of six boys and one girl. The family lived in Broad Lane, where his father worked as a stableman groom. Later, he left to work on the railways as a platelayer, maintaining the track, and the family moved to Hampshire Cottages in the London Road. After leaving school, Ernest worked as a caddy (a messenger or errand boy). It then becomes difficult to track his movements, as he volunteered for service in 1915, attesting at Hereford, joined the 6th Battalion, Shropshire Light Infantry, and went to France in September 1915. However, by the time of his death, he was with the 7th Battalion, and the records do not record the date of his transfer. The 7th suffered more casualties than any other battalion in the regiment, and men were being transferred to it to make up for the losses. In 1918, they were involved in phases of both the First and Second Battles of the Somme, and Battles of the Lys. On 16th September, the Shropshires were at Havrincourt, and moved up to Brigade Reserve on the Demicourt to Hermies road. This was often a dangerous time, but the War Diary records that on this occasion, the relief was "quiet." Two men were killed and twelve wounded the following day by enemy shelling, and on the 18th an enemy attack at 4:30pm was beaten off. Those who had been injured could not be got away until the following day, with nine men being taken to the Field Ambulance. Ernest was one of those wounded, and died on the 19th. He is buried in Ste. Marie Cemetery, Le Havre. On the same day, a new draft of 158 new men arrived, on which the War Diary commend, "of good physique, *but* required considerable further training."

William King George

William King George was born in Kensington, London in 1881, one of six children. His father, the son of a master mariner, started as a merchant's clerk in London, before setting up his own successful trading business. The family moved initially to Windlesham, and then to The Brackens, now owned by the firm Polysius, on the London Road near the Royal Foresters crossroads. This was a substantial property - as well as the main house, there was a kitchen wing, a basement, stables and lodge, and four or five servants were employed. After finishing his education, William joined the Army, obtaining a commission as an officer in the Gloucestershire Regiment, serving in South Africa during the Boer War. On the completion of his military service, he became a director in his elder brother's motor business. He married Noelle Campbell-Stewart in 1910, and had two sons. William's mother was a suffragette, but her husband was unaware of this as her name appears in the 1911 census; many women are missing from it as a protest against not being allowed to vote. At the outbreak of war, William was recalled from the Reserve, and served with the 1st Battalion of his old regiment. The battalion had gone to France just after a week after war broke out, but William did not join them until the start of the following year, and served with the rank of Captain. The battalion were at Givenchy in January. There had been heavy rain, with alternating frost and snow, turning the trenches into muddy waterways, in which men were forced to stand for hours on end, suffering rheumatism, frost-bite and ague. On the 19th, a severe thaw set in, making things even worse, water causing the parapet to collapse. The enemy's guns were very active on the 24th, and again the following day. A German deserter, who had given himself up early that morning, gave warning of a large-scale attack, which started at 7:30am. Although many of the enemy were killed, large numbers continued to advance, getting to within fifty yards of the British position, but were unable to make further progress. Five minutes after the attack started, Captains H. C. Richmond and W. K. George, both belonging to 'D' Company, were killed, and one of the battalion's machine guns was put out of action. Soon after, the enemy broke through on the left, but a counter-attack by two platoons of the Black Watch restored the position. In the Service Record file of William King George, held at the National Archives at Kew, is a copy of the letter sent to his widow, dated 19th April 1915: "The Military Secretary presents his compliments to Mrs George, and begs to inform her that a report has just been received from Army Headquarters in the Field, which states that the late Captain W. K. George was buried at Cuinchy. A cross has been erected bearing his name." This refers to his grave in the Guards Cemetery, Windy Corner, Cuinchy. William's father died in 1926, a fact recorded on a tablet inside St Martin's Church at Chavey Down, which also notes him as a benefactor, paying, among other things, for the Iron Room in North Road, the forerunner of the current church hall. Mrs King George sold The Braccens and moved away from the area in 1932.

EDWARD GOODFELLOW

The late Second Lieut. E. A. F. GOODFELLOW, 3rd Connaught Rangers, Holly Bank, Bracknell.—Killed in action.

Edward Arthur Fitzherbert Goodfellow was born in 1887 at Rawalpindi, India, where his father was a civil engineer with the Public Works Department. He was educated at Bilton Grange, near Rugby, and Eton College, after which he obtained a job as an engineer with the Burma Railway Company. One of the regulations of the Company was: "That all European and Eurasian employees shall undergo the necessary military training to make themselves efficient members of it. In the case of an outbreak of hostilities, the special work of the Burma Railway Volunteers will be to ensure that the railway communications are undisturbed, and to hold the stations." There were about 850 men in the Volunteers by 1908. At the outbreak of war, Edward returned from Rangoon on leave, with his wife Katharine, who he had married there in 1912, arriving at Liverpool on 15th April 1915. Within a month, he was granted a temporary commission in the 3rd Battalion, Connaught Rangers, a Reserve Battalion based in Galway. After a short period of training, he was appointed to the 60th Trench Mortar Battery. Often the focus of infantry grumbling, for a front-line trench mortar was certain to draw enemy fire, the Trench Mortar Batteries played an important part in gaining the ascendancy in both attack and defence. Trench mortars were used in a variety of defensive and offensive roles, from the suppression of an enemy machine gun, sniper posts or other local features, to the co-ordinated firing of barrages. Larger mortars were sometimes used for cutting barbed wire, especially where field artillery could not be used, either because of the danger of hitting British troops, or where the effect of the fire could not be observed. The Divisional Trench Mortar War Diary beings in May 1916 with a summary of the unit: "20 Division Trench Mortar Brigade was formed at beginning of 1916 ..... Much useful work was done, but batteries were handicapped by *a* shortage of personnel up to May, when large numbers of men became available owing to disbanding of Divisional Ammunition Columns, when volunteers were called for, and more than 150 NCOs and men volunteered to fill 79 places in what was then termed as the 'Suicide Club' by those who did not belong to it. Needless to say, by getting volunteers for the work, men were obtained who had their heart and soul in the job, and the use of trench mortars became a great factor in trench warfare." In the second half of February 1916, the 20th Division Artillery was at Elverdinghe, northwest of Ypres, and involved in tit-for-tat firing with that of the enemy. The 60th Brigade Infantry Headquarters Diary entry for 21st February recorded, "Our Trench Mortar Battery, which fired during *the* morning, was silenced at 2pm. The Officers were evidently blown up as no trace of them can be found." Edward was officially killed the day before, and is buried in Bard Cottage Cemetery. His widow moved to Church Road, Bracknell, to live with her parents after the war, and although Edward is listed on the Roll of Honour in Holy Trinity Church, he may have never lived in the town.

Ronald C. Gregory

Ronald Christopher Gregory was born at Bagshot in 1899, the younger of two brothers, two other siblings having died in infancy. His father worked as a gardener, and the family moved to Aspley Guise in Bedfordshire, before returning to Bracknell, living beside the railway in Mount Pleasant. Ronald was conscripted into the 1st Battalion, Royal Warwickshire Regiment, attesting at Wokingham. At the outbreak of war, the minimum age for men to be sent overseas was nineteen, but by 1918, this had been reduced by six months. Ronald would have been called up early that year, and probably arrived in France just after the German Spring Offensive. By late summer, the Allies were advancing through Flanders, and at about 10am on 30th August, orders were received from Brigade H.Q. that the battalion were to move forward into their assembly position, southeast of Remy Wood and the village, for an attack. The Regimental History records the action: "Companies dribbled forward, but the movement was observed, and a heavy Machine Gun and Artillery barrage was put down, during which 'B' and 'C' Companies became very disorganised and suffered severe casualties. The Artillery was asked to shell the opposite ridge, and hostile fire was considerably reduced. At noon, the C.O. was called to another conference at Brigade H.Q., and received instructions to attack at 4pm. Orders were issued, but owing to the difficulty of getting hold of Officers, the assembly area still being shelled, it was difficult to promulgate these effectively. Capt. E. J. A. Maunsell took his Company and elements of 'A', 'B' and 'C' forward at the arranged time. They had to cross a stream and swamp, some of the men wading through waist deep mud and water. The line of the second objective was reached without much opposition on the part of the enemy, a number of whom were shot down as they attempted to run away. Owing to delay in crossing river and swamp, the artillery barrage got too far ahead; this, along with shortage of men, prevented third objective being taken. The Battalion were relieved at about 4:30am, and came back into support. Heavy hostile shelling of Remy Village and Wood continued." 123 men from the ranks were wounded on this day, so it is possible that Ronald was one of them as he died from wounds on the 8th September, and is buried in Abbeville Communal Cemetery Extension, adjacent to two hospitals.

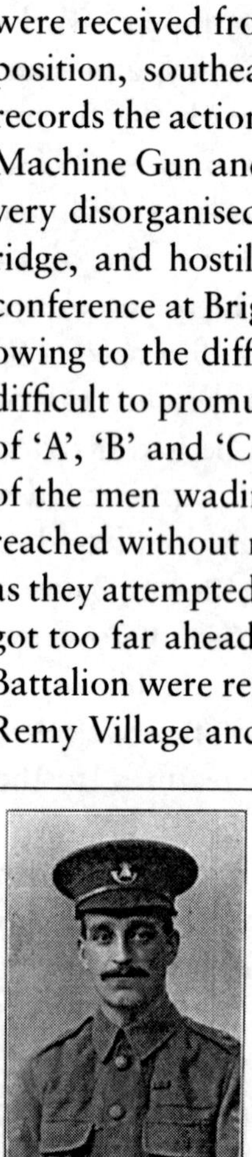
Corpl. S. G. HARVEY, London Road. Bracknell.—Died of wounds.

Sidney G. Harvey

Sidney George Harvey was born in 1883 at 11 Summerhouse Road, Stoke Newington, London, the second of four children (a fifth died in infancy). At the time, his father was employed as a coachman, but by 1901, he was working a grocer in Tottenham. Sidney, by this time, had left school, and was sharing a house in Westbourne Grove Terrace, Paddington with eight other draper's assistants. He married Jenny Green in 1906, and after the birth of their first son a few months later, moved to Bracknell, living on the London Road. Sidney worked as a postman from 1909, and five more children were born in the following years. He volunteered early in the conflict, attesting at Dalston, not far from where he grew up, and joined the 2nd Battalion, Oxfordshire and Buckinghamshire Light Infantry, where he was soon made a Corporal. Landing in France two days after Christmas 1914, the battalion were not involved in any major action until the Battle of Aubers on 9th May 1915, but it is not known whether Sidney took part. The Regimental History also records that many casualties occurred on the 17th, when the enemy shelled the trenches all day with great accuracy, causing great destruction of the breastworks, and wounding 270 men. The previous night, the battalion had assisted the 2nd Battalion, Inniskilling Fusiliers in an attack on two German trenches which had met with a lot of opposition. Sidney was probably wounded on one of these two dates, brought back to England, and died in Chatham Casualty Hospital, Kent, on 23rd June 1915. He is buried in Wokingham (St Sebastian) Churchyard, behind the church in a private grave, erected by the family; at the time of writing, the headstone of which has fallen over. He is not among the official War Graves in the churchyard; these are all men who died in the nearby Pinewood Hospital. His parents had moved to Crowthorne by 1911 (their address is given as Forest Road, just east of the High Street), and probably attended St Sebastian's Church on Nine Mile Ride.

Bandsman H. HOLLINGSWORTH, Bracknell.—Missing.

HENRY HOLLINGSWORTH

Henry John Hollingsworth was born in Enfield, Middlesex in 1881. He was probably illegitimate as he is only living with his mother in the 1891 census, although she claims to be married. But she did marry in 1895 in the Bracknell area, before going to live in Cold Ash near Newbury. Henry joined the 1st Battalion, Royal Berkshire Regiment as a bandsman, attesting on 26th September 1899 in Reading. In 1901, the battalion were stationed in Gibraltar, returned to England the following year, and then moved to Dublin in 1904. While there, he had married Margaret De Lacy in 1908, and they had had a daughter and a son. The battalion returned to Dover, but Margaret died shortly after, and Henry's two small children went to live with his mother. Henry's battalion were at Aldershot when war was declared, and ready to go to France a week later. The first train left Farnborough on the 12th, arriving at Southampton in the afternoon, embarked on the S.S. 'Ardmore' and sailed to Rouen, following which they marched three miles to their first camp for the night of the 13th. They faced the enemy for the first time at Villereuile-le-Sec, near Mons, on the 23rd, when four men were wounded. The following day, they were ordered to retire, and by evening were just outside the small town of Bavai. At 3am on the 25th, the battalion again stood to arms with orders to hold on to Bavai till the rest of the brigade had cleared it, which they did, acting as rearguard over a distance of some fourteen miles. At about 8pm, 'B' Company was ordered to return to a bridge near Maroilles being held by a party of the 15th Hussars, but were held up by congestion in the village and found it had been captured by the time they arrived. An action was launched to try and recapture it that involved an approach along a road only twelve feet across, and men immediately began to fall under heavy fire from the bridge. The advance was halted after about fifty yards and, after a reorganisation, was attempted again at a faster pace, but by now the enemy's fire was so heavy that little progress could be made, and a withdrawal was made. Five men, including three officers, were killed, 22 were missing, and a further 35 wounded, Henry being one of the latter, and died on either the following day or the 29th (both dates are recorded). After the war, when burials were being concentrated into War Cemeteries, his remains were reburied in Chauny Communal Cemetery British Extension. The body of Lancer Harry Knight was also brought in from the original burial site, and as the two bodies were mixed together, the two men have been buried in a joint grave. He was the first man from the town to die in the conflict, although William Willoughby from Crowthorne beat him to this dubious honour if the whole borough is considered. Henry's mother was back in Bracknell by 1921, when she married William Rawlins, and put his name forward for the Roll of Honour in Holy Trinity Church.

HARRY HOLLISS

Harry Lee Holliss was born in Bracknell in 1885, one of five children (a sixth died in infancy). His father had a tailor's shop in Bracknell High Street, and all five children worked there after leaving school. Harry volunteered for service, attesting at Bognor Regis, Sussex, in June 1915, and joined the 7th Battalion, Royal Sussex Regiment. The battalion had gone to France at the beginning of the month, and Harry was part of a draft that followed four months later. From February 1916, he would have been in the area of the Hohenzollern Redoubt, where underground mine warfare was very active. These were placed under enemy positions and exploded, to be followed by an infantry assault, aimed at capturing the opposing front trenches. Later in the year, the battalion saw action at the Battles of Albert and Pozieres, and were also involved in the Arras offensive in April 1917. In November, operations started on the Cambrai front. The 19th was spent in completing preparations, close to the ruined village of Epehy. The day passed very quietly except for a few shells, and the battalion left at 9.35pm for the assembly position marching via Villers Guislain and Gonnelieu. The battalion's final objective was a sunken road, about two hundred yards beyond the support trench to the Hindenburg front line. No Man's Land in the sector of the attack was 700 to 800 yards wide, and there having been little or no shelling, the "going" was very good. The destination was reached shortly after midnight, and they found the Royal Engineers had done an excellent job of marking out the assembly positions with white tape. The author of the War Diary may have been a budding author, as it now goes into great lengths about the tension of the build-up, and whether the Germans were aware of the impending attack, as the usual preliminary bombardment had not been carried out on this occasion. It was cold and damp, and the men received hot tea and rum; the officers drank "the excellent 'vin jaune superieur' of Scotland." The bad weather had prevented aerial reconnaissance, by the Germans, from seeing the build-up on the British side of the line, while the tanks to be used were halted more than half a mile back so the noise from their engines would be less obvious. Zero hour, at 6:20am, was marked by "a most terrible barrage opened from guns of all calibre, to the accompaniment of a Brocks Benefit Display of S.O.S. rockets of all colours from the German lines which had also become a mass of bursting shells." Planes, flying very low due to the mist and low visibility, and tanks, used to flatten the wire defences and provide a screen behind which the infantry could advance, were used in the attack. The element of surprise was total with very little retaliation and it was noted that troops "with rifles slung as if at a rehearsal, advanced leisurely across No Man's Land at the same speed as the tanks, and it was a strange sight to see many stop en route and light cigarettes." Everything went according to plan with little enemy machine gun fire encountered in the main, and large numbers of the enemy surrendering. The final objective was quickly gained with a total of around 120 British casualties, but notably few German ones. Harry was missing by the end of the day and his body never found, so he is listed on the Cambrai Memorial at Louverval.

The late Pte. E. HOLLOWAY, London Road, Bracknell.—Killed in action.

EDWIN HOLLOWAY

Edwin Holloway was born in Hurst in 1883, the youngest of eight children, and baptised there on 4th March. By 1901, the family had moved to London Road, Wokingham, where his father ran a shop selling fruit and fish, although this later developed entirely into a greengrocery business. Edwin worked with his father, and was also a member of the 2/4th Battalion, Royal Berkshire Regiment, a Territorial Battalion set up two months after the war started, attesting at Wokingham. This battalion was for Home Service, consisting of men who had not agreed to serve overseas, although later in the war this was changed, and all Territorial soldiers were eligible to serve on foreign soil. It is not known when Edwin joined the battalion, but training had started at Maidenhead in November 1914 with almost one thousand recruits. The first war duty they performed was providing guards for a Prisoner of War camp at The Philberds, a large house located between Holyport and the M4. The thirteen captured men there were among the first to arrive from France, and the camp later became one of the Officers' Prisoner-of-War Camps. The adjutant became suspicious when the inmates all suddenly took a keen interest in gardening, and a few weeks later, a well-constructed escape tunnel was discovered, almost ready for use. In February 1915, the battalion moved to Northampton to continue training, and two months later to Chelmsford, where their work involved digging trenches at Epping for the defence of London, and sentry duty around the roads of Essex. At the beginning of March the following year, they moved again to Salisbury Plain, and the Division was inspected by the King at Bulford on 5th May before setting off for France, landing at Le Havre towards the end of the month. The Berkshires were involved in the attack at Fromelles on 19th July 1916. This was designed as a subsidiary attack to the much larger offensive taking place further south on the Somme, but it was an unmitigated disaster with very heavy casualties and no significant gains. The following year, the Division pursued the Germans as they retreated to the Hindenburg Line. On 21st August, the battalion moved into assembly trenches at Wieltje, northeast of Ypres, for an attack the following day, part of the Third Battle of Ypres. Their role was to follow close behind the leading platoons, assaulting each enemy strong point as it was reached, either taking or blockading it, allowing the leading battalions to continue their advance. Zero was at 4:45am. The first strong point was Pond Farm which resisted two attacks but finally fell in the afternoon. Hindu Cottage, the second strong point, was surrounded as marshy ground prevented a frontal attack. A private from 'A' Company, who had lost his own platoon, managed to get into the strong point, and held nineteen Germans prisoner for forty-eight hours until relieved by an Officer from the 2/6th Gloucestershires; he was awarded a Military Medal. A third strong point, Schuler, was also taken with the capture of 76 Germans, and although in an isolated position, was also held for forty-eight hours until relieved. Three further strong points could not be reached due to heavy machine gun fire from the right, but the position reached was consolidated and the battalion finally relieved on the night of the 23rd/24th. 32 men were killed in the attack, over one hundred wounded and around eighty missing; Edwin was one of the former and is buried in the Tyne Cot Cemetery. He is also listed on Hurst War Memorial.

WALTER E. HOPE

The late Pte. W. E. HOPE, Border Regt., Orchard Cottages, Broad Lane, Bracknell.—Killed in action.

Walter Ernest Hope was born in 1882, one of eleven children. His father worked as a platelayer on the railway, and the family lived at Whitmoor Crossing, adjacent to the current sewage works. One of Walter's brothers would later become the crossing keeper there. After leaving school, Walter worked as a grocer's assistant in one of Bracknell's shops, but after the death of his father in 1903, moved to Ross-on-Wye, Herefordshire, to do a similar job. He joined the $3/1^{st}$ Battalion, Hereford Regiment, a Territorial Battalion, attesting at Hereford, where it had formed in February 1915. When it moved to Oswestry, Shropshire, in September, he was transferred to another Territorial Battalion, the $3/4^{th}$ Battalion, Shropshire Light Infantry, and finally to the 11th Battalion, Border Regiment. The records do not give the date for the transfers, so it is not possible to follow Walter's war experiences, but the Borderers had fought at the Battle of the Somme in 1916. A Sergeant writing home ten days after the first day of the Somme said: "We have had a terrible smashing up; all our officers either killed or wounded. It's been an awful time, and Workington has suffered heavily. We were one of the first Battalions to go forward, and we were mown down like grass. I don't think it will last much longer as the German losses must be terrible, and the sooner it is over the better for everyone. I hope I may never have an experience like it again." And, writing from hospital; "Many boys of the battalion are wounded and many have gone west, the first day of July .... They include my pal Hinchcliffe. I am sure of young Diamond as well, I believe. Of course you will see the list in the papers shortly. The poor old battalion got a 'biffing' at last. I was hit in both shoulders. The bullet went into the right one and came out on top of the left, so I consider myself very lucky. The machine gun fire was hellish. It simply mowed us down. But the boys still went marching on. I shall tell you more about it when I come to see you, which I hope won't be long now." The following year, Walter's battalion were involved in operations on the Ancre. Overnight on 1st April, they moved forward from Foreste on to the Rouy to Etreillers road, and after a halt for the rum ration, moved on another mile to a position some five hundred yards southwest of the village of Savy. They were in position by 5am, when the artillery barrage opened up, and rapidly moved forward and through the village, capturing it, and digging in a new position on the far side. Several German prisoners were taken, and a number of the enemy killed, all achieved in some ninety minutes. The enemy shelled their new position for an hour in the afternoon, but they continued to work on the defences all day, and later took over from the 7th Battalion, Highland Light Infantry, who withdrew. Walter was killed during the fighting, and is buried in Savy British Cemetery.

ARTHUR JENKINS

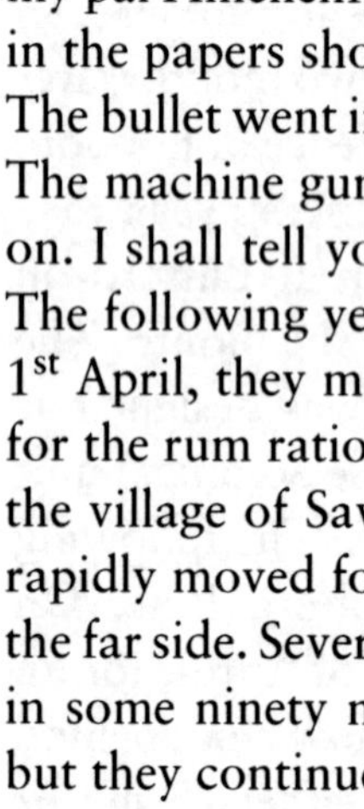

Pte. ARTHUR F. JENKINS, Mount Pleasant, Bracknell.—Wounded.

Arthur Frederick J Jenkins was born in Bracknell towards the end of 1892, the youngest of three children. At the time of his birth, the family lived in the High Street where his father worked as a grocer's porter, but by 1911, they had moved to Easthampstead Road as his father was by now working at the District Council sewage farm, then located on the east side of Longshot Lane. After leaving school, Arthur worked as a tile maker, probably at the brickworks on Skimped Hill Lane; the site is now occupied by Artlington Square. He volunteered for service in 1915, attesting at Wokingham, and joined the 6th Battalion, Royal Berkshire Regiment. Training was done at Colchester and on Salisbury Plain until July 1915, when the battalion left for Folkestone and sailed for Boulogne, arriving on the 26th. A week after their arrival, they were in trenches, receiving instruction on trench warfare, and although there were a few casualties in the next few days, it would be opposite Mametz on the 22nd when several men were killed by snipers. They stayed in the area until mid September before marching to Albert. Here there was a great deal of mining from both sides, and the battalion had over one hundred men, working four six-hours shifts every day on mining fatigues, removing and disposing of, over three thousand bags of chalk each day without the enemy being aware of what was happening. It was mid October before they went into billets at Buire and were able to enjoy such entertainments as a cinema. The rest of the autumn, winter and following spring followed a regular pattern of trenches and rest periods, although from March, training started in readiness for the coming Battle of the Somme. Five men were killed and 42 wounded during the four days' bombardment preceding the attack, largely due to the inadequacy of the dug-outs. The battalion moved into its assembly positions at 3am on 1st July, leaving the third trench empty after it was observed this was where the majority of the enemy's shells were falling. They were opposite Mine Trench, the most advanced of the enemy's defences, at the west end of which was Casino Point. A huge mine was exploded under this at 7:27am, a few men of the battalion were hit by debris, and the crater from the explosion was forty feet deep and thirty yards across. Over sixty men from the battalion were killed on that day and almost 250 wounded. The next battle the Berkshires were involved in came on the 19th. The task was to clear the northern part of Delville Wood, after the 8th Norfolk had cleared the southern end. At just after 7am, the battalion moved off, but the Germans were shelling the road to the wood, and the delay of the Norfolks getting into it held them up, and they suffered many casualties. By the time they got into the wood, they found it had not been cleared as reported, and things became very confused before a line was eventually dug, and held with difficulty, by 5pm. Fighting continued for the next two days but Arthur would play no part in it, having been killed; his body never recovered and is listed on the Thiepval Memorial.

THOMAS W. JOHNSON

Thomas William Johnson was born in 1877 in Easthampstead. He was the eldest of fourteen children, only six of whom were still alive by 1911. He spent the early years of his life at an address in Binfield, where his father worked as a labourer, before the family moved to the top of Bracknell High Street. Thomas married Rose Wise in 1898, and they had three daughters followed by a son (an older boy died in infancy). While Thomas worked at the brickworks (where Eastern Road is now), the family lived in London Road, but later they moved round the corner into Broad Lane. He joined the 8th Battalion, Royal Berkshire Regiment under the Derby Scheme, attesting a Wokingham, and was mobilised in mid June 1916. The War Diary records the training of new drafts in mid September, so it is likely this is when Thomas joined the unit. Training continued through much of October, but an outbreak of German measles at the end of the month meant they remained in isolation at Franleu when the rest of the Brigade moved on to Henincourt, only rejoining them four weeks later. In June the following year, they moved to the neighbourhood of Dunkirk, to prepare for an operation along the Belgian coast, but this was cancelled when the initial assaults in the Third Battle of Ypres failed to progress as expected. The Berkshires took part in the Second Battle of Passchendaele in 1917, suffering very few casualties. On 20th March 1918, while holding the front line near Cerizy, north-west of Moy, a warning was received of an impending enemy attack. The offensive started at 4:30am the following morning, with a powerful barrage and gas shells launched on the British front line, whilst the back areas were also heavily shelled. It was very foggy and communications had been broken by the bombardment so Battalion Headquarters knew nothing of the attack until 10am, when a report was received that the front line had been broken. The Germans began working round the flanks, opening machine gun fire on the trenches from the rear which, along with snipers on all sides, inflicted heavy casualties. By the time the mist lifted, the battalion were virtually surrounded and a withdrawal was ordered; only 182 men made it back. Fighting continued for another week by which time over 450 men had become casualties. Charles, by now a Lance Corporal, was one of those missing at the end of the day's fighting on the 21st; his body was never found, and his name is listed on the Pozieres Memorial.

Lce.-Corpl. ALBERT JORDAN, Bracknell.—Wounded.

ALBERT H. JORDAN

Ernest Albert H Jordan was born in Bracknell in 1897, and was one of eight children. His father was a travelling sewing machine agent, and the family lived in Wantage and Reading before coming to Bracknell, just before Albert was born. By the time Albert was thirteen, the family were living on the London Road in Bullbrook, and he had left school and was working as a fishmonger's assistant. He volunteered for service, attesting at Croydon in 1914, and joined the Royal West Surrey Regiment. After training in England, he went to France, arriving on 20th July 1915, and probably joined the 1st Battalion (their War Diary records a draft arriving on 1st August). Later, Albert was transferred to the 19th Battalion, Middlesex Regiment. This was a Pioneer Battalion, focussing on 'fatigue' routines such as trench digging, installation of barbed wire entanglements, and the moving of supplies and munitions. These battalions comprised men who were conscientious objectors, and those unfit for active service. This implies he had probably been badly wounded earlier in the conflict, but as his Service Record no longer exists, it is not possible to know when this occurred. He had, by now, been promoted to Lance Corporal, and was part of a draft posted to the 19th Battalion, London Regiment. On 25th August 1918, two companies moved from support to the Brown Line, which had been captured three days earlier; the rest of the battalion joined them the following day, which was described as "quiet." They spent the next two days building a new Battalion Headquarters before moving again, to trenches near Carnoy on the 29th. Even when not in the front line, men were not safe from shelling, and Albert was killed on the 28th; his name is listed on the Vis-en-Artois Memorial.

WILLIAM KING

Alfred William King, known as both William and Wilfred, was born in Bracknell on 5th August 1898, and baptised in Holy Trinity on 16th October. He was the youngest of three children of Arnold King, a cycle agent, blacksmith and mechanical fitter. The family lived in the High Street before moving to New Road, Bullbrook. William was conscripted into the 1st Battalion, Somerset Light Infantry, attesting at Wokingham, and during his time in the army, was promoted to Lance Corporal, despite his young age. Although the battalion were fighting at Arras in 1917, it was probably before William joined them, but he may have been involved in the fighting around Ypres later the same year. They were fighting at Arras again in March the following year, in the defence of Hinges Ridge, and at Bethune during the Battles of the Lys in April. In August, they were back at Arras, and on the 29th, orders were received to push forward and seize the line of the Senssee river, from its junction with the Cojeul river, as far as Moulin du Roi. The patrols came under very heavy fire from machine guns and snipers, but the enemy were forced to retire by a flanking movement. No bridge was found across the Cojeul, but a tree trunk was improvised and, after about three and a half hours, the enemy were driven back. The following day, patrols were sent out to secure a line some three hundred yards southeast of the Sensee. Both the companies involved encountered heavy machine gun fire, and it was decided to hold a line about seventy-five yards over the Sensee. Orders were received to attack at 4pm and capture Eterpigny as a jumping-off line. Considerable casualties were incurred before Zero, owing to heavy shelling of the area between the rivers. The prospect for the attack was not good as the men were tired, the majority wet through for 24 hours, and most of the senior N.C.O.s had become casualties. At 4pm, the advance began by rushes and the enemy mostly retired, pursued by fire. The objective was gained and a line established but at a cost of about 190 casualties. William was one of these, and is buried in Dury Crucifix Cemetery.

Tpr. R. J. LEGG, 4, South View, London Road, Bracknell.—Missing.

RICHARD J. LEGG

Richard James Legg, known as Dick, was born in 1880 at East Hagbourne, near Didcot, where his father worked as a platelayer on the railway. He had three siblings, as well as a half-sister from his mother's first marriage. By the age of eleven, Dick had left school, and was working as an agricultural labourer. His father died in 1896, by which time Dick was working as a railway porter at Didcot station. The family moved to Beresford Road, near Reading West station, and he and his two brothers all worked at Huntley and Palmer's biscuit factory in King's Road. In 1903, he married Ada Bourton in Oxford, and together they had seven children (one died in infancy), the last two after moving to Bracknell where they lived in London Road. Dick worked as a canvasser in the brewery trade; his mother's first husband had been a brewery labourer in Reading, and his mother latterly worked as a domestic servant for a retired brewer from Wiltshire, so there may well have been recommendations between employers within the trade. Dick joined the 1/1st Berkshire Yeomanry, attesting at Wokingham, and joined them in Egypt in 1916. They campaigned in the Western Desert during the spring, before joining the British advance on Jerusalem the following year. After two unsuccessful battles in March and April to evict the Turkish Army from Gaza, the British forces were reorganised under their new commander, General Allenby, and the third Battle of Gaza was a notable success, culminating in the capture of Jerusalem in December 1917. During this campaign the Berkshire Yeomanry were involved in two successful cavalry charges against the Turks. Towards the end of November that year, they were fighting in the Judaean Hills. On the 19th, they marched to Beit ur et Tahta, and bivouacked the night in seasonal torrential rain; soldiers only had a waterproof sheet, heavy baggage having been left behind. Next day, they continued towards Beitunia, coming under heavy machine gun fire from the village which they then attacked. About 200 Turks, ensconced behind boulders, held them up, and they were forced to spend another night on a ridge, facing the enemy, in more heavy rain. "We were so cold that it was impossible to fire any longer," wrote one soldier. The fighting continued on the 21st, but with no progress possible, and the Turks counter-attacking, driving other units back, the Regiment evacuated the ridge in the early evening and descended to Fokha, arriving at 4am next morning. Here they remained for several days, although the horses were taken back to Ramleh. A bombing raid by seven enemy planes on the 27th injured nine men and 25 horses, and damaged saddlery and equipment. Meanwhile Fokha was shelled, as was an outpost at Abu Zeitoun, which was also attacked by about six hundred Turks, supported by artillery. For four hours, the Berkshires held out against repeated advances. Despite reinforcements, by nightfall just one officer and twenty-six men of the Berkshire Yeomanry were left. Both Stanley Ewins and Richard Legg from Bracknell were killed that day; both are buried in the Jerusalem War Cemetery, two graves apart.

Henry W. Marshall

Harvey William Marshall, also known as Henry, was born in 1893 (the records state both Binfield and Bracknell as his place of birth), and baptised on 16th July at Easthampstead by the curate. This was probably at St Andrew's Church, located where Boyd Court, the Guinness Trust flats now stand, at the junction of Wokingham Road and Downshire Way. He was one of seven surviving children, having lost five siblings in infancy. When Henry was born, the family lived in Gough's Lane, and his father worked in the nearby Lawrence Brickyard, but by 1911 they had moved to Old Farm in Warfield Park; here young Henry worked driving carts around the estate, while his father looked after the cows. His records have been mixed with those of William Marshall from Brightwell (then in Berkshire, but now part of Oxfordshire), but it has been established that Henry volunteered for service, joining the 11th Battalion, Worcestershire Regiment. His training took place at Cheltenham and Longbridge Deverill near Warminster, Wiltshire, before going to France in September 1915. Two months later, the battalion sailed again, bound for Salonika, arriving on Boxing Day. It is probable that Henry manned one of the battalion machine guns, as he later transferred to the 78th Company, Machine Guns Corps. As the War Diary for this company no longer exists, it is not possible to follow his experiences during the conflict. On 25th September 1918, forward units crossed the Serbian-Bulgarian boundary, and hostilities with Bulgaria ceased two days later. The Division advanced towards Adrianople as the war with Turkey was still underway, but this also soon ceased. The 26th Division successively became part of the Army of the Danube, and then of the Occupation of Bulgaria. The unit had moved to Rustchuk, on the bank of the Danube in north-eastern Bulgaria in mid November 1918, and spent the next few weeks supplying working parties. Having survived the war, Henry died on 11th December. As well as the Spanish flu outbreak after the war, both malaria and dysentery were rife in the area. An Officer had returned from leave in England on the 1st, and may unwittingly brought the flu with him. As well as Henry, the War Diary records burials on the 6th, 8th, 9th, 13th, and 19th of the month. It also gives details of his burial: "Number 74536, Pte Marshall, H. buried at Protestant Cemetery. 1 Officer, 25 O.R. funeral party." In 1960, the graves of those buried in Rustchuk were moved to Sofia War Cemetery.

George Matthews

George Davis Matthews was born in Bracknell on 25th November 1889, and baptised four weeks later in Holy Trinity. He was the second youngest of ten children of a family living at number 8 Bay Road, Bullbrook. His father worked as a farm labourer, although the 1901 census gives his profession as a heather broom maker. Like three of his brothers, George went to work at one of the several brickworks in the area after leaving school, probably in the one on the opposite side of the London Road (where Eastern Road is now situated). He joined the Royal Navy on 29th November 1915, attesting at Southampton, when he was described as being just over 5'3" tall, with brown eyes, brown hair, with a fresh complexion, and a scar on the left side of his chest. He spent most of the next three months at the Regimental Depot in Deal, Kent, before moving to the Portsmouth Depot for a further four months, where he received a wound that required treatment for two and a half weeks. At the declaration of the war on 4th August 1914, there was a surplus of some 20-30,000 men in the reserves of the Royal Navy who would not find jobs on any ship of war, and these were formed into two Naval Brigades, plus a Brigade of Marines, for operations on land. The latter served in Gallipoli before moving to France in May 1916. The records indicate that George was assigned to the Royal Marine Brigade in June 1916, and the 2nd Royal Marine Battalion three months later. It was the exploits of the Royal Marine Light Infantry in the defence of Antwerp in 1914, when those that failed to escape back to England, fled to the Netherlands, but were captured and interned, that no doubt caught the imagination of many future recruits, reading of their adventures in their local papers. George joined his battalion in France at the start of October 1916, and took part in the Battle of the Ancre the following month. Next year, the battalion were involved in the Arras Offensive in the spring, and the second Battle of Passchendaele in the late autumn. He came home on leave at the end of the year, telling his mother he felt it would be his last visit as he felt his luck could not hold out much longer. In late March 1918, under the assault of the German Offensive, the battalion fell back some forty miles, suffering heavy casualties. On 2nd April, the 1st and 2nd Battalions, RMLI, marched from Forceville to Toutencourt, and to Engelbelmer on the 3rd, where they bivouacked round the village and were subjected to intermittent shelling. On the 5th, Engelbelmer was heavily shelled and drenched with gas, and at 9am, 7th Battalion, Royal Fusiliers were attacked, and minor breaks occurred which were at once restored by counter-attacks. Early in the afternoon, 1/RMLI moved up into support. The situation in Aveluy Wood was obscure, but by 7pm, patrols of 1/RMLI had discovered two gaps in the line which were closed after mixed fighting. In the early morning of the 6th, 2/RMLI moved into a position of readiness, northwest of the Wood. At 2:30am the line was intact, but later the position again became less defined, and at 7:45am, 2/RMLI came up in support of 1/RMLI. About 9:30am, a counter-attack was successful in re-establishing the line. The 7/Royal Fusiliers withdrew after dark, and the two RMLI battalions remained in the line until the afternoon of the 7th. George was badly wounded by flying shrapnel in the counter-attack, with one arm cut right off, and left unconscious An officer helped the stretcher-bearers get him back to a Field Hospital, where he died later the same day; he is buried in Doullens Communal Cemetery Extension.

JOHN H. MERRETT

John Herbert Merrett, known as Jack, was born in Bracknell in 1899. He was one of six children, a seventh dying in infancy. The family lived at Ramslade Cottages, Broad Lane, next to The Blue Lion pub. His father worked as Head Gardener at the nearby Ramslade House, and laid out the grounds there. John was conscripted into the Training Reserve in 1917, attesting at Wokingham, and was trained in Dorset. With the introduction of conscription at the beginning of 1916, this had replaced the system whereby each regiment had its own training battalion. The official compliment of the Training Reserve was over 208,000 men. Initially assigned to the Worcestershire Regiment, he was later transferred to the 1st Battalion, Shropshire Light Infantry. As it is not known when the transfer took place, it is not possible to follow John's experiences in the war. In early March 1918, the Shropshires were in camp near Vaulx, training and forming working parties. On the 14th, unusual enemy activity was reported, and the battalion stood to for four hours, but nothing happened. According to the War Diary, the Battalion Headquarters staff continued to be uneasy about the situation for the next six days, but Major Lees was still allowed to leave for six months Home Duty on the 20th. The next day, the German Offensive began with a very heavy bombardment of the trenches at 5am. The Shropshires and other units attempted to hold the onslaught at the Haig Line, inflicting heavy losses on the attackers before retiring to it. The vast majority of the battalion, under Col. H. M. Smith, were surrounded, and fought to the last; very few facts concerning this are known as so few of them survived. Desperate fighting continued on the next day as the British attempted to hold the line, but by 3pm, the Germans had outflanked them, and were reported to have broken through at Bois de Vaulx. Three counter-attacks were mounted, but all three were beaten off. The British were forced back, first to Vaulx, and then ordered to reform behind Vraucourt. Only 77 men from the battalion were left after the two days of fighting. Although John's official date of death is the 22nd, it is likely the paperwork lagged behind the action during this period. His body was never recovered, and his name is listed on the Arras Memorial.

George Morton

George William Morton was born at Chavey Down in 1894, one of six children. According to his baptism record at Holy Trinity, he was born on 9th February, but baptised on 25th January! The family lived on South Road, Chavey Down, with his father working as a domestic gardener, but by 1911, his occupation was listed as carpenter's labourer. After leaving school, George worked for a time as a general labourer, but then appears to have moved north and joined the 1st Battalion, Royal Highlanders, enlisting in Edinburgh in April 1912. The battalion were at Aldershot when war broke out, and crossed the Channel to Le Havre ten days later. They took part in the Battle of Mons, the Battle of the Marne, the Battle of the Aisre, and the First Battle of Ypres in 1914, the Battles of Aubers and Loos in 1915, as well as the Battle of Albert at the beginning of July 1916. By the middle of August, the battalion were at Bazentin. An attempt to take the German Intermediate Line on the night of 16/17th August having failed, instructions were received to attack dawn on the 18th. The assault was to begin at 4:15am, after a two minutes' intense bombardment. However, the 1st Camerons had occupied part of the Intermediate Trench later on the 17th, and the Highlanders were ordered to relieve them in the front and support trenches, but this was delayed by a barrage, and they were not able to move forward until 8pm. Further heavy shelling meant the battalion were only able to reach its position five minutes before Zero. There was a thick white fog that morning which made conditions extremely difficult. The advance began at 4:15am, and at once came into the enemy's barrage. 'A' Company could not discover any trench, although they advanced another seventy yards to look for it. They came into a heavy fire of rifle grenades, bombs and artillery. The trench had been crossed by this Company, but had been shelled out of recognition. In front of 'B' Company, on the right, the trench existed in better condition, and was defended by two lines of bombers. The front line was dealt with and the trench entered, but then came under attack from the second line. The

British second line followed the first, about twenty-five yards behind, but portions of it lost direction and the line was broken up by heavy shell fire. The reminder reached the objective with the first line. When the assault had reached a point about seventy yards behind the Intermediate Line, attempts were made to re-organise it. Parties had lost touch and sense of direction, and it was not possible to see more than a few yards; there were no definite trench lines for men to form on, as they had expected. Eventually, all withdrew to our front trenches in small parties. The casualties were seven officers and 140 other ranks. George was killed but his body never recovered, and he is listed in the Thiepval Memorial.

HERBERT NORMAN

Charles Herbert D. Norman was born in Bracknell on 21st December 1893, and baptised in Holy Trinity on 19th January the following year. He was the youngest survivor of ten children, two of whom had died young. Both his parents had come from the east of the country, and their first three children were born at St. Neots, Huntingdonshire, before the family moved to Bullbrook in around 1880. Herbert's father worked locally as various labouring jobs, but Herbert must have decided he wanted a more adventurous life, and joined the Army at Aldershot. He appears in the 1911 census as a Private in the 3rd Battalion, Dorsetshire Regiment, at the Depot Barracks in Dorset. This was a reserve battalion that remained in the UK for the whole of the war, but Herbert was a member of the 1st Battalion at the outbreak of hostilities, arriving in France with them five days before Christmas 1914. The battalion took part in the Second Battle of Ypres in 1915. Later in the war, Herbert was fighting with the 2nd Battalion, Leinster Regiment. It is not known when he transferred, but the Leinsters had faced the German Spring Offensive of 1918. The Division suffered very heavy casualties in June of that year, and returned to England for reorganisation, before returning to France on 1st August. If Herbert had been in England, recovering from injuries received earlier, he may have joined the new unit at this point. On 14th October, the Battle of Courtai began. The battalion were in their assembly position at 5:35am, and 'A', 'B' and 'C' Companies advanced in the first wave, penetrating over 4000 yards. However, dense fog and smoke from the intense barrage laid down, led to gaps in the advancing line, and many machine guns were passed over, which continued in action. German Field Batteries, unconscious of having been passed, also continued firing until charged by 'D' Company. The objective was reached, and although the enemy was expecting the attack, they offered no great resistance. "Captured big," recorded the War Diary, "14 Officers, 249 other ranks, 60 machine guns, and 11 guns." Seventy men in the Division were wounded in the attack, one of them being Herbert. He died later the same day, and is buried in Duhallow A.D.S. Cemetery.

JOHN B. OLYOTT

John Barnes Olyott was born in Bracknell in 1884, and baptised in Holy Trinity on Boxing Day. The name Olyott originates in East Anglia, and John's father was born in Norwich, before moving to London, and then coming to Bracknell by 1881 after his marriage two years earlier. He worked in the town as a plumber. John was the second of four children. The family lived in London Road, but after his father died, when John was only six years old, they moved to Church Road where his mother took in lodgers. After leaving school, John worked for a time as an ironmonger's apprentice before moving to Nottingham, to continue work in the same trade.

He was conscripted into the 8th Battalion, Northumberland Fusiliers attesting at Nottingham. Although the battalion had served in Gallipoli and Egypt, they were in France by the time John joined them in 1916. They took part in some phases of the Battle of the Somme that year, as well as Operations on the Ancre, the Battle of Messines, and several of the confrontations in the Third Battle of Ypres in 1917. Overnight on 14th/15th August, the battalion moved into a very muddy front line, and into the assembly positions on the east side of Steenbeer twenty-four hours later. At Zero, two platoons suffered heavy casualties from rifle and machine gun fire from a German strong point, and the first line of 'W' Company lost heavily soon after as well. A gap had developed on the British barrage, but this was filled with rifle grenades and Lewis guns, and proved very effective. The enemy surrendered their front line, and after heavy hand-to-hand fighting, their second and third lines were also captured. The right was enfiladed by three machine guns from the direction of Mon du Hibou, the Brigade on this flank not being up, but these were silenced with Lewis guns. The left advanced to within three hundred yards of the objective, killing the occupants of a strong point en route, but then lost direction, heading toward the cemetery; they then withdrew to a hundred yards west of the objective in the rear of the cemetery as the barrage was creeping backwards and forwards, preventing them from going any further. The battalion were relieved on the night of 17th/18th, but had suffered over three hundred casualties. Around forty men had been killed, with a similar number missing; John was one of the latter, and his name is listed on the Tyne Cot Memorial. A solider in another unit, who was to die a few days later, had written home, describing the area: 'We have not been in the trenches for about a fortnight now, but up till then we had four days in and four out. It was a fairly quiet part of the line that we were in, though of course at times it was rather warm, such as rapid firing, and a few shells flying over, but we soon got used to them. We used to hear at home that the Germans couldn't shoot, but can't they? I wouldn't give them half a chance if I knew it. At present we are billeted at a large village some miles behind the firing line, doing some training, and it is very trying, as the weather is so hot, but I dare say we shall have it still hotter before long. The woods and country back here are looking grand, but as you get nearer the firing line the villages and towns are battered about dreadful, and at some of them there are churches in ruins which at one time must have looked splendid and quite beautiful. We all have the same wish as you, that it was all over and that we could get back home again, but I am afraid that that will not be for some time yet. It is quite amusing trying to make the French people understand different things we want, but in most shops they are picking up English wonderful, and can quite understand, but that is chiefly where troops have been billeted."

THOMAS OLYOTT

Thomas Charles Olyott was John's elder brother, born two years earlier, and baptised on Boxing Day that year in Holy Trinity. He worked as a carpenter in the building trade after serving an apprenticeship locally. He married Ethel Lewis in Shobden, Herefordshire, on 29th December 1909, but the couple returned to Bracknell to live in Easthampstead Road, and had three children. His wife was already six months pregnant with their third child when Thomas signed up under the Derby Scheme, and joined the Royal Engineers, attesting at Ascot on 9th December 1915. He was 5'6" tall, weighed thirteen stones, and had a pulse rate of 78. He was mobilised in September the following year, posted to the 2nd London Division, a Territorial

Force, and remained in the UK until late May 1917. His Service Record shows he was a skilled carpenter and joiner, and also trained as an electrician before serving overseas; these skills were utilised in the 423rd Field Company, Royal Engineers. As well as performing construction and maintenance work, the Field Companies, which were attached to the fighting portions of a Division, also saw action and took part in the fighting. Many kinds of trade were required in the army, and Field Companies would typically contain farriers, shoeing smiths, trumpeters, blacksmiths, bricklayers, carpenters, clerks, masons, painters, plumbers, surveyors, draughtsmen, wheelwrights, engine drivers, sappers, and batmen. At the beginning of April 1918, Thomas's unit were in billets at Beuvry, and working on concrete shelters in the forward area. Two men were killed and four wounded by a shell on the 2nd. They continued to work on the shelters for the next few days, and moved to billets at Gorre on the 8th.The following day, the Germans launched an attack along the whole Division front. There was a heavy bombardment on the back areas, with Gorre being very heavily shelled. By 11am, the enemy artillery was reported to be very active, wounding three men, and three hours later, another two in the ration party were injured, and two horses stampeded. Soon after, the unit moved from Gorre Wood to Mespleaux Farm, but this came under attack next day, with several direct hits. On the 11th, the men were heavily whizz-banged (these were German 77mm shells that travelled faster than sound; the shell went over with a whizz, followed by the bang). At 8am, the enemy put down a barrage on the rear line, and a machine gun barrage on the front and support lines. This was followed by a very effective attack, and the British were forced to retire to the support positions. A further advance was held up by rifle and machine gun fire from the 423rd Company and others, and "very heavy casualties inflicted on enemy." Thomas was wounded, probably during the fighting, and died in 23 Casualty Clearing Station, a few miles south of Lillers, on 12th April; he is buried in Lapugnoy Military Cemetery. His wife Ethel, meanwhile, had returned to Shobden, and after receiving news of her husband's death, moved to Monmouth, to where his personal effects were sent, comprising letters, photos, a pipe, pipe cleaner and tobacco pouch, a match box cover, metal watch and strap, diary and pencil, his wallet, and a souvenir note, value 25 centimes.

JOHN F. QUICK

John Firman Quick was born, according to the registration of his birth, towards the end of 1867, at Westminster, London, although he claimed to be born at Gravesend, Kent, when joining the army, and at Plumstead, near Woolwich, in the 1911 census. His early life is a mystery as he does not appear in either the 1871 or 1881 censuses, but he was apprenticed to William Aldridge, a bootmaker living in Turnham Green, West London, from 1882 until 1887. It seems likely he was illegitimate, possibly with a mother from Ireland, working in service, who returned with her young child to her home country, and a soldier as a father (there was a military barracks in Gravesend from 1862, and the Royal Artillery were based at Woolwich). On 3rd December 1889, John joined the Shropshire Light Infantry at Kilkenny in southern Ireland, when he was described as being just over 5'3" tall, weighed eight and a half stones, with brown eyes, dark brown hair, a fair complexion, and scars on his forehead and left groin. He served until March 1896, when he was transferred to the Army Reserve, with his consent, before completing the seven years for which he had signed. Two months later, he married nineteen-year-old Mary Line in Hammersmith, London. At the outbreak of the Boer War in October 1899, John was recalled, and fought in South Africa, taking part in campaigns at Paardeburg, Driefontein, Johannesburg, and in the Cape Colony. He was promoted to the rank of Lance Corporal in February 1901, but demoted back to private six months later. Returning to England, he was discharged in August the following year, having now completed his service, his discharge papers stating he had "no relatives." He married again (using the name John Frederick Quick) at St George Hanover Square Register Office in London, on 1st August 1903, to Amelia Edwards, with the first of three children being born four months later. The youngest child was born in Sunbury, Surrey, in 1912, but by 1915, John and his family had moved to 3 Hampton Cottages, New Road, Bracknell; this is the address given when he attested at Wokingham on 11th August of that year. At forty-six, he was too old for active service, but joined the No. 4 Remount Depot, 54th Remount Squadron, Army Service Corps. This was based at Arborfield Cross, where around two hundred men trained horses and mules, from both Britain and abroad, for the conflict. He was appointed Lance Corporal in February the following year, but again, the promotion only lasted for less than twelve months before he reverted to being a private. His service record explains the reason: "When on active service, conduct to the prejudice of good order and military discipline in serving drink to another NCO and bringing him home drunk." Later the same year, on 3rd November, John reported to the Medical Inspection Hut, complaining of feeling unwell, and died two days later from chronic bronchitis. The coroner agreed with the findings, and issued the death certificate without the need for an inquest. John was buried in Larges Lane Cemetery on 8th November 1917. The relatives had made no arrangements for the grave to be marked, and it was later given an official Commonwealth War Graves headstone, the only one in the cemetery from the First World War. It is located at the far end of the burial ground, just to the left of the main path. The Reading Mercury of 19th November 1917 contained a report of his burial: "On Thursday afternoon, at the Bracknell Cemetery, the internment of Private John Firman Quick took place. The deceased, an old soldier, rejoined the Army at the outbreak of war, and has been serving in the Army Service Corps, attached to the Remount Depot at Arborfield Cross. After returning from his home in Bracknell on Monday, he reported himself sick, and after examination by the regimental doctor, expired almost immediately. He was accorded a military funeral, the body being conveyed to the cemetery by Army wagon from Arborfield, an officer and about a dozen of his comrades following."

FREDERICK V. RANCE

Frederick Victor Rance was born at Bracknell on 21st June 1897, one of six children. His father worked on the railway, before running a laundry in Broad Lane. After leaving school, Frederick worked as a builder's labourer for a couple of years before being conscripted and joining the navy in November 1916. He was 5'5" tall, with dark hair, grey eyes and a fresh complexion; he also had a scar on his chin. After three months' training, he joined HMS 'Dido', a depot ship at Harwich before transferring to HMS 'Hecla' in September, another depot ship which was based at Buncrana, Lough Swilly, County Donegal. In July 1918, he moved to a third depot ship, HMS 'Apollo', based at Devonport, Plymouth. While there, an accident claimed his life on the 16th August 1918. A report from the Court of Enquiry into the death recorded, "this man .... accidentally fell overboard and was drowned. No blame attributable to anyone." His body was never recovered, and his name is listed on the Portsmouth Naval Memorial.

GEORGE T. RANCE

George Thomas Rance was Frederick's older brother, being born four years earlier, also in Bracknell. On leaving school, he worked as a domestic gardener until joining under the Derby Scheme, attesting at Reading, and joined the 5th Battalion, Royal Berkshire Regiment. He was mobilised in January 1916, and training would have lasted no more than three months before the new men would leave these shores. The War Diary records some drafts arriving at the end of April and in May, so George would have been in one of them. On July 1st, when the first attacks of the Somme Battle were in progress, the battalion were marching from Franvillers to Henecourt Wood. At 5pm an order was received for the 12th Division to relieve the 8th near Albert, a relief which was not completed until the following morning. The battalion found itself in front-line trenches with orders to take the village Ovillers la Boiselle the following day. An intense bombardment was due ten minutes before Zero, to be followed by a barrage falling on the village church. At the last minute, plans were changed and the bombardment started a full hour before Zero, drawing a heavy fire in response, causing many casualties on the waiting men, and when they crossed No Man's Land. Although the enemy's front trench was reached quite easily, things became more heated and confused as the attackers pressed forward. It was still dark, making it difficult to distinguish friend from foe or locate damaged trenches, while the bombardment had failed to damage the German dug-outs, leaving them free to emerge and face the British. At first, the battalion fell back to the German front-line trench, but even this became impossible to hold due to attacks from both flanks and a further withdrawal was made to a sunken road between Albert and Ovillers, and the men dug in. Although only four men were killed in the fighting, over one hundred were missing and twice that number wounded; George was one of the missing and his name is recorded on the Thiepval Memorial.

ARCHIE RICHARDSON

The search for Arthur, known as Archie, Richardson is complicated by the fact that two of them were born within twelve months of each other, both in Warfield. However, a reference to "Popeswood, Binfield" in the Reading Mercury points to him being born in 1879, the son of Moses Richardson, a "drainer of land" in the 1881 census. The family were living in Clay Lane (now Park Road), near The Boot public house and, at that time, Arthur was the youngest of eight children, although a younger sister was born after the family had moved to Binfield Road. His father died when Archie was twelve, so his mother moved to Bracknell High Street and took in laundry to support the family. After leaving school, Arthur worked in one of the local brickworks, before joining the 1st Battalion, Royal Berkshire Regiment, attesting at Reading in 1902. The battalion spent time in Gibraltar and Ireland, but had returned to England and was at Aldershot when war was declared on the 4th August. They departed for France on the 12th, landing at Rouen the next day. From here their first action would be in the withdrawal from Mons, followed by the Battle of the Marne, the Battle of the Aisne, and the First Battle of Ypres. The Berkshires later spent the winter in and out of trenches, although the battalion did not take part in the Christmas truce. It is not possible to follow Archie through the war as, at some point, he was transferred to the 2nd Battalion. For the last nine days of March 1918, the battalion were involved in heavy fighting against the German Spring Offensive, and the War Diary only records the phrase "took part in enemy offensive operations" for each day as they fought desperately to halt the onslaught. The battalion had been billeted at St Martin-au-Lert for over a week, but on the 22nd, they proceeded to Guillaucourt by train and then marched to Chaunes. At around midnight, they received orders to move to the left bank of the Somme, between Roncy-le-Grand and Pargny, which was done under heavy fire. All day on the 23rd, they remained in reserve, but on the 24th were in the front line. Early the next morning, they were ordered to attack, but the Germans launched their own at 6:15am, the British line was thinly held, and a gap developed. By mid afternoon, the Berkshires had withdrawn to Omiecourt, having suffered heavy casualties. They continued to fall back over the next few days, mounting the occasional ineffectual counter-attack, until they were at Castel on the 31st. At 2:30pm came the news of a breach in the line at Moreuil Wood, and the Berkshires were sent to recover the situation by capturing an outlying copse, which they achieved. In front was high ground held by the enemy, making their position very dangerous, and with his men very wet and weary, Major Griffin requested they be relieved, which was done under cover of darkness. Just over three hundred men from the battalion were casualties for this period, but it was two days later before the records were updated, so Archie's date of death is recorded as 2nd April 1918. His body was never found, and he is listed on the Pozieres Memorial.

ERIC W. ROE

The late ERIC W. ROE, a drummer boy 2nd Grenadier Guards, Bracknell.—Killed in action.

Eric William Roe was born at Bracknell on 14th July 1893, and baptised in Holy Trinity on 2nd October. He was one of five children (a sixth died in infancy), and the family lived in the London Road. Bracknell was obviously a tight-knit community at that time, and young Eric was having a "sleep-over" with a neighbour's family in the 1901 census. His father worked as a foreman with a local printing firm, but Eric joined the army, attesting at Reading, and joined the 2nd Battalion, Grenadier Guards as a drummer boy in 1909, aged just sixteen. He then trained as a musician, before becoming a professional soldier. The battalion were at Chelsea Barracks when war was declared and went to France immediately, arriving at Le Havre on August 15th, and fought in the Battle of Mons and the subsequent retreat. The Battle of the Aisne took place a month later and the Regimental History records the action in some detail. "The morning of September 14th broke cold and wet. A thick mist hung over the valley of the river – fortunately this made artillery observation by the enemy impossible, and enabled the men to cross the river without coming under shell-fire. During the night, the Royal Engineers had managed to build a pontoon bridge over the river at Pont-Arey, and at 5:30am the brigade moved off to this point. As this bridge was the sole means of crossing all arms, there was naturally some little delay, and during the period of waiting Colonel Feilding sent for all the commanding officers; he explained the dispositions he had made, and instructed them to make Ostel their objective. The 2nd Battalion Grenadiers was to form the advance guard to the Brigade, and Major Jeffreys received orders to secure the heights about La Cour de Soupir, and to push on and make good the cross-roads at Ostel, about a mile farther on. Accordingly the Battalion moved off, crossed the river, and marched to Soupir, without opposition. At Soupir the road ran uphill through a dense wood, and it was impossible to see very far ahead. Progress was necessarily very slow, and the advanced guard had orders to move with the utmost caution. No. 1 Company, under Major Hamilton, formed the vanguard, and half of No. 2 Company, under Captain Symes-Thompson, was sent as a flank guard to the left, where the ground rose steeply above the road, and the trees became very thick. About half-way, the vanguard came into touch with the German outposts. At the same time, they were joined by some men of our 4th Brigade, who had gone too far to their left, and in consequence had narrowly escaped being captured by the enemy. Word was sent back by Major Hamilton that he was not at all happy about his left flank, which was on the high ground towards Chavonne, and Major Jeffreys despatched the rest of No. 2 Company to support Captain Symes-Thompson and strengthen that flank. Two platoons of No. 1 and one platoon of No. 2 were sent off to the left, and having got in touch with the cavalry on that flank, took up a position in the woods above Chavonne, where they remained for the rest of the day. Meanwhile, the leading men of the advanced guard, under Lieutenant Cunliffe, pushed on, and near La Cour de Soupir ran right into the enemy, who were in superior numbers. All the men were taken prisoners, and Lieutenant Cunliffe was wounded. But the rest of the advanced guard were also pressing forward, and soon the positions were reversed. Faced with the alternative of capture or retiring before a stronger force, the German officer in command decided on the second course. This meant perforce abandoning the prisoners; but there was one thing at any rate that a German officer still could do. Remembering the teachings of his Fatherland, that the usages of war were a mere formula, and the most dastardly crime excusable if any advantage could be got from it, he deliberately walked up to Lieutenant Cunliffe, who was lying wounded on the ground, pulled out his revolver, and shot him dead. As to what eventually happened to the German officer, there is some conflict of evidence. Some of the men of the Battalion swore that they recognised him among the prisoners who were led away that evening. Another story, which was generally believed at the time, is that Captain Bentinck, with a company of Coldstream, happened to come up just in time to see this cold-blooded murder, and that the men were so infuriated that they bayonetted the German on the spot. But this version can hardly be true, for the Coldstream did not arrive till a good deal later. Shells were now screaming through the trees with monotonous regularity, and the hail of bullets grew ever thicker as the advanced guard came up to La Cour de Soupir. It became evident that the Germans were not only in strength at the top of the hill, but were advancing across the open ground against our left flank, and at the same time trying to surround the advanced guard by working through the woods on the right flank. No. 3 Company, under Captain Gosselin, was sent off to the right with instructions to clear the enemy off some rising round and protect the right flank. This it succeeded in doing, but found vastly superior numbers opposed to it, and could not make any further progress. It was here that Lieutenant de Vouex was killed, being hit through both lungs by a chance shot in the wood. Urgent appeals from the firing line induced Major Jeffreys to send two platoons of No. 4 to help No. 1 Company, and one to the right for No. 3, while the remaining platoon, with the machine guns, under Lieutenant The Hon. W. Cecil, was posted on the edge of a clearing in case those in front were driven back. The advanced guard had now done its part. It had ascertained where the enemy was posted, but if an advance was to be made, it was clear that it would have to be strengthened considerably. Colonel Feilding therefore sent the 3rd Coldstream up to the left of the road and the Irish Guards to the right. Pushing through the woods and picking up platoons of No. 1 and No. 2 Companies Grenadiers, these troops came up to the hard-pressed No. 1 Company on the open ground near La Cour de Soupir.

Here the German's attempt to cross the open was effectively stopped by our rifle-fire, and the whole of their firing line was wiped out. But, even with these reinforcements we were still outnumbered, and an advance remained impossible. By now the firing line was fairly well established behind the banks of some slightly sunken roads running north and east of La Cour de Soupir; it was composed of Grenadiers, Coldstream, and Irish Guards, all mixed up together, as they had come through the woods by companies or platoons, just as the situation demanded. Though the German shells were still crashing into the trees and searching the woods, our own guns were answering back, in spite of having hardly a tenth of the ammunition. But while a satisfactory foothold had been obtained here, Sir Douglas Haig found that there was a gap between First and Second Corps. Being very hard pressed, with no reserves available, he sent back for help to the Commander-in-Chief, who at once placed the Cavalry Division at his disposal. On foot, the cavalry was despatched to the left, to prolong the line, occupied by the 4th Brigade, and succeeded in repelling the German attacks.

A steady fire was being kept up by the 4th Brigade at the German front line, which was lying down close in front of it in a mangel and beet field, and therefore very hard to see. The German fire suddenly began to slacken, and the moment seemed to have arrived for a charge, when, without any warning, the men in the German leading line ran forward with their hands above their heads in token of surrender, and at the same time white flags appeared in various parts of the line. At once a large number of our men leaped up and ran to meet them. Major Jeffreys and Major Matheson, fully alive to the possibilities of danger, shouted and yelled to them to stop, but the men ran on, eager to capture so many prisoners, and soon British and Germans were mingled together in a confused mass. At this point the German supports opened fire on them all, mowing down friend and foe alike, and killing a large number of both sides. Most of those who were unhit dropped down at once where they were in the root field, and when it got dark many of the Germans walked into our lines and surrendered. It must be added there is no evidence that this treachery was deliberately planned. It would seem that the leading line had had enough, and genuinely meant to surrender; the supports had no such intention, and there is thus perhaps some justification for their action. But it was a lesson to the 4th Brigade which it never forgot. Thenceforth the white flag was looked on with suspicion, and whenever it was used, not a man moved from his place. After a hurried consultation between Major Matheson, Major Jeffreys, and Major Lord Bernard Lennox, it was agreed that, while Major Jeffreys held the enemy in check in front, the other two should take some men with them, and try to work round the German flank. This operation took some time, but evidently it surprised the Germans, who were holding a ridge about 500 yards in front of our firing line. Many of them could be seen running from right to left across the front, and offered a fine target for our men posted at the edge of the wood – the shooting was good and hardly a man escaped. The difficulties of the situation were now borne in on Major Jeffreys and Major Matheson. It was getting dark, and they could get no orders from Brigade Headquarters, as the telephone wires had all been cut by bursting shells. Signalling was out of the question owing to the density of the woods. Meanwhile, the Germans were still shelling the road, and it seemed only too probable that the orderly who had been bringing instructions from the Brigade had been killed on his way. The men were dead-tired, having had nothing to eat all day, and Major Matheson, who had found it a very hard matter to get through the wood to the right, came to the conclusion that no advance could be made in this direction without reinforcements. Therefore it was decided that the only thing to do was to re-sort the battalions and to dig in where they were. A point of junction was arranged, and the much mixed battalions were reorganised; digging started, and the men, tired out as they were, set to work with a will, and soon produced a trench. Thus was the beginning made of that long line of trenches which was to eventually stretch from the Argonne to the Belgian coast, and which formed the battleground of the two armies for years to come. Converted into a dressing-station, the farm of La Cour de Soupir was filled with wounded, British and German. The ground in front of the trench was covered with dead and wounded Germans, but though as many stretcher-bearers as possible were sent out, it was not easy to find them in the darkness. Shelling began again at dawn before all the German wounded could be brought in. Behind the farm was a deep quarry with several caves in it; here the men not actually required for the firing line were stationed – comparatively safe except for an occasional shell from a German howitzer. On the 15th, Sir John French made an endeavour to strengthen the line, and consequently there was no need for the 4th Brigade to advance. All day it was shelled, and had to meet vigorous counter-attacks. It was holding a line which was really too long for it with its scanty reserves, and it is inexplicable why the enemy did not take advantage of this and drive it back to the river. The morning was spent by the 2nd Battalion Grenadiers in improving the trenches. About noon it was heavily shelled, and as the enemy seemed to have the range of the trench, the men were withdrawn into the wood, a certain number being left to keep watch. They proceeded to watch, not without some quiet satisfaction, the empty trench being plastered with shrapnel that did no harm to anyone. More parties were sent out at dawn next day to collect the wounded, some of whom must have been lying out between the lines for nearly two days. A good many were brought in, but the work had to be stopped as soon as it was light, as the Germans deliberately shelled our stretcher parties. About 11am, a shell set fire to a large stack, on the right of the farm, occupied by Captain Ridley and two men – they had been posted on top of it to snipe the German fire observation post, more than 1100 yards away. Helped by the blazing rick to locate the farm, the German artillery now began to plaster it with common shell, shrapnel, and H.E. *(high explosives)*. As this violent shelling seemed to portend an attack, the trenches were fully manned, with the result that there were many casualties. One shell landed right in the trench and killed Lieutenant Welby and the men near him. Although our gunners replied gamely, they could not compete with the lavish German expenditure of ammunition. A report having come in that the enemy were advancing, Major Jeffreys ordered No. 2 Company to come up from the quarry, and line its northern edge, so as to be available as a support. It had hardly been there a quarter of an hour when an 8-inch high explosive just missed the farm, and, grazing the roof, pitched right on the edge of the quarry. A terrific explosion followed, and out of the 103 men who had been brought up, only 44 were left, all the rest being killed or wounded. In the front trenches, meanwhile, shelling went on incessantly, and there were many counter-attacks, directed against the part of the line held by the Coldstream. During the evening two companies of Oxfordshire Light Infantry were sent up to take over the trenches next morning." The dressing station for casualties was well in the rear, and there were not enough horse ambulances to deal with the volume. As a drummer, Eric may have been tasked as a stretcher-bearer. These played a very dangerous role as they crept around the battle ground at night, trying to bring in both British and German wounded, under shelling. Eric was killed during this period and is buried in Vailly British Cemetery.

FRANK SARGEANT

Frank Frederick Sargeant was born in Easthampstead in 1886 and baptised in the church there on 9th May. He was the youngest of seven children and was only three years old when his father, who worked as a bricklayer, died. By now, his two eldest brothers were doing similar jobs, and the family continued to live near Easthampstead Church, but after they married and left home, Frank and his mother, who was now taking in washing, moved to Mill Lane. Frank also worked as a bricklayer after leaving school, marrying Maud Studd on 20th May 1912, with a daughter and a son being born by 1916. Although his service record still exists, it was damaged by fire and water when the building housing all the papers burnt down in 1940, making parts of it illegible. He joined up under the Derby Scheme, attesting at Wokingham on 7th December 1915, giving his address as London Road, and was mobilised in June the following year. He joined the 1/1st Battalion, Hertfordshire Regiment, a Territorial Battalion which initially stayed in England, but was posted on 2nd December, moved to Halton Camp near Wendover, Buckinghamshire two days after Christmas, and left Folkestone for Calais on 2nd January 1917. At the end of July, the Hertfordshires took part in the Battle of Pilkem, part of the Battle of Ypres of that year. The attack started at 3:50am on July 31st, but his battalion were in reserve at the start and only left their bivouacs at 6am, and after moving several times, were ordered to be ready to attack at 5pm. This order was then cancelled and they moved back a couple of hundred yards, but came under heavy shell fire and moved into adjacent trenches. Frank was killed during the shelling and his body not found; his name is listed on the Ypres (Menin Gate) Memorial. Although he lived in Bracknell, his mother still lived in the parish of Easthampstead, and he is listed on the Roll of Honour in both churches.

ALBERT R. SEARLE

Albert Edward Searle was born in Sunningdale in 1894, the elder of two brothers. The family had moved to Stanley Road, Bracknell, by the end of 1897, where his father worked as a clerk for a firm selling corn and coal, and Albert joined the same firm on leaving school. He was already a member of the 1/4th Battalion, Royal Berkshire Regiment, a Territorial Battalion, when war broke out, having attested at Wokingham. They had started their annual training at Marlow two days earlier, but immediately brought back to Reading. All the men were invited to volunteer for foreign service, with the majority heeding the call. Much of the training took place in and around Chelmsford, before they arrived in France at the end of March 1915, where they spent their first night on a hill overlooking Boulogne, shivering under a thin blanket and awoke to driving snow. A week later they were receiving instructions on trench warfare, and on the 15th April occupied a position on the front line for the first time. He would then have seen action at Ploegsteert, Bethune and Pozieres. In the first twelve months, the battalion lost around four hundred men, but Albert had survived and was promoted to Lance Corporal. After a period of respite from fighting, when they practised using rifles and received training in the use of bombs, they moved to Varenneson on 10th August 1916. This took longer than scheduled as the roads were in poor state and they had to make a detour; they continued over the next couple of days to Bouzincourt and then Ovillers. On the 13th, they were in reserve to the 4th Oxfordshires who were holding a trench captured the previous day. At 9:30pm, the Oxfordshires reported the Germans were trying to bomb them out of the trench and the Berkshire men were ordered to assist them in an attack. After various delays, the attack commenced at 5:10am, by which time it was getting light. There was also some confusion as to precisely when the attack should start with the result that two companies of the Berkshires started before the rest, and a lack of supporting shell fire allowed the Germans to stand up in their trenches and fire at the oncoming men. None of the British got to within a hundred yards of the German positions and were pinned down, sheltering in shell holes. It was only when a British plane, observing the action, returned and signalled to the artillery to start firing, that men were able to return the trenches. There were 140 casualties, almost half being killed. Albert was wounded and died the next day, and is buried in Warloy-Baillon Communal Cemetery Extension.

HENRY SMITH

John Henry S Smith was born in Olney, Bedfordshire, in 1896, the middle of three brothers. His father was a wicker basket maker, and the family had moved to Leighton Buzzard by 1911, before coming to Bracknell. It is not clear whether Henry actually lived in the town as he joined under the Derby Scheme, attesting at Luton, and joined the Bedfordshire Regiment, probably the 2nd Battalion. This meant he probably arrived in France just before the Battle of the Somme, when the battalion captured Montauban and Trones Wood. The Machine Gun Corps was formed earlier the same year, but it is not known when Henry actually transferred, as both units are listed on his Medal Card. Towards the end of March 1917, Henry's unit was at Bellacourt, and spent most of the time in training. The War Diary entry for 2nd April reads: "Shelling started again at 8am when a dozen H.E. *(high explosives)* put over, these dropped near a battery about fifty yards behind the railway. Early morning, enemy machine gun fired bursts at our aeroplanes. Enemy artillery fairly active on the left, searching for our batteries, and shelling the sunken road. Our front line on the left not shelled during the morning. The point where the road cuts the railway, and battery, shelled continuously throughout the morning. Battery shelled during the night, but all shells fell short. At 9am, an enemy aeroplane flying at great height came over to observe. Enemy then lengthened range, and shells dropped beyond the battery. Shelling ceased around midday. Casualties: 1 killed." The one casualty was Henry; his body was never recovered, and he is listed on the Arras Memorial.

STEPHEN SONE

Stephen Isaac Sone was born at Chavey Down on 5th March 1896, and baptised in Holy Trinity three months later. He was one of seven children (another died in infancy). The family lived in North Road, Chavey Down, where his father worked as a brickmaker and general labourer. The Sone family were one of the first in the 'new' village of Chavey Down, and in later years, Stephen's father, known as Nobby, was an odd-job man at the bakery (at the junction of Longhill Road and North Road), and used to hide his tips under a flower pot outside the shop! After leaving school, Stephen worked a garden boy, along with his older brother Ben, possibly at one of the nearby estates of Warfield Park or Lily Hill. At the outbreak of war, the two brothers immediately volunteered, looking for adventure and excitement, going to Hounslow to attest. Initially they were in the 5th Battalion, London Regiment (a training unit), before being transferred to the 1st Battalion, Royal Highland Regiment, and went to France on 1st December 1914. The first major action he saw would be the Battle of Aubers on 9th May the following year. The British artillery started firing at 4am, with the enemy replying about an hour later. The battalion were in position just over two hours later, by which time an earlier assault had been unsuccessful and a counter-attack was anticipated. A second attack at midday was postponed to 2pm, and then for another two hours. There was heavy hostile shelling just before the 'off', a few minutes before 4pm. The total distance to the German trenches was three hundred yards, and was covered in about two minutes, despite a hold-up due to some of the wire not being cut. Initially the attack was a success, but the Germans fought back and wrought havoc with bombing in the trenches, and by 4:42 pm, the message for "attacking troops are to be withdrawn under cover of artillery fire to breastworks" was received, and this was accomplished over the next hour and a half. The battalion were back in billets just before midnight, but the losses had been heavy, with more than fifty men killed, nearly 250 wounded, and over 150 missing. Ben was wounded, but Stephen was one of the missing, and his name is recorded on the Le Touret Memorial.

VICTOR THURMER

Victor Charles Thurmer was born towards the end of 1897 at Chavey Down, the younger of two brothers, although two others siblings died in infancy. His father worked as a general labourer, and the family lived in North Road. On leaving school, Victor worked as a grocer's assistant before being called up, attesting at Wokingham in May 1916. A small part of his service record survives, but only enough to tell us he was 5'4½" tall, weighed less than 7½ stones, and was posted to the Royal West Kent Regiment five days after attesting. While in Kent, he spent time with the 2/1st Kent Cyclist Battalion. This unit was based at Canterbury, and would have been tasked with guarding key points and patrolling the coastline to deter invasion and to catch spies. One blemish on his record occurs in June when he was late on fatigues, and received a punishment of three days – probably confined to barracks, but the record is illegible at this point. Later he was transferred to the 11th Battalion, and crossed the Channel to France on 4th January 1917. The following June, the battalion were involved in the Battle of Messines when nineteen huge mines were exploded under German lines. On 31st July, an attack was launched, the objective being to capture Hollebeke and clear the ground across the Comines Canal, just east of Battle Wood (southeast of Ypres). No Man's Land had been under very heavy shell-fire while the 11th Battalion were forming up for the attack. Luckily, the battalion escaped fairly lightly, and when the British barrage stopped at 3:50am, it went forward so rapidly that the enemy's counter-barrage came down well behind it and failed to do any damage. Oblique Trench was the objective of the leading companies, but mist, uncut wire, and the stubborn fight put up by the Bavarians delayed the advance, and only after strenuous fighting was the trench at last cleared, on which 'A' and 'B' Companies began consolidating 150 yards further on. 'C' and 'D' Companies then passed through, but found it hard to get on in the face of the machine gun fire from houses along the Hollebeke road. A small group got well forward, worked round the village and proceeded to bomb dug-outs and capture prisoners, but being quite without support, had to come back to escape being cut off. In the meantime, Colonel Corfe had come up to the front himself, and had found that the next battalion to the right had failed to capture the village, and that the advance was held up by machine gun fire from pill-boxes around Hollebeke Church. Despite the heavy fire from machine guns and rifles, they worked forward into the village, cleared pill-boxes, mopped up cellars and dug-outs systematically, and successfully established themselves in the ruins. Some sixty prisoners were taken and many casualties inflicted on the enemy, who put up a stubborn resistance. By 11:30am, Captain Rooney was able to report that Hollebeke had been cleared. The remainder of the battalion now came forward to assist in consolidating a line east of Hollebeke and only one hundred yards short of the final objective. According to the Regimental History, "this day's attack had been carried out under more than ordinary difficulties; the ground, naturally marshy, had been reduced to a frightful condition by the combination of an unusually high rainfall and a stupendous bombardment. It had been all but impossible to get forward in the mass of churned-up mud and water. Consolidation in such a state of things was equally difficult. The only compensation was that the ground presented equal obstacles to a counter-attack, which the exhausted survivors of the attack would have been hard pressed to repulse with their rifles and Lewis guns mostly choked with mud. But though the 11th, now less than three hundred strong, remained in position till the night of August 4th under heavy shell-fire and persistent rain, no counter-attack developed, and at last a battalion of the 39th Division arrived to relieve it." Victor was a casualty of this attack; his body was never recovered and his name is listed on the Ypres (Menin Gate) Memorial.

PERCY G. TREBLE

Photo] [Khaki Studio
The late Lce.-Cpl. PERCY GEO. TREBLE, London Road, Bracknell.—Killed in action.

Percy George Treble was born at Reading in 1892, the middle of three boys. His father worked as a farm bailiff, so Percy and his brothers grew up on farms at Checkenden and Mapledurham, but on leaving school, Percy worked as a clerk before moving to Bracknell. He volunteered for service, attesting at Reading, and joined the 8th Battalion, Royal Berkshire Regiment. Much of his training was done at Reading, as well as at Sutton Veny near Warminster, Wiltshire. The battalion went to France, landing at Le Havre, on 7th August 1915. New boots had been issued on leaving Warminster, and the three days of marching that followed, caused a lot of footsores to some of the men. On the 17th, they were in trenches for the first time. Most of the next month was spent in billets, with short periods in the front line trenches, before they were involved in their first major action, an attack on the German position east of Hulluch on 25th September 1915. The War Diary records the action: "At 5:50am, an intensive bombardment began, the enemy's artillery at once replying, though they inflicted little damage and caused few casualties in the front-line trenches. Simultaneously with the bombardment, the gas company began to operate the gas cylinders which were in the front-line trench, and there then occurred several casualties from poisoning, caused it was supposed, by leakages in the cylinders. Use of the gas ceased, and smoke bombs were thrown from the front-line trenches, proving entirely successful in screening the advance. At 6:30am, the fire of our artillery lifted, and Battalion advanced in quick time, to assault the first line enemy Trenches. The advance was opposed by heavy artillery and machine gun fire, while the wire in front of the German trenches was found to be scarcely damaged, and it was in cutting a way through this obstacle that most of the regiment's heavy casualties occurred. Shrapnel and machine gun fire combined to play havoc in the ranks, and an additional disaster was the blowing back of the gas on the wind into our own ranks. However, after a struggle, the German first line was penetrated, and the trench found to be practically deserted, the enemy apparently, having deserted it earlier in the day, merely leaving behind sufficient men to work the machine guns. Mainly overland, but with some men working up the communication trench, our line advanced successively to the second and third German lines, and met with but slight opposition. From the third line, a further advance was made, and an enemy Field Gun captured. A fourth line German trench was also seized, but being in so incomplete a state that it afforded little cover from rifle fire and none whatever from shrapnel. The line was ordered to be withdrawn to the 3rd German line trench, and this position was occupied until the Battalion were relieved. At the point, when the Battalion were negotiating the German wire, about fifty men became separated from the remainder of the Battalion and attached themselves to the Gordons advancing and taking the German guns in the fourth line German trench. They then advanced and occupied the road west of Hulluch, but were unable to advance further owing to our artillery fire, which was falling short, so waited for support to come up, in the meantime starting to dig themselves in. At 3.30pm, the Germans counter-attacked, driving in our flanks, and as the support had not yet arrived, they were compelled to retire, holding a position about one hundred yards west of the road. The Berkshires numbers were reduced to about half. On receiving news that the supports were coming up, they again advanced to the road and proceeded to place in a state of defence. At 11.30pm, the Germans again counter-attacked in large numbers, driving in our right flank. We retired to the position we had before held in the afternoon, but the Germans continued to push the counter-attack. Our support line then opened fire and we were caught between the two fires. We then made our way as well as possible to our supporting line (the German fourth line). Only six of the Berkshires returned safely." At some stage during the day, Percy was killed; his body was never found and his name is recorded on the Loos Memorial.

Richard L. Trodd

Richard Lawrence Trodd, also known as Lawrie, was born at Odiham in Hampshire in 1888, the youngest of four children. His father worked in the brick manufacturing trade and by 1901, the family had moved to Church Road, Bracknell. Later his father worked as a commission agent (a salesman earning his wage from commission on the sales he achieved), with Richard acting as his clerk. During his time in Bracknell, Richard won prizes at the local Sports Days for sprinting. He married Anne Spiers, who had been working in Bracknell as a shorthand typist, early in 1914, the marriage taking place in her home town of Gravesend in Kent. Richard joined the 5th Battalion, Royal Berkshire Regiment, under the Derby Scheme, attesting at Wokingham towards the end of 1915, and was mobilised in May the following year. The War Diary records several drafts arriving in September, one of which included Richard. For most of the autumn and winter, the battalion were engaged in routine trench warfare in and around Arras, until being relived just before Christmas. There are very few casualties recorded in the War Diary for December, apart for two men being wounded on the 4th, and one on the 11th. The last of these three was Richard who died in the nearby 41st Casualty Clearing station later the same day, and is buried in Wanquetin Communal Cemetery Extension.

William Watson

William Edward Hinds was born at Llanflyllin, near Oswestry, in north Wales, in 1899. He was the youngest of four children, a fifth dying in infancy, and the only one not born at Sunningdale. By 1901, the family were living back in Sunningdale, but using the surname of Watson; they later moved to Chavey Down. His father, who had joined the army in 1891, but was discharged after three months due to persistent bouts of rheumatism, worked as a hotel coachman, possibly at The Royal Foresters on the Ascot Road. William was conscripted into the 13th Battalion, King's Royal Rifle Corps, attesting at Wokingham in 1917. He arrived in France the following spring, although the precise date is not known. In August, the battalion were involved in the Battle of Albert, part of the Second Battle of the Somme. On the 22nd, the Germans were in retreat. Late that evening, the battalion moved up to relieve one of the Naval Division battalions, during which it ran into gas shelling, one shell falling into the middle of a platoon, laying several men out. At 4am the next morning, an attack on Gonnelieu was underway. The enemy barrage was heavy, and there was also very heavy machine gun fire. Zero hour was at 11am and the attack commenced, progressing rapidly. Several hundred enemy prisoners and many machine guns were captured, and the final objective gained at 1:30pm. The position was subject to heavy shelling with numerous counter-attacks. William lost his life in this action, and is buried in Gomiecourt South Cemetery.

Henry Wilkes

Henry Charles Wilkes was born at Bracknell in 1898, the eldest of four children. His father worked as a groom in Staffordshire, Warwickshire and Yorkshire before appearing in the 1911 census at Bagshot, by which time he had progressed to working as a carman (a horse and cart delivery man, the forerunner of a modern-day van driver). Later, he would move again to Northamptonshire. Henry was living in Windlesham by the time he joined the 1st Battalion, Royal Berkshire Regiment, under the Derby Scheme, attesting at Wokingham, and was mobilised in January 1916. The War Diary does not mention the arrival of new drafts of men, so it is not known when Henry joined the Berkshires at the front. The battalion were not involved in the Battle of The Somme, and it was July 27th before they were involved in a serious attack again. They had gone into the front line near Delville Wood three days earlier, and the attack started on this day with a bombardment at 6am, lasting just over an hour. Two hundred yards of ground was gained and they dug in. At 8:10am, the advance resumed until they finally reached Princes Street, their objective, running east/west through the middle of the wood. They had encountered considerable rifle fire, but it was not very accurate and did little harm. However, enfilading machine gun fire caused some problems for the consolidating parties. This was followed by high-explosive-shell fire for the remainder of the day, preventing any supplies of food or water reaching the men. More shelling and fire continued the next day, and it was quite late before the battalion could be relieved. 37 men were killed during the course of the two days with a similar number missing. Henry died on the first day and is buried in London Cemetery and Extension, Longueval.

Henry Winter

Charles Henry Winter was born at Warfield Street in 1890, and baptised at the local church on 28th September. He was one of six children and by 1901, the family had moved to Chavey Down, where they lived next door to the church. His father worked as a plumber and painter, also doing some signwriting. As Charles was named after his father, he started to use his middle name to avoid confusion when he started work, labouring on the roads. He volunteered for service, attesting at Southampton, and joined the 7th Battalion, Rifle Brigade, and was with the first group of the battalion that went to France, landing at Boulogne on 19th May 1915. The battalion were involved in the Battle of Hooge a couple of months later, when the Germans used flame-throwers for the first time. Like Henry Wilkes, he was also involved in fighting in and around Delville Wood. For him, the attack was on 18th August, though limited in objective. The Regimental History describes the fighting: "A bombardment began on the day before, and thickened on the 18th until at Zero hour, 2:45pm, it became intense, and the infantry crept up under it in readiness to assault, five minutes later. The right company, 'A' Company, captured its section of Orchard Trench, but the task of 'D' Company on the left was far more difficult. From a jumping-off trench indifferently sited and in rear of those on the right, they had to secure two hundred yards of Wood Lane that ran forward at an angle from Orchard Trench. Success was necessarily dependent upon support on the left, but this was held up at the very outset. 'D' Company in the ensuing delay lost the barrage; and though the southern end of Wood Lane was captured and retained, the remainder held out. A block was built thirty yards up the road and there, and in Orchard Trench, the 7th Battalion, reinforced now by 'B' Company of the 8th Battalion, remained until midnight of the 19th/20th August, when it was relieved and went back to Montauban. The casualties for so small an operation had been heavy; six officers and 264 other ranks, of whom one officer and 62 other ranks killed." Henry was wounded and died three days later in one of the hospitals at Boulogne, and is buried in Boulogne Eastern Cemetery.

THOMAS WOODLEY

Thomas Woodley was born at Drayton, between Didcot and Abingdon, in 1877 (at that time part of Berkshire). He was one of eight children and spent most of his childhood in Oxfordshire, where his father worked as a farm labourer. By the age of thirteen, Thomas had left school and was doing similar work, but by 1900 had moved to Berkshire, and married local girl Emily Gaines. In the census the following year, they were living in Sunninghill, and he was working as a delivery driver, with a horse and cart, for the railway. But the job did not last, and Thomas moved his family back to Botley, near Oxford, to continue farm work. By now he had three children to support, but a further four had died in infancy. He was conscripted in the 12th Labour Battalion, Devonshire Regiment, attesting at Reading, and went to France in June 1916. The Labour Battalions, later to become the Labour Corps, as well as being trained infantrymen, were used for building and maintaining roads, railways, canals, buildings, camps, stores, dumps, telegraph and telephone systems, as well as for moving stores for both men and animals. They often contained men, not considered fit enough to fight in the front line, but who were able to perform labouring jobs in support of the fighting men. In January 1917, Thomas's unit was at Montauban. Although the month started sunny and dry, the weather deteriorated, with snow and severe frosts. Arthur Dease, the son of an Irish Colonel, was in his forties, but served as an ambulance driver, and wrote a series of letters to his mother during the war. He made various references to the weather and conditions in January 1917: "We are back from the muddy front once more & confess am not very sorry. At present in a small town, cold snow, dreary & very uninteresting.... it is snowy & very slushy & beastly generally. Much colder here than on the Somme .... a great many colds & coughs & throats about. This is the dreariest climate, never see the sun by any accident & it rains or snows .... Bitter cold continues, hard frosts & clear days, ground like iron & all lightly covered with snow. This country reminds me of Alberta, Canada." Most of the men in the Devonshires were working on improving and repairing roads in the area, and the War Diary records, "men make very little progress as ground is so hard." One man was wounded on the 17th, and enemy planes dropped bombs near their camp during the night a week later. Figures at the end of the month suggest around 10% of the battalion were in hospital during the month, mostly affected by the conditions. Thomas died in the 39th Casualty Clearing Station on 29th January, and is buried in Allonville Community Cemetery. Within a few months of her husband's death, Emily married Sidney Goddard, and the couple moved to Hope Cottages, London Road, Bracknell. When the local Roll of Honour was being erected in Holy Trinity church, she put Thomas's name forward for inclusion, although he does not appear to have had any connection with the town.

HARMANSWATER UNITED REFORMED CHURCH

Bracknell Congregational Church stood in Bracknell High Street in a position now occupied by the Nat West Bank. It was demolished in 1968. A War Memorial, unveiled on 5th November 1919, is now in St Paul's United Reformed Church, Harmanswater. It lists nine men who made the "supreme sacrifice," and a further 35 who "served with the colours."

G. ALMOND
See Holy Trinity, Bracknell

P. BOWYER
See Ranelagh School

H. HOLLISS
See Holy Trinity, Bracknell

F. RANCE
See Holy Trinity, Bracknell

G. RANCE
See Holy Trinity, Bracknell

R. SARGEANT
See Easthampstead

V. SARGEANT
See Easthampstead

A. SEARLE
See Holy Trinity, Bracknell

V. TAYLOR
See Easthampstead

RANELAGH SCHOOL

The Roll of Honour in the hall at Ranelagh School contains the names of fifteen Old Boys.

PHILIP BOWYER

Philip Daniel Bowyer was born at Warfield in 1896. He was one of four children (a fifth died in infancy), and the family lived near The Three Legged Cross. His father worked as a coachbuilder and wheelwright at the nearby garage. Philip had joined the Berkshire Yeomanry, a mounted arm of the Territorial Force, before the war, and spent two weeks in the summer most years, training at Churn Camp, five miles south of Didcot. The Berkshire Yeomanry went there again at the end of August 1914 to prepare. On arrival of the Brigade Headquarters, it was found that no provision had been made for encampment of troops, and men had to bivouac in the open for the first few days; luckily, the weather was fine. No water was available, but within a few days, cast iron pipes had been laid to bring water to the camp from Blewbury, a short distance to the northeast. In the second half of September, the training began. They remained in Reading until April 1915, when they sailed for Egypt, and were based at Abbassia, Cairo, where they remained for the next few months. The Berkshires arrived in Alexandria early in the morning of the 14th August, having travelled overnight by train. There, they boarded the S.S. 'Lake Michigan' for "an (exact) destination known only to those of a high rank, packed like sardines in a troopship, so overloaded that many of the men had to spend the whole of the .... voyage on deck." The ship arrived at Mudros on the 17th, having sailed a circuitous route to avoid enemy submarines, but did not land; the men were transferred to another ship and continued to Gallipoli. On arrival, they were met by a steam launch towing six boats, each capable of holding fifty men, and went ashore at Suvla Bay in these. Frank Millard, a Reading man, wrote to his parents of the landing: "[We] reached Gallipoli quite safely on August 18th, and although we have been here but 36 hours, we have had quite an exciting time. We did not actually land under fire, but had just disembarked and were carrying our maxims and ammunition off the landing place, when I heard a long whistling, followed by a report. I didn't know what it was at the time, but was soon informed by a Naval officer, who simply said 'Grease - they're on you,' when 'yours truly' picked up two boxes of ammunition, and 'greased' and that quickly." After getting settled, the men were taken off to build a road, before returning to have a swim, which was interrupted by some enemy shells falling in the sea. The next day Frank told his family, "We are not fed badly, and even in this short time we are becoming quite good cooks. Our little dugout consists of a hole scraped in the ground about a foot deep, with a few stones stacked on the earth outside, and some bushes stacked round it. Its outward appearance is very pretty, but inside it might easily be more comfortable. However, things will improve as we go on, so why worry? I don't think we shall be out here long, so you may see me home sooner than you expect." He omitted to mention that two men had already been wounded. On the 20th, there was speculation of a move, and at 8pm, they moved along the coast towards Lala Baba. The rate of march only averaged about one mile per hour, due to frequent halts to allow supply carts to pass both ways along the very narrow road. The 2nd Mounted Division, of which the Berkshire Yeomanry were a part, were the reserve for an attack on Scimitar Hill on the 21st. The Berkshires led the Troop Column towards Chocolate Hill and came under heavy shrapnel fire while crossing a plain, which they later discovered was aptly named 'Shrapnel Valley'. But despite several men going down injured, "there was not the slightest disorder .... the formation of the regiment was perfect." One man described it was "just like being in a hail-storm." They reached the shelter of Chocolate Hill at 4:45pm, with orders to attack the Turkish trenches just 45 minutes later, while it was still daylight. The earlier attack had failed to reach its objective, and the Yeomanry were required to move forward, uphill over unknown territory, in mist and smoke from burning shrubbery which hid their objective, with snipers shooting from trees on both sides. "We got within 800 yards of them, and then down came the shrapnel and shells." By now, they had fixed bayonets, and after pausing some one hundred yards from the Turkish line, a charge was called for. There are several accounts of what happened from then on. "How did the charge begin? Well, an officer shouted, as far as I can recollect, 'Come on, lads! We'll give 'em beans!' That is not exactly according to drill-books and regulations as I know them; but it was enough. It let the boys loose, and they simply leapt forward and went for the Turkish trenches." "The final charge is impossible to describe. As soon as we got over the gully, there was a fusillade of shells and rifles, and machine guns seemed all around us. It seemed impossible to live through, and that was where we had most casualties. We, or what was left of us, took two lines of trenches." "Although there had been many casualties, the Regiment then swept over the ridge into the enemy's trenches, Major Gooch being the first man in. Part of the ground captured was held by the Regiment, with other Yeomanry, until early the next morning, when, under orders, a retirement was conducted in good order, as the position was considered untenable in the daytime." ".... owing to enfilade fire down the left, the trench could not be held, and after about ten minutes had to be evacuated." "Our Brigade, with the Berks doing the leading, got right on top of the hill we were set to capture, by means of two bayonet charges after continual rushes, but the order came that all Yeomanry were to retire to a certain spot. It did seem a pity after what we had done and given." "Personally I got it coming back, but came across several wounded and did what little I could to relieve them, arriving at our trenches about 10 a.m. on Sunday morning. I was just in time for the roll call, and when hearing the figures it was as much as I could do to keep my pecker up." An unknown trooper would later write home: "Sorry to say, the Berks Yeomanry got rather badly cut up: cannot seem to find any of my pals." Philip was killed in the assault, and is buried in Green Hill Cemetery, one of only nine men from the Berkshire Yeomanry whose bodies were recovered for burial. He is also listed on the Roll of Honour inside Warfield Church.

JOHN CALLINGHAM

See Easthampstead

WILLIAM DIAPER

See Easthampstead

CYRIL FRANKLIN

Cyril George Franklin was born in 1899 at Chobham, Surrey, and was the eldest of three children. His father was a schoolmaster, and later the headmaster, at Valley End School. After attending Ranelagh, Cyril was conscripted into the 5th Battalion, London Regiment, attesting in London, although he listed his place of residence as Windlesham. The battalion were heavily involved in the German Spring Offensive at Arras in March 1918, and would be fighting around Arras in August. They had been in the front trenches at Beaurains earlier that month, and were relieved on the 16th. Starting the following day, they made their way to Arras, making some of the journey by train and bus. Late on the 19th, there was gas shelling in which Cyril was wounded. He died two days later, and is buried in Ligny-St. Flochel British Cemetery, Averdoingt.

The late 2nd Lieut. O. O. GOSWELL, Queen's Westminsters, 24, Barkham Rd. Wokingham.—Killed in action.

OWEN GOSWELL

Oliver Owen Goswell was born on 2nd March 1898 at Faringdon, Oxfordshire (but part of Berkshire until the boundary change of 1974). His mother was the matron of the local workhouse, but his father died when Oliver was only two years of age; previously both parents had been employed on the staff at the workhouse in Cheltenham. Presumably it as thought the workhouse was not a suitable place for the young boy to grow up as by 1911, Oliver was living with relations in Barkham Road, Wokingham, the town where his father had been born in 1859. He was conscripted into the 15th Battalion, London Regiment, attesting in June 1916 at Swindon, where he worked for the Inland Revenue. He had already applied for a commission in the Army Service Corps at the start of the year, while still a student, but was informed there were no spare places. After seven months in the Army Reserve, he was mobilized in February 1917. He was six feet tall, and weighed almost twelve stone. After producing two letters from his employer, offering no objection to him, as a Civil Servant, from applying for a commission, he was accepted at No. 6 Officer Cadet Battalion at Balliol College, Oxford. As in the Second World War, there were protected occupations (known as Starred Professions), which were considered necessary for the war effort and the running of the country; workers in these professions were exempt from being called-up. The list of Starred Professions was updated as the war dragged on, and more men were needed at the front. As an example, attendants at Broadmoor were exempt until June 1918, although some still volunteered to serve. Owen was granted a commission at the end of October. He was attached to the $2/16^{th}$ Battalion, London Regiment, and sailed from Folkestone on 26th January 1918, arriving in Alexandria precisely one month later. Jericho had been captured at about the same time, and occupation of the Jordan Valley began. At the end of April, the battalion were ordered to attack line running from El Haud to Wari Arsenayet. Deployment was completed by 8pm, but the War Diary notes that the moon was almost full, and the men were visible from almost half a mile away. The enemy were holding a ridge with precipitous approaches and strong advance posts, but their artillery barrage and rifle and machine gun fire were all ineffective. The advance posts were quickly driven in, and 'A' and 'C' Companies advanced up the spurs leading to ridge. 'B' followed suit, but came under very heavy machine gun and rifle fire at close range from the enemy's main position. The position was cleared with bayonets, and captured by 4:15am, with more than seventy prisoners-of-war, and four machine guns being captured. The line was then subject to heavy machine gun fire from both flanks, as the enemy held strong positions on the dominating hills, north of Arseniyet. Owing to the difficulty in locating the enemy machine guns, and the inability to call for artillery support because of a broken telephone wire, it was impossible to advance any further that day. The enemy shelled the front line heavily all day, killing twenty men, and wounding more than eighty others. Owen was one of two officers killed; his body was never recovered, and his name is listed on the Jerusalem Memorial. The list of Owen's personal effects, returned to his mother, is extensive: a haversack, pyjama suit, three pairs of pants, a holdall, breeches, puttees, handkerchief, towel undervest, a pair of braces, slacks, field boots, slippers, and a 50 centime note. In addition, there was a valise with a large assortment of military clothing and toiletries, as well as books, letters, photos, postcards, writing pads, notebooks and a cheque book. Despite all these items, Owen's mother wrote to the war Office in February 1919, enquiring after a watch, obviously an item of great sentimental importance, but despite searches and enquiries, it was "lost." There was also confusion over whether he had left a will, as his Customs and Excise Office initially claimed he had left one, but further investigation found this not to be the case. At the time of his death, Owen's mother had retired, and was living at Winnersh. A short article in the Reading Chronicle of 18th May 1918, tells of the death of Owen: "Second Lieutenant O. O. Goswell of the Queen's Westminster Rifles, was killed in Palestine aged 20. The only son of the late Owen Goswell and Mrs Goswell. Mrs Goswell is the Matron of Farringdon Union, the deceased was well known in Wokingham, and was a scholar at the Council school where he won a scholarship, completing his education at Rasleigh (sic) College, afterwards entering the civil service. For many years he resided with his uncle H. Goswell of Barkham Road, and made many friends."

RICHARD GOULDING

Richard Cecil Goulding was born in October 1899 at Brading on the Isle of Wight. He was the eldest of four children (including a pair of twins), with a younger sister dying in infancy. His father worked away from home as a butler when Richard was born, but as the family grew, he took a job as a hotel waiter, and the family moved, first to Camberley, and then to Crowthorne, where he worked at the Waterloo Hotel. Richard attended Crowthorne School and Ranelagh School in Bracknell, appearing on the Roll of Honour in both establishments, was a member of the Crowthorne Boy Scouts troop, and also sang in the village church choir. Not wanting to miss out on the 'excitement' of war, he joined the Guards Band of the King's Royal Rifles on 1st December 1914, attesting at Winchester, and claimed to be almost sixteen year old. He was just 5'2" tall, weighed less than seven stone, with blue eyes, fair hair, and a fresh complexion, and recorded his profession as musician. His young age was soon discovered, and a letter from his parents to the authorities the following June agreed to his serving in the band, although he would not be eligible to serve overseas until he reached the age of nineteen. In October 1916, he was transferred to the 5th Battalion, based at Sheerness, Kent, performing coastal defence and other home duties, where he remained until February 1918, although correspondence reveals there were still questions about his age, compounded by the pay office granting him proficiency pay before the due date, an error picked up and corrected by the Colonel of the Regiment. Richard served in France with the 13th Battalion until September 1918, when he was wounded and admitted to hospital for treatment, before rejoining his battalion on 19th October. On 4th November, they made an attack through the village of Louvignies-lez-Quesnoy at 6:15am. Although faced with a heavy enemy barrage, it mostly fell behind them, and caused little trouble. Enemy machine gun fire was troublesome from the orchards and hedges to the west of the village, but with the aid of a tank, they moved slowly forward, although it was not until dusk that they captured both the village and a nearby ridge, on which the Germans had made a determined stand. Richard, now with the Lewis Gun section, was one of the day's casualties, and is buried in Beaurain British Cemetery. In July the following year, his father wrote, asking if there were any personal effects to be returned, but only one letter was found, and forwarded to the grieving family. Richard's name is also listed in the lych gate at Crowthorne.

Kenneth Grant

Kenneth Henry Grant was born on 30th November 1896 at Wimbourne, Dorset, the youngest of four children. His father worked as a domestic gardener, and the family soon moved to Sunningdale, and then to Lock's Ride in Chavey Down. Kenneth must have been very intelligent, as he first attended Ranelagh School from 1908 to 1914, before going to Reading University. His studies there were interrupted when war broke out, and he applied for a commission on 23rd June 1915, having been a member of the University O.T.C. since the day after war had been declared. He was almost 5'11" tall, and weighed nearly ten and a half stone. Kenneth was posted to the 10th Battalion, Seaforth Highlanders, a Training Unit based at Dunfermline in Scotland, and then attached to the 8th Battalion, which he joined in early June the following year. On 26th August, the battalion were in Gourlay Trench, midway between Bapaume and Albert, having relieved 9th Battalion, Black Watch in the front line at 3am. The War Diary makes two mentions for the day, "situation quite normal" and "day and night quiet." It then goes on to say that Lieutenant Grant was killed in action, another officer wounded, and two other ranks were killed, with another sixteen wounded, but gives no further details. To get some idea of the amount of paperwork generated during the course of the war, the file for the battalion at The National Archives, Kew, contains no fewer than 51 appendices, containing maps, orders, messages and orders for this month alone. Over four months after his death was reported, Kenneth was buried in Villa Wood Cemetery, north of Mametz Wood. After the Armistice, over one thousand graves in the vicinity, including Kenneth's, were moved to Flatiron Copse Cemetery, Mametz.

Frederick Harris

See Easthampstead

Maurice Kenward

Maurice Kenward was born in 1899 at Kilburn, London, the younger of two brothers. His father worked as a stationer's assistant, but died before Maurice was three years old. His mother moved to Sunningdale, along with her elderly parents and spinster sister, and worked as a confectioner while her son attended school; meanwhile Maurice's older brother was placed in an orphanage in Purley, Surrey. After attending Ranelagh School, Maurice was conscripted into the 5th Battalion, London Regiment, attesting in London, although still living in Sunningdale. The battalion were heavily involved in German Spring Offensive at Arras in March 1918, and would be fighting around Arras in August. Before that, they were in the front line at Baurains from the 7th. There was some light shelling on the 8th, and also on the 9th around the Battalion Headquarters in the afternoon. The War Diary records that one man was wounded; that man was Maurice, who died the next day. His grave was not found after the war, so his name is listed on the Vis-en-Artois Memorial.

ARTHUR LOXLEY

Arthur Harry Loxley was born on 15th August 1898 at West Horsley near Guildford, the elder of two boys. His father was a farmer at Wix Farm, East Horsley in 1901, but by 1911 had made a complete career change, and was working as a coal merchant, living in Wellington Road, Wokingham, and earning enough money to employ a domestic servant. Arthur attended Ranelagh School, and then may have taken a post as a legal clerk as he joined the Inns of Court O.T.C. in June 1915. The Inns of Court Officer Training Corps was based in Berkhamsted, and was originally part of the London Territorial Force, consisting mainly of men connected with the law courts. The subjects covered were drill, musketry (although limited by a shortage of suitable ranges), entrenching (but little in the way of trench warfare, apart from bombing), map reading, field exercises in open warfare (designed to instil leadership and initiative), and lectures, which covered a whole range of subjects from sanitation, through tactics, to the history of the war. After only three months, he applied for a commission, adding two years to his age. He was 5'6" tall, and weighed ten stone, and was accepted. However, his subterfuge may have been discovered, as he did not join his unit, the 4th Battalion, North Staffordshire Regiment, until October 1916, and was attached to the 6th Battalion, Yorkshire Light Infantry to go to France. Although 'other ranks' were required to be nineteen to serve overseas, for Officers the age was a year less! The Regimental History records the action of the early spring in 1917: "The Germans retreated to the Hindenburg Line, a well-prepared defensive position, capable of being held with fewer men, bringing the Allies forward over ground with no supporting infrastructure. At the beginning of April, as the British moved cautiously forward, the Yorkshires were in billets in Berneville, preparing for Battle of Arras. Trenches representing the first and second objectives had been marked out on the ground, alongside the Arras to Doullens road, and frequent practise attacks were carried out. At the same time, lines of assembly trenches were being dug, east of Beaurains, the enemy offering no opposition. On the night of the 7th, the battalion proceeded through Arras to the caves at Ronville, where they remained until 8pm the next evening. Under the paving of Arras, lie impressive chalk quarries, dug since the Middle Ages. In six months, around 450 members of the New Zealand Engineers Tunnelling Company linked up the quarries to create an underground network of caves, where 24,000 soldiers could be quartered, waiting for the offensive to start. The Yorkshires took up their position in assembly trenches; during move and time in the trenches, such good discipline was maintained, the enemy were unaware they were occupied until attack started. From midnight, nine small parties of men went out and cut the German wire in front of the first objective. They were continuously sniped and machine gunned, which caused a few casualties. At 5:30am, the attack commenced well to the north, gradually worked south. Six tanks reached the assembly trench at 7:15am, and twenty minutes later, the artillery barrage started, and the leading waves left the assembly trenches. The first objective, Pine Trench, was taken by 8am without difficulty and with only slight casualties, and the capture of 35 Germans. The attack continued to Fir Alley Redoubt, a triangular system of very strong, deep trenches, very heavily wired. The defences had not been much damaged by the bombardment, but under cover of the barrage, the men got through the wire and captured the Redoubt. Again, the enemy offered only slight resistance, and another 25 prisoners of war were taken, with another six later being brought out of a dug-out. The Redoubt was taken by 8:15am. Two platoons were left to consolidate, the rest followed the barrage lift to attack Telegraph Hill trench. Some casualties occurred during the advance from machine gun fire from Neuville Vitasse and shells, but Telegraph Hill trench was taken within half an hour. Again, resistance was slight, and more prisoners were taken. Another two platoons were left to consolidate, and the rest pushed on to Covell Switch. Both this and Telegraph Hill trench part of Hindenburg Line, consisted of a very deep and wide trench with a few deep dug-outs (mostly in course of construction). Covell Switch was taken ten minutes later, and another 85 prisoners taken. Some Germans on the right gave some trouble, but were pushed back by a bombing attack. At 1:30pm, 150 of the enemy attempted a counter-attack, but were driven off." The attack continued on the following day, but Arthur would take no part in it, having been killed. He is buried in Tilloy British Cemetery, Tilloy-les-Mofflaines.

Terence Mackay

See Easthampstead

Arthur Myatt

Arthur Foster William Myatt was born at Walworth, London in 1893, the elder of two boys. His father worked as a domestic coachman. The 1901 census recorded Arthur visiting Brighton with his mother and brother, but his father is still in Kensington and, presumably, working. His father died the following year, and by 1911, the three of them were living in Howard Road, Wokingham. Arthur had finished his schooling, but was a 'pupil teacher student' at Reading University. He was conscripted into the Army in February 1916, attesting at Maidenhead, and joined the 15th Battalion, London Regiment. The battalion fought in phases of the Battle of the Somme later that year, as well as the Battle of Messines, a phase of the Third Battle of Ypres, and at Cambrai in 1917, where they captured Bourlon Wood from the Germans and then held off several counter-attacks. Arthur was awarded the Military Medal for bravery which was recorded in the Reading Mercury: "Local Schoolmaster wins Military Medal. Lance-Corporal Arthur Myatt, City of London Regiment, Civil Service Rifles, has just been awarded the Military Medal for an act of great gallantry. On a night in June his company was holding a front trench. On being relieved Lance-Corporal Myatt and his chum were the only fit men left. All night, with their Lewis gun, they held off the enemy, beside attending to the wounded. Mr Myatt is a well-known local schoolmaster, and was educated at Palmer School and Culham College." On 1st December, ten men of the battalion were wounded while being relieved in the front line trenches; Arthur was one of them and died two days later. He is buried in St Sever Cemetery Extension, Rouen. His name is also recorded on the Roll of Honour at Reading University.

William Scribbins

William Howard Scribbins, known as Howard, was born in Crowthorne on 6th November 1899, the eldest of three children. His father worked as a clerk, and later steward, at Wellington College. By 1911, Howard was attending Ranelagh School in Bracknell, a co-educational, fee-paying grammar school, although only part-time. He joined the Royal Flying Corps on 17th November 1917, and was based at Farnborough. He was appointed Flight Second Lieutenant at the end of July the following year. On 22nd August 1918, while flying an Avro RE8 from Number 1 Training Depot Station at Stamford, Lincolnshire (now RAF Wittering), Howard was killed in an aeroplane accident, and is buried in Crowthorne churchyard, on the north side of the church. The Reading Mercury of 31st August 1918 carried a report of his burial: "The death, the result of a flying accident, of Flight Lieutenant William Howard Scribbins, RAF, has occasioned much regret in Crowthorne, both he and his parents having been so very well known in the district. Much sympathy is felt for his parents, Mr and Mrs Scribbins of Wellington College, who had the sad experience of witnessing the accident that terminated their son's career. The deceased was only 18 years of age, and after passing through various courses in his training with continuous success, had recently been appointed instructor. He was buried with Military Honours in Crowthorne Churchyard on Monday." William's name is also listed in the lych gate at Crowthorne.

Frederick Swain

Frederick James Swain was born in 1898 at Tunbridge Wells, Kent, and had one younger brother. His father was working as an ironmonger's assistant at the time of 1901 census, by which time the family had moved to Lewisham. Ten years later, the family had moved again, with Frederick's father now having his own grocery business in Rose Street, Wokingham, and it is likely young Frederick worked in the shop until he was called up, joining the 25th Squadron, Royal Flying Corps, in 1917. In October of that year, the Squadron moved to Boeseghem, southwest of Hazebrouck, where its activities increased dramatically. Instead of operating over an area limited to the extent on one Army Front, its duties involved the Fronts covered by all the British Armies. Its work consisted of long-range reconnaissance, photography, and bombing of distant targets outside the Army area. In addition to the strategic raids, the Squadron also bombed tactical targets. During these patrols, the formations were protected by escorts of Bristol Fighters. During the first two months of 1918, the Squadron did less bombing, and made an increasing number of photographic reconnaissance. On 27th February 1918, Frederick and his pilot, Lieut. Maurice Dickens, were testing a DH4 a two-seat biplane, day-bomber (Serial Number A7733) which crashed into sea (it was thought to have been shot down). This type of plane was considered to be the best single-engined bomber of the First World War; even when fully loaded with bombs, its reliability and impressive performance made it highly popular with its crews. The plane and the pilot's body were salvaged four months later, but Frederick's body was never found, and he is listed on the Arras Flying Services Memorial. His name also appears on the War Memorial erected in Wokingham Baptist Church.

Edmund Toy

Edmund Charles Toy was born at Christow, Devon, on 26th July 1899. His parents both came from Littlehampton in Sussex, but his father worked firstly as a railway cashier in Devon (1901 census), and then as a Public Works contractor's manager in Swansea (1911 census). At some time after this, the family moved to Ascot which brought Edmund to Ranelagh School. In 1914, after a massive fund-raising effort, Crystal Palace was bought for the nation, just days before the outbreak of war. The trustees immediately offered it to the Admiralty for training facilities, and over 125,000 men passed through it. Edmund went there in the summer of 1917 and qualified as a Probationary Flight Officer. It was probably during this period that he obtained extra qualifications in magnetism and electricity from Regent Street Polytechnic. He then went to the Royal Naval Air Services Training School at Manston, Kent in August for six months, before spending a further three months at the Officer and Aircrew Selection Centre at Cranwell. This was followed by a posting to Freiston, Lincolnshire, where he piloted a Sopwith Camel, and was commissioned a Second Lieutenant in July 1918. In this month, he also joined 213 Squadron, based at Bergues, just south of Dunkirk. His last flight was on 25th August 1918, flying his Camel (Serial Number B6358). He was last seen in combat with five enemy aircraft, ten miles south of Ostende. Edmund's body was never found, and he is listed on the Arras Flying Services Memorial.

BRACKNELL BOWLING AND SOCIAL CLUB

Bracknell Bowling club was situated in Stanley Road, off Bracknell High Street. It merged with Bracknell Social Club in 1970, and moved to its current premises on Church Road soon after. The Roll of Honour, a framed list of 33 members of the Club who fought in the war including three who were killed, hangs in the Club foyer.

B. E. Carr

Bertram Edward Carr was born in 1877 at Brighton. He was the second of nine surviving children, two others dying young. His father was a Baptist Minister, moving frequently to new posts, and the family lived in Lincolnshire and Leicestershire, before settling in Bath, Somerset. Bertram, by now, had left home and was making artwork from metal. In the 1901 census, he was visiting a family in Mortlake, and married their daughter Winifred at Richmond Register Office on Christmas Day 1906. After the birth of their first child, they moved to Bracknell, where three more children were born; of their children, two daughters survived, but two sons both died in 1914. Bertram worked as a shop assistant in an ironmongery in the High Street. He enlisted under the Derby Scheme in December 1915, attesting at Wokingham, and joined the 14th Battalion, London Regiment. By now, he had become manager of the shop, and was living in Stanley Road, a step away from the High Street. As his service record survives, we know he was about 5'6" tall and weighed ten and a half stone; the physical inspection to gauge his suitability for active service was performed by Doctor Fielden, a well-known and respected local physician who lived at the top of the High Street (the clock from his house is now in the office building opposite The Old Manor). Bertram was mobilised in January 1917 and, after four months of training, sailed from Folkestone to Boulogne, arriving on 10th May, joining his unit the following month. He was wounded in July and spent a month recovering before returning to active service. On 19th November, the battalion were at Beugny, awaiting orders. These arrived early in the morning, three days later, and they moved to the British front line in front of Louvereval. The 3rd Army attack on the Hindenberg Line was already in progress, and they were to continue the attack, commencing at 6:00am the next morning. However, the adjacent Brigade failed to get forward, leaving them in a deep valley and under enfilade fire from Germans on higher ground. They remained here until the early afternoon, when 'D' Company and the Stokes Mortars managed to cross the valley and surround the German garrison firing on them, capturing nearly eighty of them. A counter-attack developed from the west, preceded by heavy shell fire, but after managing to get bombs forward to 'B' Company, it was repulsed. Bertram was killed during the fighting, and is buried in Moeuvres Communal Cemetery Extension. As the village and cemetery remained in German hands until September 1918, it was presumably they that found and buried his body. Almost half the burials there are of unknown men. Bertram was initially one of these, but has subsequently been identified and is now listed, along with thirty others, on a Special Memorial in the cemetery.

R. LARCOMBE

George William Larcombe was born at Beaminster, Dorset, in 1881. He came from a family of twelve children, but five died in infancy. Like his father, George was a farm labourer. He married Lilian Holborn in 1909. He was conscripted into the 14th Battalion, Gloucestershire Regiment, attesting at Dorchester, and was mobilised in March 1916. The battalion were not involved in any major action until mid July 1916, one of the phases of the Battle of the Somme. Later in the month, on the 26th, the Gloucesters took their turn in the trenches at Billon Wood, near Maricourt. They were in the support trench, and spent most of their time working on communications trenches, coming under bombardment for an hour and a half on the 29th. They were relieved next day at about 1:30pm, but just before the relief started, the trench and roads were heavily bombarded with High Explosive and gas shells. The War Diary records the casualties as "slight"; but George was one of them. His body was not recovered, and his name is listed on the Thiepval Memorial. His widow remained in the Bracknell area and remarried in 1924.

L. TRODD

Laurence Richard Trodd - see Holy Trinity, Bracknell

BRACKNELL DISTRICT WORKING MEN'S CLUB

Bracknell Working Men's Club was also located in Stanley Road, off the High Street. The AGM, held on Monday February 7th 1921, resolved to place "a memorial in the Club to those who had fallen in the Great War." The memorial, which has been lost, listed 117 men, twenty of whom were killed in the conflict.

H. BAKER
See Holy Trinity, Bracknell

H. BELCHER
See Easthampstead

S. W. BROWN
See Holy Trinity, Bracknell

J. CALLINGHAM
See Easthampstead

ALF. DAVIS
See Holy Trinity, Bracknell

E. T. DAVIS
See Easthampstead

S. H. EWINS
See Holy Trinity, Bracknell

W. GILKERSON
See Easthampstead

H. HOLLISS
See Holy Trinity, Bracknell

E. HOLLOWAY
See Holy Trinity, Bracknell

C. LANGLEY
See Easthampstead

R. A. LEGG
See Holy Trinity, Bracknell

JOE LEWIS

Joseph Frederick Lewis was born on 6th September 1887 at Sunningdale, and baptised there 13th November. He was one of six children, two of whom were born in Ireland, which was not to gain its independence until 1922. His father was working as a domestic coachman at the time, but later got a job as a stud groom, probably at Warfield Hall where Sir Charles Brownlow was breeding horses, and the family moved to Newell Green. After leaving school, Joseph worked in domestic service, and appears in the 1911 census as a footman at Tyringham House, Newport Pagnall, one of fourteen servants working for an American banker, his wife and infant son. He volunteered for service, attesting at Wokingham on 31st August 1914, joined the 1st Battalion, Royal Berkshire Regiment, and went to France at the end of November. The battalion were in training when his draft arrived, and he would not be in the front trenches until three days before Christmas. The battalion were involved in the fighting at Neuve Chapelle and Loos in 1915, and the Battle of Delville Wood the following year. The Reading Mercury reported him to be invalided and wounded, but gives no indication as to when this occurred. The Berkshires had not been involved in any major action since the end of August 1916, and the War Diary for the first few days in November records the enemy artillery as being very active, with one man wounded on the 2nd, and another on the 5th. Joseph, with the rank of sergeant, died of wounds on the latter date, so it is probable that he was one of the men referred to. He is buried in Euston Road Cemetery, Colincamps.

F. LOVEGROVE
See Easthampstead

S. LOVEGROVE
See Easthampstead

The late Sergt. H. J. PINNELL, Station Road, Bracknell.—Killed in action. Aged 22.

J. PINNELL

Henry John Pinnell, known by his middle name, was born in 1893 at Sandhurst, but grew up in Bracknell. He was the eldest of five children, another two other dying in childhood. His father worked as a baker and confectioner, a business John joined after leaving school. By now, the family had moved from Wokingham Road to Station Road. He was already a member of the 1/4th Battalion, Royal Berkshire Regiment, a Territorial Battalion, when war broke out, having attested at Wokingham. They had started their annual training at Marlow two days earlier, but immediately brought back to Reading. All the men were invited to volunteer for foreign service, with the majority heeding the call. Much of the training took place in and around Chelmsford, before they arrived in France at the end of March 1915, where they spent their first night on a hill overlooking Boulogne, shivering under a thin blanket and awoke to driving snow. A month later, they were in the front line for the first time. Through the rest of the year and the first half of 1916, they took their turn in and out of the line, with the occasional raids to break the monotony, but were not involved in any major actions. Nor were they involved in the great Battle of the Somme on 1st July, but received orders for an attack two days later, but this was cancelled at short notice, much to the disappointment of the men. On 20th July, they were at La Boiselle, and preparing for an attack three days later. The 4th Oxfordshires led the attack, and just before 4am, the Berkshires moved forward to support them. Their entry proved decisive, and the enemy were forced back. During the afternoon, the captured positions were heavily shelled, but there was no counter-attack, and the Berkshires were relieved at 10:30pm that evening. 25 men were killed, and just over one hundred wounded. John, now a Sergeant, was one of those killed, and as his body was never recovered, his name is listed on the Thiepval Memorial.

H. RIXON

See Easthampstead

C. SARGEANT

See Easthampstead

L. TODD

See Holy Trinity, Bracknell

R. TODD

See Easthampstead

OTHER GRAVES

There are two other graves in Larges Lane Cemetery of men who were war casualties, but who are not listed in Holy Trinity Church.

HARRY MILLS

Joseph Henry Mills, see Easthampstead

LIONEL RAINFORD

Lionel Rainford was born 16th October 1891 in Sicily, where his grandfather was the Vice Consul, and his father involved in viticulture. In the 1901 census, Lionel was living with his mother in lodgings in Richmond, Surrey, while his two elder sisters were attending a convent school in Worthing. In 1903, they all visited their father, who by now had moved to Australia and was employed as a civil servant, advising on the growing of vines, and treatment of their diseases, publishing several books and papers on the subject. By 1911, Lionel had left school and was working as a political enquiry clerk, living with his mother and sisters in Hammersmith. His mother listed her profession as electrolysist, a practitioner of the pseudo-science of treating minor ailments with low voltage electricity. She died in 1927 from accidental electrocution. Lionel joined the Royal Naval Air Service on 3rd November 1914, acting as a motorcycle messenger. His Naval record describes him as 5'9" tall, with grey eyes, brown hair, and a fresh complexion. He was based at Eastchurch, Isle of Sheppey, Kent, which was the Royal Navy Air Service base for training and experimentation in naval aviation. It later became the base for aircraft defending the Medway Naval bases, London and the Thames Estuary, during the war. The RNAS was merged with the Royal Flying Corps in 1918 to form the RAF. On 16th December 1914, his body was found beside the road at Bottle Bridge (outside the 'Three-Legged Cross' on the Maidenhead road). An inquest was held the following day, and reported in the Reading Mercury under the headline "Naval Air Mechanic's Death. An inquest was held on Thursday on the body of a Naval air mechanic, who died as a result of a motorcycle accident. The unfortunate cyclist crashed into the wall of Bot Bridge, Warfield. This bridge is rather narrow, both in width and length. The verdict was 'Accidental death'." The coroner found the cause of death to be a fractured skull. The Reading Mercury of 26th December reported on the funeral: "Amidst a torrential downpour of rain, the remains of the unfortunate air mechanic Lionel Rainford, whose sad death was reported in last week's paper, were borne to rest on Saturday, when his comrades paid him a fitting tribute. The body had lain at the residence of Dr Feilden, and thence it was carried on shoulders of his comrades to Holy Trinity Church .... The cortege then formed up, and the coffin was borne by two rows of Naval Air Brigade men, and was followed by an armoured car fitted up as a bier .... The detachment of Naval Men present, numbering about 150 .... and motor dispatch riders, acted as bearers ... *a* firing party of twenty fired three volleys, *while* buglers played the Last Post." The grave, with a marble surround, is located by following the main path to the far end of the cemetery, then turning left. It is further along on the left, at the junction with a grass path, behind a small shrub. The inscriptions read: "Lionel Rainford R. N. Air Service aged 23 killed serving his country December 16th 1914."

EASTHAMPSTEAD

ST MICHAEL AND ST MARY MAGDALENE CHURCH

The memorial cross in the churchyard, listing 65 names, was unveiled on 14th February 1920. A memorial tablet inside the church, with the same men arranged by regiment, was donated by Lady Haversham, of South Hill Park, and unveiled on 2nd July 1921. The parish included Priestwood, and a daughter church, dedicated to St Andrew, stood on the site now occupied by Boyd Court.

MATTHEW JOHN ALLWRIGHT

The birth of Matthew John Allwright was registered in 1898, but he may have been born at the end of the previous year as he was baptised on 6th January in St Andrew's Church. He was the second of seven children, and grew up in Waltham Cottages, Binfield Road. His father worked in one of the local brickyards, probably at the local one on Skimped Hill Lane, now the site of Arlington Square. Matthew joined the 7th Battalion, Berkshire Regiment under the Derby Scheme, attesting at Wokingham. By the time he had completed his training and was ready for action, the battalion were in Salonika in Greece. Much of the time there was fairly monotonous, with spells in the front line, where work on the trenches seems to have been the main activity recorded in the War Diary. Malaria and dysentery were a greater threat than the enemy. The circumstances of Matthew's death are not entirely clear. He was initially buried in the German Cemetery at Skopje which implies he had been taken prisoner as some point. On 8th May 1917, the Battalion were in Christmas Ravine, just west of La Tortue, when the British artillery was bombarding the enemy all day. Two companies were ordered to join an attack in the early hours of next day, while the remaining two companies remained in support. Some casualties were incurred from enemy shells during the advance, and more when they occupied the front line trenches, which were subject to heavy trench-mortar fire. Attempts at a further advance were checked, partly because any forward trenches were too shallow to offer any cover against enemy fire which was becoming increasingly heavy. Eventually, the Berkshire men were forced to retire, but the situation was somewhat confused, with some retreating and some staying in place. By the end of the day, the battalion had lost fifteen men killed, over 130 wounded, and nine missing. Matthew was reported as a Prisoner of War in the Reading Mercury of 25th July 1917. A request to the Red Cross for news of him had been made by his relatives before this date, so could well have been one of those reported missing. He died on 31st October, either from wounds or, more likely, of disease. Another five men, from different regiments, were also buried in the German Cemetery, probably after having been treated in a German Hospital. When bodies were being consolidated into War Cemeteries after the war, these six graves could not be located, so a memorial to each was erected in Skopje British Cemetery.

WILLIAM BARKER

William Barker was born in 1884, one of four children. The family lived in Station Road where his father worked as a blacksmith. William's mother died when he was only eleven years old, and his father was later admitted to Berkshire County Lunatic Asylum at Cholsey, near Wallingford, where he remained until his death in 1935. After leaving school, William worked as a labourer in one of the local brickyards, but later moved away from the area. By 1911, he was a lodger at an address in Godalming, Surrey, working as a plasterer. At the outbreak of war, he volunteered for service, attesting at Reading, and joined the 5th Battalion, Berkshire Regiment. Initial training was done in Kent before marching to Aldershot, through snow, at the end of February 1915. Three months later, the battalion left by train for Folkestone and sailed for Boulogne. At some point, William was transferred to the 1/5th Battalion, Northumberland Fusiliers; this may have been in February 1918, when a reorganisation of the 13th Division took place. On 8th April, the Fusiliers marched to Le Sart, halting at 4:30am the following morning under heavy bombardment. At 10am, they continued to Chapelle Duvelle, and three hours later, were ordered to move further forward to Trou Bayard. Merville and Estaires were both being shelled, and roads around the former were blocked. By 4pm, the battalion were in position, with orders to counter-attack if the enemy crossed the nearby river Lys. Shelling was still heavy, and the sound of heavy machine gun fire reached them from south of Estaires. By 9:30pm, they had taken up strong points during a quiet spell, and although the shelling was not so heavy, the enemy seemed to be close. Just before midnight, reports were received the Germans had crossed the river near Bas St Mur, but had been driven back by the 40th Division. One shell must have landed near William, as he died on the 9th; his body was never recovered, and his name is listed on the Ploegsteert Memorial.

HARRY BELCHER

Harry Belcher was born toward the end of 1893, and baptised on 13th March the following year, probably at St Andrew's Church, as the family lived in Binfield Road; later they moved to Priestwood Terrace in Downshire Way. He was the youngest of seven surviving children, another dying young, supported by his father who worked as a carpenter. After leaving school, Harry worked as a grocer's assistant. He was already a member of the 1/4th Battalion, Royal Berkshire Regiment, a Territorial Battalion, when war broke out, having attested at Wokingham. They had started their annual training at Marlow two days earlier, but immediately brought back to Reading. All the men were invited to volunteer for foreign service, with the majority heeding the call, but Harry chose, for whatever reason, to stay in England until 1916. The Berkshires were not involved in the great Battle of the Somme on 1st July, but received orders for an attack two days later, but this was cancelled at short notice, much to the disappointment of the men. They were not involved in an attack again until the 23rd, when about one third of them were wounded. His first winter abroad was bitterly cold, but the battalion were in billets after Christmas, training with bombs and Lewis Guns. In February they moved back into the trenches, but with overnight temperatures registering twenty degrees of frost, digging was impossible, and water froze in the buckets as it was being carried forward to the trenches. Mild spells were invariably accompanied by fogs and mists, masking the German withdrawal to the Hindenburg Line, all buildings and infrastructure being destroyed as they went. By 4th April 1917, the Brigade was ordered to prepare for the capture of the three villages of Ronssoy, Basse Boulogne and Lempire. Snow fell all day, obscuring the attempts of the Company Commander to see the lie of the land. The Battalion moved forward from Villers-Faucon at 2am, and were in position two hours later, east of Templeux Wood. There was just under a mile to cover to reach Ronssoy, but it contained small coppices, lanes and ditches, all of which were thought to contain enemy outposts. The attack went remarkably well and, despite some enfilade fire on one company early on, little resistance was met, as the Germans were not anticipating it; some were just sitting down to breakfast when the Allies arrived in the village and fled, leaving their soup, coffee and sausages to be enjoyed by the British. British artillery fire, unfortunately, came down on some of the battalion on the east of the village, causing a few casualties. By the end of the day, nine men had been killed, around forty wounded, and another two were missing; one of these was Harry and his name is recorded on the Thiepval Memorial.

The late ALFRED BRANT, High Street, Bracknell.—Killed in action.

ALFRED BRANT

Alfred William Brant was born in 1885 in Binfield, and baptised in the local church on 7th February the following year. He came from a large family, being the second youngest of ten children with three more dying in infancy. The family lived in the area around Moss End Farm where his father worked, travelling round the local area with a cart, selling vegetables. Alfred also worked, off and on, as a farm labourer (in the 1901 census, his occupation is listed as "at home," despite being sixteen years of age). In 1910 he married Fanny Bye with a daughter being born at about the same time, and several more children following in the next five years. He volunteered for service, attesting at Chertsey, joined the Royal Engineers, and arrived in France towards the end of August 1915. He appears to have had a spell in the infantry, fighting with the East Surrey Regiment, but returned to the Royal Engineers, and was with 79th Field Company in the 18th (Eastern) Division at the time of his death. As well as performing construction and maintenance work, the Field Companies, which were attached to the fighting portions of a Division, also saw action and took part in the fighting. Many kinds of trade were required in the army, and Field Companies would typically contain farriers, shoeing smiths, trumpeters, blacksmiths, bricklayers, carpenters, clerks, masons, painters, plumbers, surveyors, draughtsmen, wheelwrights, engine drivers, sappers, and batmen. The unit was at Boezinge towards the end of November 1917, working on drainage, a bridge over the Steenbeck, and the erection of Boezinge Canal and Baboon Camps. On the last day of the month, they undertook work during the night, erecting camouflage screens in the vicinity of Angle Point and Aden House. During this work, one sapper was killed, and another six men wounded. The mortality was Alfred, and he is buried in Bleuet Farm Cemetery.

The late Pte. OWEN BROMLEY, Nine Mile Ride, Wokingham.—Killed in action. Aged 19.

OWEN BROMBLEY

Owen Brombley was born early in 1900 and baptised 11th March the same year. He was the youngest of thirteen children, although one brother died at the age of seventeen. His father worked as a carter at one of the farms on the Easthampstead Park estate, and the family lived on Nine Mile Ride. Owen was conscripted into the Devonshire Regiment, attesting at Wokingham, but was later transferred to the 8th Battalion, Berkshire Regiment. As he would have had to be eighteen years of age before he was called up, and then done his training, it would have been about the middle of 1918 before he reached France. The Regimental History mentions a draft of men joining the battalion on 7th September, so this may be when Owen joined them. This transfer was not without incident, with the accidental explosion of a shell at Mericourt Station, which killed 21 men outright, four died subsequently, and a further 31 were wounded. The next week was spent in training at Montauban, but by the 16th, the battalion were in the front line trenches, east of Ste. Emilie, and received orders for an attack on the 19th. The assembly posts were reached at 8:15 that morning, with Zero set for 11am. 'A' and 'B' Companies got held up by machine gun fire, but eventually reached their objectives. 'C' Company also succeeded, but only after a severe bombing fight. 'D' Company was kept back, but later moved up into Lempire village after reports that it was still held by Germans, but found it clear by the time they got there. The battalion held the same positions the following day, and although nothing is mentioned in the War Diary, this is the date in the records when Owen was reportedly killed. As his body was never recovered, he may have perished on the previous day; his name is recorded on the Vis-en-Artois Memorial.

RICHARD BROMBLEY

Richard Brombley was one of Owen's older brothers, being born in 1896 along with his twin sister Winifred, and baptised on 14th June. By the time of the 1911 census, he had left school and was working as a garden boy, probably on the Easthampstead Park estate like his father. He volunteered for service, attesting at Wokingham, and joined the 8th Battalion, Berkshire Regiment, coincidentally the same battalion as his brother would join later. Most of his training took place in Reading, but at the beginning of May 1915, the battalion moved to Sutton Veney, near Warminster, and three months later, left Southampton, bound for Le Havre. They were in trenches for the first time on 17th August, receiving instruction on trench warfare, before spending about a month in billets, training and supplying fatigue parties for various duties. On 25th September, they were involved in their first attack, as part of the Battle of Loos. Gas was used on the enemy, but leaking cylinders caused some problems for the British troops as well. The battalion continued to see action for most of the remainder of the year, and the start of 1916. Although there only six casualties for the whole of February, numbers started to rise in March and April. There is nothing in the War Diary recorded for April 26th, but this is the day when Richard was killed, probably due to shelling or sniping. His body was never recovered, and his name is listed on the Arras Memorial.

The late Pte. JOHN CALLINGHAM, son of Mr. and Mrs. Callingham, Bracknell, who died as the result of being badly gassed and burned.

JOHN CALLINGHAM

John Callingham was born in 1899, and baptised on 28th February the same year. He was one of five children, but the only boy in the family. His father was the foreman at a plant nursery on the Bagshot Road, opposite the Sports Centre. John was initially conscripted into the Worcestershire Regiment, attesting at Wokingham, but was later transferred to the 1st Battalion, Berkshire Regiment. This was possibly at the beginning of April 1918 when the Regimental History notes, ".... the reinforcements, which arrived whilst the battalion were in the throes of changing sectors, were all young and inexperienced soldiers."

Despite this, they were back on the front line by the 14th, and in and out of the trenches for the rest of the month. Casualties appear to be remarkably light for the next few months, with many men only receiving slight wounds. The War Diary also records a bad outbreak of influenza in early July, when the battalion were in Brigade Reserve near Monchy. On 21st August, they were near the village of Ayette, south of Arras, with orders to begin an attack at 4:55am. The attack was supported by six tanks, but the morning was quite misty, making it difficult to keep direction, and the tanks soon got into difficulty. Apart from some isolated machine gun fire, there was little resistance and the attack was completed successfully. They were relieved the following day and then marched for an attack on Ervillers on the 23rd. The battalion assembled for attack under shell fire, and moved off at 11am through a German barrage. This caused a few casualties, but the German infantry offered little resistance, and surrendered as the British came at them. For the rest of the day, the British were under artillery and machine gun fire from a nearby ridge. A further attack was made the next day; the result was a success but there were again casualties, mainly from machine gun fire. On the 25th, the battalion were relieved. During these four days, 24 men were killed, two hundred wounded, and 35 sent to hospital, suffering from the effects of gas. John became another casualty, dying on the 26th, and is buried in Mont Huon Military Cemetery, Le Treport, which served several nearby hospitals.

George Chaplin

George Chaplin was born in 1885, and baptised in the local church on 12th July. He was one of nine children, with another dying in infancy. The family lived in East Lodge on the South Hill Park estate, where his father worked as an agricultural labourer. The lodge was located on the Bagshot Road, behind the large Sainsbury's store by the roundabout at the top of Birch Hill. South Hill Park was owned by Sir Arthur Hayter, MP for Wells, Bath, and then Walsall, who was also a local magistrate. Hayter served as Lord of the Treasury and then Financial Secretary to the War Office under Gladstone, and was raised to the peerage as Baron Haversham in 1906. As well as South Hill Park, Hayter owned a London residence at No. 9 Grosvenor Square, where the young George was employed as a hall boy after leaving school. This was the lowest ranked male servant in a household, and he would have been expected to work up to sixteen hours per day, seven days per week. His duties would have included emptying the chamber-pots for the higher-ranking servants, cleaning boots, laying the table, assisting in the cleaning of the servant's hall, and running any errands required by other members of the staff. However, there was scope for moving up the hierarchy of below-stairs staff, and by 1911, he had moved to Mill Hill, Beaconsfield, and was working as a footman. Four years later, he held a similar position at Overstone House, Northampton, a massive building with over one hundred rooms, owned by Lady Wantage, but only used for winter hunting parties. George volunteered for service, attesting at the nearby village of Moulton on 7th July 1915, and joined the 7th Battalion, Northamptonshire Regiment. At his physical examination four months later, he was described as being 5'7" tall, and weighing nine and a half stone. It was noted he had "flat feet but quite suitable for an infantry regime." He was called up on 2nd March 1916, but not before marrying Ruth Peppitt at Overstone Parish Church five days earlier. After four months' training, he went to France on 14th June. The first major action he would have seen came at Guillemont on 18th August. Rain fell and the ground was heavily cratered, making movement difficult. Zero was set for 2:45pm and was preceded by a long bombardment. The 7th Northamptons were to the north of a track to Guillemont, and heavy machine gun fire prevented most of them from reaching the German lines, but the left company managed to gain a foothold. There was some desperate fighting, and with reinforcements from the 9th Battalion, Sussex Regiment, this was held, and consolidated later with the help of Engineers as darkness fell. George was killed at some point during the day, and is buried in Delville Wood Cemetery, Longueval.

HENRY CHAPLIN

Henry Chaplin was one of George's younger brothers, being born in 1889, and baptised on 11th August. He was still living at home when the 1901 census was taken, and the family had left East Lodge and moved to Gormer Cottages, still on the South Hill Park estate, located on Nine Mile Ride near the stream that runs under the road and into the Park's South Lake. By 1911, Henry had left home, and was working as an assistant gardener at Grey Friars, South Ascot (on Brockenhurst Road). His employer, Harry Keppel Brooke, was the youngest son of the Second Rajah of Sarawak. He had probably moved to Sussex by the time war broke out, as by then, he was a member of the 1/4th Battalion, Royal Sussex Regiment, a Territorial Battalion, having attested at Chichester. This battalion moved to Bedford in May 1915, and later the same year, Henry was transferred to the 1st Garrison Battalion, Bedfordshire Regiment. His new battalion moved to India in February 1916, and remained there for the duration of the conflict. It was made up of men considered unfit for active service but still being able to serve in a less combative environment. Henry died on 24th June 1916, and is buried in Landour General Cemetery, India. The town contained a British Military Hospital, specialising in the treatment of tropical diseases from early in the twentieth century, so it likely Henry died from one of these. His name is also listed on the Madras 1914-1918 War Memorial, Chennai, which records the names of those buried in civil cemeteries, whose graves it may not be possible to maintain in perpetuity.

JOHN CHAPLIN

John Chaplin was the third brother in the same family who died in the War. He was born the year after Henry, but not baptised until 26th November 1893, along with a younger sister. Like his elder brother George, he worked as a hall boy in the Grosvenor Square residence of Sir Arthur Hayter, one of the twelve staff employed to run the house. As he attested in Maidstone, Kent, he had probably left the employ of Sir Arthur by the outbreak of war. The records show he was initially a member of the Huntingdonshire Cyclist Battalion, a Territorial unit providing home defence. However, there was also a Kent Cyclist Battalion, so it is possible he had joined them before, and then moved to Huntingdonshire and became a member of the Cyclists there. The Cyclist Battalions provided a mobile infantry that could also work on signals, scouting and similar activities. The battalion remained in England throughout the war, but John was transferred to the 2/1st Battalion, London Regiment, and saw service overseas, probably arriving in France at the beginning of 1917. The battalion were involved in the pursuit of the Germans as they retreated to the Hindenburg Line in March, and fighting in May, June and September. On 26th October, they were at Poelcapelle for the beginning of the First Battle of Passcchendaele. A very heavy barrage came down at 2am, making the ground well nigh impassable. Zero was at 5:40am, when it was still raining and very dark, so nothing could be seen from Battalion Headquarters for at least an hour. Then, small parties were seen, running in all directions. Wounded men began to come back, bringing conflicting stories of success, and small parties of prisoners were being conducted to the rear. At 9am, information was received that the 2/3rd London Regiment were losing ground, and at 10:30am, they requested support, with an SOS signal showing at their Headquarters soon after. 'C' and 'D' Companies were sent up in support, found the defence line, east of Poelcapelle, and started to consolidate it. While doing this, they came under heavy shelling, machine gun, and rifle fire, "but officers and men showed great coolness and determination." Reports were also received that enemy strong points had been captured, but these turned out to be incorrect, although it is possible that some were gained but then lost again. The battalion suffered more than one hundred casualties in the fighting; John was one of eight men missing by the end of the day; his body was never found, and his name is listed on the Tyne Cot Memorial. With John's death, his parents had now lost all three of their sons.

SAMUEL CHAPLIN

The late Pte. SAM CHAPLIN, Nine Mile Ride, Easthampstead.—Killed in action.

Samuel Chaplin, known as Sam, was born in 1873, and baptised 13th April, but was not related to George, Henry and John. He was one of twelve children, although four had died by the time of the 1911 census. The family lived on Nine Mile Ride, and his father worked on one of the farms belonging to Easthampstead Park. Sam never married and was still living with his mother in 1911, his father having died five years earlier. Sam also worked as a labourer on the Easthampstead Park estate, but volunteered for service in 1915, attesting at Guildford, and joined the 7th Battalion, West Surrey Regiment. His mother had died at the beginning of the year, and he may have volunteered immediately after. The first men of the battalion crossed the Channel towards the end of July, but Sam arrived in France a month later, the War Diary reporting a draft of 28 men arriving on the 31st and going straight into the front trenches, remaining there for four days. There was no major action for the battalion until the Battle of the Somme the following year. They were based near Montauban, a village in German hands, which it was their objective to capture. The days preceding the attack, in which the enemy positions were relentlessly bombarded, had mixed effects. In front of the West Surreys, it was pretty effective; the enemy trenches were badly damaged and lightly held, and the Royal Flying Corps reported large explosions at the enemy dumps. Just before 7:30am on 1st July, two mines laid by one of the Royal Engineer Tunnelling Companies were blown, which was the signal for the lead units to advance from the British front trenches. Units in the centre were held up by fire from craters in No Man's Land, the results of mine warfare in the area in May. The enemy had occupied the craters and built some strong points, which had survived the bombardment. Undamaged machine guns fired from these when the battalion began to advance. Gradually, as the day wore on, the enemy were driven back and the pressure on the battalion eased, but it was not until 5.15pm that Montauban Alley was taken. The enemy artillery, having been badly damaged in this area, did not greatly interfere with the work of evacuation of the wounded, bringing up of supplies, and consolidation of the ground won, which now began in earnest. However, enemy shellfire falling on the area intensified and stayed heavy, causing many casualties and making relief and re-supply very problematic. 174 men from the battalion were killed during the day, 284 wounded, and a further 56 were missing. Sam was one of the latter; his body was never found and his name is recorded on the Thiepval Memorial.

Pte. ALFRED JAMES CLARK, R.M.L.I., 2, Jessamine Cottages, Binfield Road, Bracknell.—Sick.

ALFRED CLARKE

Alfred James Rance was born on the 13th August 1896 or 1897 (the records vary). His birth is registered under his mother's maiden name of Rance as his parents did not marry until 1902, by which time Alfred had two younger siblings, as well as an older sister, who was born with a curved spine. He spent his early childhood in Bray, where his father worked on a local farm. By 1911, his father was not fit enough to work, and was in the infirmary of the Maidenhead Workhouse, on the site now occupied by St Mark's Hospital, where he died a few months later. The rest of the family had moved to Bracknell, and were living on the Bagshot Road. Young Alfred, just fourteen years of age, was working as a farm labourer, his mother was taking in laundry, while his elder sister Nellie was in domestic service. He joined the 2nd Battalion, Royal Marine Light Infantry at Southampton on 17th November 1915. He was just over 5'3" tall, with brown eyes, dark brown hair, a fresh complexion, and a scar on his left wrist, possibly received from his new job as a sawyer. After spending a week at Deal, he was moved to Portsmouth for training. While there, he passed a drill in musketry, and was then posted to Ireland for a couple of weeks to suppress the Easter Uprising. This was a short-lived insurrection by Irish Republicans lasting two weeks, aimed at ending British rule and the establishment of an independent Irish republic. Alfred crossed to France towards the end of September 1916. The battalion took part in the Battle of the Ancre two months later, losing over one hundred men, and the Battle of Gavrelle Windmill at the end of April 1917, again with heavy casualties, as well as many men being taken Prisoner of War. On 26th October, they took part in the Second Battle of Passcendaele. The Regimental History describes the position: "The ground was in a terrible state with the rain and mud, combined with the enemy, making attacks almost impracticable. The Paddebeck, a muddy stream, ran across the front of the Brigade, making the ground still more difficult. Men who wandered from the recognised paths were liable to drown in the mud, and objectives were almost unrecognisable. At 5:10am, the barrage opened and the battalion, who had been in position since 2am, advanced with great difficulty. The 1st Battalion managed to keep well up to the barrage and gained all their objectives, but suffered heavy casualties from enfilade fire on their left. After passing through them, the 2nd Battalion were to attack, but were only able to make headway on the flanks. They considered they were on their objective, but it was very difficult to recognise the positions. The enemy counter-attacked heavily in the afternoon, forcing back those had crossed the Paddebeek. All positions on the near side of the stream were consolidated, and at 5pm on the 27th, they were relieved." Alfred was wounded at some point during the fighting, and died in 47 Casualty Clearing Station on 28th October; he is buried in Dozinghem Military Cemetery.

Pte. H. COLE, King's Liverpool Regt., Church Villas, Binfield Road, Bracknell.

HORACE COLE

Horace Cole was born in 1898, and baptised on 2nd August, one of eight children. His father worked as a brickmaker at one of the local brickworks, possibly the one sited where Arlington Square now stands, the family living in Old Bracknell before moving to Binfield Road. Horace was conscripted into the Norfolk Regiment, attesting at Wokingham, but later transferred to the 4th Battalion, Liverpool Regiment. The Division had been heavily involved in the fighting in 1918, and after a period of route marches and Company training at Zeggarscappel, were back in action at the end of the month. On the 23rd, Horace's battalion were at Montay, moving northeast through the forest towards Croix, and then Englefontaine, which was captured three days later, a distance of about five miles. After this they were relieved, and went into billets at Montay. Sickness had been a problem during the three previous months, with the War Diary recording the numbers succumbing to various diseases such as measles, scarlet fever, tonsillitis, venereal disease, scabies, and pleurisy, although the largest numbers were from lung problems, the result of being gassed. The records indicate that Horace also died of illness on 28th October, but his name appears on the Vis-en-Artois Memorial; this probably indicates his grave could not be located after the war.

The late Signlr. WM. B. COLE, Seaforth Highlanders.—Killed in action.

WILLIAM B. COLE

William Barnett Cole (some records list his middle name as Barnest) was born in 1896 in Holloway, North London, one of five children. His early childhood was spent in Lewisham, where his father worked as a Detective Sergeant in the Metropolitan Police. After he retired from the police force, the family moved to Reading Road, Wokingham, where he ran a grocery business. After leaving school, William worked as a milk boy, assisting with deliveries. He volunteered for service, going back to Edmonton to attest, joined the Royal Field Artillery, and went to France in the middle of December 1915. It is not known why or when William transferred to the infantry, so it is not possible to follow his war experiences. On 8th October 1917, his unit, the 7th Battalion, Seaforth Highlanders, marched to Esquelbecq station, and were on a train by 5:30am. Their destination, Siege Camp, was reached by 11am, but the stores and equipment took nine hours to arrive as there was only one ramp available for offloading it from the train. The War Diary describes the accommodation as a "filthy insanitary camp *but* with good accommodation tents, protected by low walls against bomb splinters." Various officers and N.C.O.s went to the front line next morning to look at the area and reconnoitre routes. Late on the 10th, they reached their positions in the front line. They had been late setting out as the two-day rations were late arriving, and later, when they found their Lewis guns en route, the limbers (carts) supporting them had been destroyed by heavy fire. There was another delay as they arranged to carry the guns, and search the area for scattered ammunition. Already, they had lost three men, one having fainted through fatigue, one who had had a fit, and one wounded. The 11th was spent under fire in the trenches, with the Battalion Headquarters being "much shelled" and found to be too small to accommodate all the staff and ancillaries. The men moved to their assembly positions at 10pm for an attack next day, the First Battle of Passchendale. At this point, heavy rain started, and "it could not have been a worse night for the men, who shivered in shell holes and in the open throughout." The weather was so bad, that one Company continued to wear their greatcoats for the attack. The barrage started two minutes early at 5:23am, but was "patchy and thin." On the right, some of the men got caught in it, with some N.C.O.s being lost for the fighting. Zero was at 5:30am, but it was three hours before any news was received, and then it turned out to be incorrect. But already it was recognised things were not going well, the men from various units being mixed up, having lost direction, and with strong enemy resistance from several strongpoints. More inaccurate messages filtered back, and the men came under sniper, shell, and machine gun fire from various directions. To make matters worse, the Division on the left had failed to get forward, and fire was coming from that quarter as well. At 1:30pm, they were ordered to withdraw, and the 1st New Zealand Rifle Brigade passed through, but their attack too was cancelled by 4pm. Conditions for an attack had been dreadful, and there were logistical problems as well. The heavy ground, inaccurate information coming back, delays (some messages took six hours to cover one mile), and Brigade orders that were later judged as unrealistic, all contributed to the failure of the attack. The battalion had over 250 casualties, including 44 deaths, and thirteen men missing. William was one of the latter, and his name is listed on the Tyne Cot Memorial. At the time of his death, William's parents were living in Wokingham Road, Bracknell, so he is listed on a memorial here, rather than in Wokingham.

The late Lance-Corporal WILLIAM COLLINSON, Bagshot Road, Bracknell.—Killed in action.

WILLIAM COLLINSON

William Collinson was born in 1889 at Benson, Oxfordshire. He was an only child, although a younger brother died in infancy. His father was an unskilled labourer, moving between jobs, with the various census entries recording the family living near Wallingford, Bisham, and at High Elms, Bracknell, now the site of The Elms Recreation Park near the Met Office roundabout, where he worked as a domestic gardener. William married Ellen Howard locally in 1907, but had joined the Army, serving with the North Staffordshire Regiment, as the birth of a daughter the following year was listed in the military registers at Aldershot. But a son, born in 1909, is registered locally again, and by the 1911 census, the family were living on the Bagshot Road, with William working as a carter on a local farm. But he was soon in the army again, attesting at Wokingham, and joining the 1st Battalion, Berkshire Regiment. The battalion had recently had a tough time at Richebourg l'Avoue, losing over four hundred men killed, missing or wounded when William joined them as part of a draft from England in late May 1915. He would have seen action at Loos later that year, and spent his share of time in the front trenches, but the battalion were not involved in the first day of Battle of The Somme, and it was July 27th before they were involved in a serious attack again. They had gone into the front line near Delville Wood three days earlier, and the attack started on this day with a bombardment at 6am, lasting just over an hour. Two hundred yards of ground was gained and they dug in. At 8:10am, the advance resumed until they finally reached Princes Street, their objective, running east/west through the middle of the wood. They had encountered considerable rifle fire, but it was not very accurate and did little harm. However, enfilading machine gun fire caused some problems for the consolidating parties. This was followed by high-explosive-shell fire for the remainder of the day, preventing any supplies of food or water reaching the men. More shelling and fire continued the next day, and it was quite late before the battalion could be relieved. 37 men were killed during the course of the two days with a similar number missing. William was one of the latter, and his name is recorded on the Thiepval Memorial. His widow remarried in 1917, had a further two children with her new husband, and died in 1956.

Pte. PERCY COOPER, Wilts Regt., Easthampstead Road, Bracknell.—Wounded.

PERCY COOPER

Percival Valentine Cooper was born at Erith, Kent in 1893, and was one of seven children. His father, originally from Wokingham, was a traction engine driver, and Percy's parents married in the town. Their first two children were born in Bracknell, but they then moved to Erith, before returning to Bracknell by the time of the 1911 census, living at a house called "Englemere" in Easthampstead Road. Percy, by now, was working as a labourer at the Down Mill Brickyard, a site now occupied by the Bracknell Business Centre on the Western Industrial Estate. He also played football for Bracknell Wanderers, who later became Bracknell Town Football Club, and was a member of the team that won the Ascot and District League First Division title in 1912. He was conscripted into the Somerset Light Infantry, attesting at Reading, but later transferred to the 1st Battalion, Wiltshire Regiment. In the first three months of 1918, the Allied Forces faced the German Spring Offensive that threatened to win the war. On March 21st, Percy's battalion were at Achiet Le Grand, east of Fremicourt. On this morning, the Germans were shelling the area at 5am, and one landed in their camp, killing more than fifty men. Later in the morning, they moved to the north-west of Fremicourt, and went into the line in the evening. After a cold night, they spent the day consolidating their position and getting up stores and rations. A few more casualties were caused by further shelling. On the 23rd, the enemy attacked twice, but were beaten back on both occasions. Heavy casualties were inflicted by both sides, especially by the Wiltshires' Lewis gunners. The night is described as 'lively' in the War Dairy, "owing to the enemy continuously trying to creep up and cut the wire." More shelling continued on the 24th, directed by enemy aeroplanes; "the absence of our planes was noticeable," complains the War Diary. The British artillery retaliated, but much of it fell short, causing casualties to their own side. In the afternoon, there was another heavy bombardment, before the enemy attacked at 4pm. Fighting was in progress but the attack, for all intense and purposes, had been beaten back when the Commanding Officer received a message by telephone to withdraw at once. The two companies on the right did so at once, leaving the other two in the air; they attempted to withdraw but were practically annihilated by machine gun fire. Over four hundred men from the battalion lost their lives in the four days of fighting, Percy being one of the casualties on the 24th. His body was never found and his name is recorded on the Arras Memorial.

The late Lieut. E. T. DAVIS (Tom), The Orchard, Wokingham Road, Bracknell.—Killed in action.

E. TOM DAVIS

Edwin Thomas Davis, known as Tom, was born in 1895, the middle of three boys. His father worked as a builder, plumber and decorator, with Edwin's older brother joining his father in similar work. The family initially lived in Binfield Road, before moving to Wokingham Road. After leaving school, Edwin worked in the High Street as a grocer's assistant. He volunteered for service, joining the 14th Battalion, London Regiment in November 1914, and went to France the following March. The battalion took part in the Battle of Aubers and the Battle of Loos later that year. On 20th January 1916, Tom gained a commission in the 2/24th Battalion, London Regiment, as a temporary Second Lieutenant, and not only was this later confirmed, but he was then further promoted to Lieutenant. His new regiment fought in the Battle of the Somme in 1916, but left France and moved to Salonika, Greece, arriving on Christmas Day. Here, it was hoped to inflict major defeats on the Bulgarian army and effect a wide break-through in the Balkans. In April the following year, they fought on the Battle of Dorian, but the attacks were beaten by constant Bulgarian fire and counter-attacks, with heavy casualties. In June, they moved again, to Egypt and on into Palestine. By now, Tom was with the Machine Gun Corps as they took part in the Third Battle of Gaza at the beginning on November, and the capture and defence of Jerusalem in December. On Christmas Day, the Londons and their machine guns were at Beit Iksa, five miles north of Jerusalem, and in contact with the Turks. Information was received the enemy would attack on the 27th, so the guns were manned during both day and night. The attack came in the early hours, and by 7:30am, the Londons had beaten off three assaults, but were then forced to retire as the Turks had captured some high ground and were able to enfilade their position. This was despite the British guns mounted in the northern outskirts of Beit Hannina finding good targets in the attacking forces. There were more than sixty casualties during the fighting, Tom being one of two officers killed; he is buried in Jerusalem War Cemetery, Israel.

The late Rfn. W. DIAPER, Mill Lane, Easthampstead. — Killed in action. Aged 17.

WILLIAM S. DIAPER

William Stanley Diaper was born in 1898, and baptised in the local church on 12th June, when he was given the names David William Stanley. He was the second of five children; the middle initial on the Roll of Honour distinguishes him from an older cousin with the same name. The family lived in a cottage on Mill Lane near Mill Pond, and William's father worked as a plumber on the Easthampstead Park estate. After leaving school, William worked as an electrician's mate, before volunteering to fight, attesting at Wokingham on 19th March 1915. Men had to be nineteen to serve abroad, but many younger boys, eager for adventure, added a year or two to their age to be included; William was one of these, adding two years to enter the Army. He joined the 1st Battalion, Rifle Brigade, and after barely two months' training, went to France on 1st June. Just over a month later, on 6th July, his battalion were involved in a difficult minor mission. The Regimental History, written in 1926, describes it as "a brilliant example of organisation by a subordinate commander and of careful adherence to the commander's plan by the troops engaged. Moreover .... it furnishes a complete condemnation of the methods of local attack practised by both the Allied and German Armies in the early years of the War." The Battalion were near the Yser Canal where a communication trench, which ran through No Man's Land, linked the two trench systems. Both sides maintained posts in this, separated by one barricade; the locality was known as International Trench. At 6am, the assaulting companies went over the top. The Regimental History describes the action: "The distance to be traversed was less than fifty yards, but within five minutes of Zero, all the officers were out of action. After a further five minutes, 'I' Company, despite heavy machine gun fire which caused a number of casualties, were on the objective, and two platoons were digging in. This party had passed through a trying experience, for a 9-inch howitzer shell, intended for an enemy machine gun, scored a direct hit on the British parapet as they were leaving and caused "indescribable confusion." A party of Royal Engineers, attached for the purpose, began to join up the International Trench with the old German front line, and two parties of Somerset Light

Infantry began digging two communication trenches and a fire trench. But despite the hedges and some natural cover, the work was directly overlooked from the Pilckden defences, from where heavy fire was opened and maintained. Meanwhile, the assault had resolved itself into a number of bombing forays, in which the 1st Battalion proved themselves too much for the enemy. The digging went steadily forward behind the screen of bombers, who continued to be engaged with the enemy until early the following morning. Bombs and machine gun ammunition were ceaselessly hurried forward and even more speedily used up (it subsequently transpired that every bomb had been used up and further bombs borrowed from the French). The trench and dug-outs were choked with German dead and littered with letters and parcels; evidently the mail had just arrived. Some kind of a meal had also been in progress, for there was an abundance of hot coffee which was eagerly consumed by the raiders, who in addition, fortified themselves with cigars. Thirty prisoners were captured, together with two machine guns, two trench mortars, and a considerable amount of trench stores. A counter-attack was attempted at about 7:30am, but was broken up by the artillery. But the enemy machine gun fire continued with unabated accuracy, and by 11am, the casualties were becoming severe. The consolidation was steadily persisted in, despite a second half-hearted threat of counter-attack, once again broken up by the guns. At 1pm, heavy shelling began. Soon afterwards there was a sharp revival of bombing by the enemy on both flanks. At 3pm, a more deliberate counter-attack developed on the left, but was easily driven off. Half an hour later, the shelling had become so severe that the old British front line had to be evacuated. The captured trenches received their share of the bombardment, under cover of which another attempt was made at counter-attack on the left, the enemy endeavouring to work along a communication trench instead of advancing over the open; this attack was also checked and defeated. This was the last attempt at recapturing the position; shortly after 5pm, the firing died down, and late at night, the captured ground was handed over to the 2nd Battalion Lancashire Fusiliers. But the gain of some seventy-five yards of ground had been made at the expense of four officers and 33 other ranks killed, a further four officers plus 176 other ranks wounded, and 37 missing." William was one of the casualties and is buried in Talana Farm Cemetery.

ARCHIE GILKERSON

The late ARCHIE GILKERSON, 1st class stoker, H.M.S. Princess Irene, Bracknell.—Lost at sea. Aged 27.

Archie Gilkerson was born in Wokingham on 2nd July 1887. His father had married three times (his first two wives had both died), and Archie had seven siblings, as well as three older half-siblings. His early childhood was spent in Billingbear Road, Wokingham, where his father worked as a bricklayer, but by 1901, the family were living at No. 3 Temperance Cottages, Binfield Road. Archie was now thirteen years old, but had already left school and was working as a storeman's assistant. By 1911, he was a general fitter when, on 21st February, the signed on at Chatham, Kent, for five years' service in the Royal Navy. On enlistment, he is described as being a little over 5'2" tall, of dark complexion, with brown hair, grey eyes, and had a scar under the knee of his left leg. It must be remembered that ships were powered by steam engines at this time, and Archie worked below decks as a stoker. His initial training was done at the Sheerness Dockyard, before he was allocated to HMS 'Natal' for over three years. His first trip on this ship was to India, as the 'Natal' was an escort to the RMS 'Medina', carrying the newly-crowned King George V to the Delhi Durbar. On his return, he married

Bracknell girl Alice Bowyer in 1914, probably in Camberley where she worked as a domestic servant. Early the following year, the 'Natal' underwent a refit at Cromarty, so Archie was back at base. On 27th May, he was on board HMS 'Princess Irene', anchored off Sheerness, where priming of mines was being carried out, prior to laying them a few days later. Just after 11am, there was a huge explosion, and the ship was totally destroyed, all but one of the 377 men on board being instantly killed, and most of the bodies never found. Two people on shore were killed by flying debris, and fallout from the explosion reportedly landed in Maidstone, some twenty miles away. The cause of the disaster was thought to have been due to a faulty primer, although evidence at the Official Enquiry showed that the work of priming the lethal mines was being carried out by untrained personnel, and in a great hurry. Archie's body was never found, and his name is listed on the Chatham Naval Memorial.

EDWARD GILKERSON

Edward John Gilkerson was born on 21st January 1895, and was a younger brother of Archie. The family were already living in Binfield Road when he was born, so he grew up in Bracknell. After leaving school, he worked for a time as a moulder in an iron foundry, before joining the Navy at Portsmouth on the day before his 17th birthday. His naval papers describe him as being 5'4" (a year later he had grown by two inches), having a fair complexion, with brown hair and blue eyes, as well as small scars on his left knee, and a ship tattooed on his right forearm. After his initial training, he spent four months aboard HMS 'Implacable', part of the Home Fleet. This would have mainly been patrolling around the coast, including coastguard duties, although there would have been one or two spells further out to sea. This was followed by another spell of training in engineering and mechanics, before returning to sea on HMS 'Bulwark', a pre-Dreadnought Class battleship, also mainly involved in work within coastal waters, until June 1914. When war broke out, he was back in training at a shore-based gunnery school, undertaking training which lasted until June the next year, after which he joined HMS 'King George V'. This was a Dreadnought Class battleship and the flagship of Vice Admiral Sir Martyn Jerram. The 2nd Battle Squadron, including HMS 'King George V', sailed from Scapa Flow on 15th December, in an attempt to combat German warships that were bombarding towns on the east coast of England. The ship also took part in the Battle of Jutland, but was on the edge of the action, firing just nine shots at the German Battlecruiser SMS 'Derfflinger', all of which missed their target! But if Edward had been on the fringes of the action until now, he was about to be in the centre of it. The German fleet was based at Bruges in Belgium. This was six miles from the coast, and linked to the open sea by two canals, one to Zeebrugge, opening into the North Sea; the other, smaller one, to Ostend, allowing access to the English Channel. Submarines, in particular, were a menace to British shipping. Towards the end of 1916, a plan started to be formulated to block the two canal entrances, thereby sealing the German boats in. Intelligence reported there were 28 German destroyers and nearly forty submarines there. Although both exits would need to be attacked simultaneously, the larger operation would be at Zeebrugge. A diversionary attack on the Mole (harbour breakwater) would form part of the plan. Although the Mole itself was heavily fortified, it was connected to the mainland by a steel viaduct; if this was destroyed, the Germans would not be able to bring furthers defenders on to the Mole when the attack began. It took almost twelve months from the first draft for agreement to be reached at all levels, highly detailed plans to be worked out, and officers chosen for the mission to be picked. Volunteers were then sought from all sections of the navy, the only stipulation being they be "unmarried, single men, of very good character." They were unlikely to return from the operation. Edward's service history was exemplary, and he was chosen to take part, one of no more than six from each ship supplying volunteers. There now followed several months of strict discipline and intensive training with, in theory, no contact with anyone outside the training base (although some men did find ways of leaving for a few hours in the evenings, no doubt to sample the local watering holes and other pleasures). Secrecy was also key, and many of the original volunteers fell by the wayside as a result of the harsh regime. Early in March, the remaining men were inspected by Winston Churchill, Minister of Munitions, who then addressed them, "You are going on a daring and arduous stunt from which none of you may return, but every endeavour will be made to being back as many of you as possible." He then gave them the opportunity to drop out, without any consequences or blemish on their records; every man stayed. Later, the King visited as well. The operation would need to take place at high tide, combined with a night with no moon and an onshore wind (for an effective use of smoke screens); only five nights out of every two weeks were candidates on account of the tides. After one postponement, the armada set sail on 11th April 1918 and got within sixteen miles of Zeebrugge, but then the wind changed direction, and the action had to be called off. Two nights later, it was abandoned again, as strengthening winds and heavy seas would have made an already difficult mission even more hazardous. The element of surprise, and a possible delay of a further three weeks before conditions were right, meant there was a real possibility the whole enterprise would be cancelled. The force set sail again just before 5pm on April 22nd, "and those with chivalrous and romantic imaginations realised the attack would take place in the early hours of St George's Day." The two aborted missions had exposed some flaws in communication, and other details which were rectified on this occasion, but it was later found the Germans had moved a marker buoy, critical to the positioning of some of our boats, causing some to be in the wrong place early in the approach. The wind changed at a critical moment, so the smokescreen was not entirely successful, but a later report noted that no better conditions occurred before, or for some considerable time later. Edward was a gunner on board HMS 'Vindictive.' This ship was obsolescent at the start of the War and had been used mainly in foreign waters, but had been adapted and equipped for this operation, including the installation of an extra deck at a suitable height to access the Mole for the diversionary attack. In the event, she came to a halt three ships' lengths away from the Mole and had to be rammed by another boat to get into position, but was in place only a minute after the allotted time of midnight, despite being hit by many shells, causing heavy casualties on board. When the marines and seamen did get onto the Mole, they discovered that there were German machine gun positions and barbed wire between them and the guns. They also came under fire from a German destroyer docked on the other side of the mole. The foretop guns were soon put out of action, and the superstructure of the 'Vindictive' almost destroyed. The landing parties suffered very heavy casualties, but still succeeded in distracting the Germans at a crucial moment. The connecting viaduct was rammed and destroyed, and two of the three blockships were able to reach their target positions. They were sunk in the entrance to the inner harbour, although they did not manage to block it entirely. The Germans were later able to dredge a new channel around the blockships, and the port was very quickly back in use. By 1:10 am, the 'Vindictive' had taken the survivors off the Mole, and the remains of the flotilla returned to Britain. The cost was high with 176 men killed, over four hundred wounded, and almost fifty missing. The mission failed to prevent German submarines from using the harbour, but the attack, and a later one at Ostend, did raise morale in Britain at a crucial moment in the war. So many outstanding actions of bravery occurred during the operation that eight nominations could have been made for the award of a Victoria Cross. However, military regulations only allow for two such recommendations from any one operation, so the names of those nominated were subject to a secret ballot. Although Edward's Service Record bears the stamp: "Participated in ballot for V.C. granted for operations against Zeebrugge & Ostend, 22-23 April 1918," his name did not appear on the ballot list, the implication being a clerk was stamping the records of all those who took part in the raid, regardless of whether they returned alive or not. Although the provision for awards by ballot is still included in the Victoria Cross warrant, this method had not been used since the Zeebrugge Raid. Edward's body was brought back on the HMS 'Vindictive' and buried in Dover (St. James's) Cemetery in a special plot, dedicated to the victims of the raid. The epitaph on his grave reads: "He died willingly."

William Gilkerson

William Thomas Gilkerson was a brother of Archie and Edward, and was born at Wokingham in 1890. After leaving school, he worked as an assistant in a shop selling stationery. He also played football for Bracknell Wanderers, who later became Bracknell Town Football Club, and was a member of the team that won the Ascot and District League Second Division title for the first time in 1914. He volunteered immediately when war broke out, attesting at Wokingham, and joined the 2nd Battalion, Royal Berkshire Regiment. The Battalion were in India at the outbreak of war, and did not get to France until November; William was part of a draft that arrived a month later, probably one of the forty men who arrived two days before Christmas. If he had gone into the trenches the next day, he would have been part of the Christmas Truce when British and German soldiers met in No Man's Land, exchanged presents, sang carols, and played football (although the Berkshires took no part in the game). The Battle of Neuve Chapelle, on 10th March the following year, was the first large-scale organised attack undertaken by the British army during the war. William's battalion were involved in the attack, with almost one hundred men were killed or missing, and over two hundred wounded. This was soon followed by action at St Eloi, and the capture of Hill 60 in April. Towards the end of April, the battalion took their turn in the front trenches, and the War Diary records one man being wounded on the 21st, and two on the 24th. William was probably one of these, dying of wounds on the 26th, and is buried in Merville Communal Cemetery.

Thomas Glew

Thomas Glew was born in the village of Buxted near Chichester, Sussex, in about 1877, although no registration for his birth has been found. The first record of him is in the 1881 census, when he was living with his unmarried mother, Susan, who is acting as housekeeper to Mark Turner, a farm labourer, ten years her junior. Mark and Susan married a few months later and moved to Sunninghill, Mark's place of birth, with a further seven children being born, although some of them died before reaching adulthood. On leaving school, Thomas worked as a domestic gardener, and appears in the 1901 census, living in the lodge at Richmond House in Surrey, before moving back to a cottage in Oriental Row, Sunninghill. He had married Harriet Cooper in 1900, and they had four sons, the youngest being born in 1909. Thomas volunteered for service, attesting at Wokingham on 12th January 1915, and joined the 9th Battalion, Berkshire Regiment. This was a Reserve Battalion, based in Dorset between Dorchester and Wareham, and later re-organised into the 37th Training Reserve Regiment when conscription started in 1916. He was transferred to the Royal Military Police in late September 1916, who were responsible, among other things, for the transport of prisoners-of-war. This probably means he was considered unfit for overseas service, but was still able to carry out military duties in the UK. By the end of the war, there were approximately 25,000 men in the Military Police. Thomas died 5th January 1919 in the Third Southern General Hospital, Oxford, of a heart attack. By this time, his widow and children were living at 6 Searle Street, Bracknell, a small street running on the north side of the pub opposite Bracknell railway station, and is buried in the churchyard at Easthampstead church with a Commonwealth War Graves Commission headstone.

EDWARD S. GOOCH

Edward Sinclair Gooch was born in Richmond, Surrey in 1879. His father had worked as a civil engineer with several railway companies, including the London and Southwestern Railway, Bracknell lying on one of their lines, where he was Locomotive Superintendent. After he retired, he came to live at Cooper's Hill, near the railway station, where he died in 1900. Edward was privately educated at Eagle House School at Sandhurst (where his name appears on the Roll of Honour in the school chapel), and Winchester School, after which he went to Reading University. He obtained a commission with the Lancashire Fusiliers in 1898, before transferring to the 7th Hussars two years later, and fighting with them in the Boer War. He married Eva Everard in Scotland in 1903, with a daughter being born the following year. They lived in Richmond, Surrey, employing seven servants, and had another house in Scotland. By 1904, Edward was a Major with the Berkshire Yeomanry, a territorial force of part-time cavalry, formed primarily for home defence. As well as military duties, he was involved with the local Boy Scouts at home, and was Assistant County Commissioner and Honorary County Secretary for Inverness-shire. The Berkshire Yeomanry remained in Reading until April 1915, when they sailed for Egypt, and were based at Abbassia, Cairo, where they remained for the next few months. The Allies had landed on the Gallipoli peninsular on 25th April 1915, in an attempt to break the stalemate then clogging the Western Front. The intention was to knock Turkey, an ally of Germany, out of the war, and open up a supply route to and from Russia via the Black Sea. But the fighting at Gallipoli quickly degenerated into the same trench deadlock, and by August 1915, more men were needed. Another front was opened on the Gallipoli peninsula, with landings at Suvla Bay to the north of Anzac Cove (held by the Australians and New Zealanders). The Berkshires arrived in Alexandria early in the morning of the 14th August, having travelled overnight by train. There, they boarded the S.S. 'Lake Michigan' for "an (exact) destination known only to those of a high rank, packed like sardines in a troopship, so overloaded that many of the men had to spend the whole of the .... voyage on deck." The ship arrived at Mudros on the 17th, having sailed a circuitous route to avoid enemy submarines, but did not land; the men were transferred to another ship and continued to Gallipoli. On arrival, they were met by a steam launch towing six boats, each capable of holding fifty men, and went ashore at Suvla Bay in these. Frank Millard, a Reading man, wrote to his parents of the landing: "[We] reached Gallipoli quite safely on August 18th, and although we have been here but 36 hours, we have had quite an exciting time. We did not actually land under fire, but had just disembarked and were carrying our maxims and ammunition off the landing place, when I heard a long whistling, followed by a report. I didn't know what it was at the time, but was soon informed by a Naval officer, who simply said 'Grease - they're on you,' when 'yours truly' picked up two boxes of ammunition, and 'greased' and that quickly." After getting settled, the men were taken off to build a road, before returning to have a swim, which was interrupted by some enemy shells falling in the sea. The next day Frank told his family, "We are not fed badly, and even in this short time we are becoming quite good cooks. Our little dugout consists of a hole scraped in the ground about a foot deep, with a few stones stacked on the earth outside, and some bushes stacked round it. Its outward appearance is very pretty, but inside it might easily be more comfortable. However, things will improve as we go on, so why worry? I don't think we shall be out here long, so you may see me home sooner than you expect." He omitted to mention that two men had already been wounded. On the 20th, there was speculation of a move, and at 8pm, they moved along the coast towards Lala Baba. Earlier, the Commanding Officer, Lieutenant Colonel H.G. Henderson was admitted to the Field Ambulance at Suvla, an old injury from the Boer War preventing him from continuing. As the next senior officer, Edward relinquished command of the 1st Squadron, and took temporary command of the Berkshire Yeomanry until the regimental second-in-command, Major Wigan, could arrive from Mudros. The rate of march only averaged about one mile per hour, due to frequent halts to allow supply carts to pass both ways along the very narrow road. The 2nd Mounted Division, of which the Berkshire Yeomanry were a part, were the reserve for an attack on Scimitar Hill on the 21st. The Berkshires led the Troop Column towards Chocolate Hill and came under heavy shrapnel fire while crossing a plain, which they later discovered was aptly named 'Shrapnel Valley'. But despite several men going down injured, "there was not the slightest disorder .... the formation of the regiment was perfect." One man described it was "just like being in a hail-storm." They reached the shelter of Chocolate Hill at 4:45pm, with orders to attack the Turkish trenches just 45 minutes later, while it was still daylight. The earlier attack had failed to reach its objective, and the Yeomanry were required to move forward, uphill over unknown territory, in mist and smoke from burning shrubbery which hid their objective, with snipers shooting from trees on both sides. The Commanding Officer of the Dorset Yeomanry described the formation of the plan to get to the enemy line. "We now reached the top edge of the wood, and closed up to Gooch's squadron, all lying down in a dry ditch. Hurndall (Berks Adjutant), Gooch and self then discussed the situation. In front of us, in the now fading light, we could see a grassy plateau, with a few bushes dotting it, and, rather below a slight rise in the ground, a dark line, spitting fire - evidently the trench. We decided we would dump in the ditch all the picks and shovels, form two lines, Berks leading and Dorsets in support, and as soon as we heard Lord Longford's cheer would charge the trench. As there were several machine guns on the parapet, the prospect did not seem very bright." By now, they had fixed bayonets and a charge was called for. There are several accounts of what happened from then on. "How did the charge begin? Well, an officer shouted, as far as I can recollect, 'Come on, lads! We'll give 'em beans!' That is not exactly according to drill-books and regulations as I know them; but it was enough. It let the boys loose, and they simply leapt forward and went for the Turkish trenches." "The final charge is impossible to describe. As soon as we got over the gully, there was a fusillade of shells and rifles, and machine guns seemed all around us. It seemed impossible to live through, and that was where we had most casualties. We, or what was left of us, took two lines of trenches." "Although there had been many casualties, the Regiment then swept over the ridge into the enemy's trenches, Major Gooch being the first man in." "Gallant Major Gooch, who was in command of the regiment, was badly wounded with revolver in hand on the brink of the enemy's trenches." From the Commanding Officer of the Dorset Yeomanry: "Presently we heard cheering and shouting, followed by strange cries, prayers to Allah, and shrieks. We got up, and doubled on to the plateau, but on getting half-way across, it was obvious the attack was doomed to failure: men fell like rabbits, from the machine gun fire; Gooch was hit in the head .... a few Turks could be seen bolting down a trench to our right, but at the same time we could see their reinforcements coming down from a trench on the hill above. There were no signs of the other Brigades on our right, who at this critical moment might have turned the balance in our favour." An account survives of the critical moment: "Major Gooch led 'A' Squadron up Hill 70 and on entering the Turkish trenches, was confronted by three Turks. He grasped the middle one by the throat and shouted. Corporal Thomas rushed up and bayoneted one, and Lieutenant Blyde shot the third. Corporal Thomas's brave action undoubtedly was largely instrumental in saving Major Gooch from being instantly killed, though unfortunately he subsequently died of his wounds in the head." Thomas, himself shot through the lungs in the attack, would receive the Distinguished Conduct Medal for his actions. Although the costly attack had been successful, the captured ground could not be held. "Part of the ground captured was held by the Regiment, with other Yeomanry, until early the next morning, when, under orders, a retirement was conducted in good order, as the position was considered untenable in the daytime." ".... owing to enfilade fire down the left, the trench could not be held, and after about ten minutes had to be evacuated." "Our Brigade, with the Berks doing the leading, got right on top of the hill we were set to capture, by means of two bayonet charges after continual rushes, but the order came that all Yeomanry were to retire to a certain spot. It did seem a pity after what we had done and given." "Personally I got it coming back, but came across several wounded and did what little I could to relieve them, arriving at our trenches about 10 a.m. on Sunday morning. I was just in time for the roll call, and when hearing the figures it was as much as I could do to keep my pecker up." An unknown trooper would later write home: "Sorry to say, the Berks Yeomanry got rather badly cut up: cannot seem to find any of my pals." On 8th September, it was reported: "Major E. S. Gooch ....wounded on the 21st August 1915 arrived back in England," and on the 21st: "Exactly one month after the battle, Major Edward Gooch died of wounds received. He was in hospital in London (Lady Ridley's Home). Major E. S. Gooch, aged 36, had previously served in the 7th Hussars. He joined the Berkshire Yeomanry in 1903, and had commanded the 'A' (Windsor) Squadron since 1910." Soon after the news reached Gallipoli, Corporal Charlish of the Windsor Squadron wrote to his parents: "We have just had the news through that our well-loved Major Gooch has died of wounds in England. I was just about four yards from him when he was shot through the head in the charges. All the regiment regrets his loss, and has sent a letter of condolence to Mrs Gooch, every member signing it." Edward was buried in Fort William (St. Andrew) Episcopalian Churchyard, close to his Scottish home, and listed on the Fort William War Memorial. Among the other men fighting with the Berkshire Yeomanry that day, were Lieutenant William Niven (also killed), the father of 1960s British film star David Niven, and Frederick Potts of Reading who, badly wounded himself, dragged a badly injured comrade back to the British lines, using a shovel as an improvised sledge; the journey of six hundred yards took 48 hours. He received the Victoria Cross from King George V at Buckingham Palace in December 1915.

HENRY T. GRANT

Henry Thomas Grant was born in 1894 in Folkestone, Kent. He was one of seven children in a family living in a cottage in the town in North Street. This road is close to the beach and harbour, where his father worked as a fisherman. After leaving school, Henry worked as an errand boy for a tailoring business, before leaving his home town for work. He was conscripted into the Army early in 1916, and joined the Army Service Corps. His Service number suggests he was employed as a driver, or possibly an electrician, maintaining vehicles. It is not known when Henry went to France, but he was in England in early 1917, when he married Jessie Cole, a 23 year-old domestic servant from Twyford, in the Easthampstead registration district. He was at the G.H.Q. Anti-Aircraft Gunnery School in Germany in 1919, which came under the Royal Garrison Artillery, and died on 13th February, probably as a result of the flu epidemic. He is buried in Cologne Southern Cemetery. His widow was probably still living in the Easthampstead area, and put his name forward to be included on the local memorials.

ALBERT HANCOCK

Albert Henry Hancock was born in Bracknell in 1884, and baptised at Holy Trinity on 7th December. He was the second youngest of six children. The family lived in Binfield Road, but after the death of his father, a carpenter, in 1894, Albert, his mother and two brothers, moved in with one of his elder married sisters. After leaving school, Albert worked in the brick trade, firstly as a carter in one of the local brickworks, but later as a labourer at Bramshott, near Liphook, in Hampshire. He was conscripted into the Royal Garrison Artillery, attesting at Aldershot, and was mobilised in March 1916. At the time of his death, Albert was with the 113th Heavy Battery, but as his service record does not exist, it is not possible to know how long he was with them. Heavy Batteries of the Royal Garrison Artillery were equipped with heavy guns, sending large calibre high explosive shells in fairly flat trajectory fire. The usual armaments were 60 pounder (5 inch) guns. As British artillery tactics developed, the Heavy Batteries were most often employed in destroying or neutralising the enemy artillery, as well as putting destructive fire down on strongpoints, dumps, stores, roads, and railways behind enemy lines. At the beginning of October, they were shooting with aeroplanes acting as observers, who would report back on whether they needed to alter their range, and inform them of successful hits. On the 2nd, they scored direct hits on two German gun positions; these were followed by explosions. Although a full complement was six guns, they were operating with only four until two more arrived from Calais on the 6th. However, three of their current guns were then condemned, and sent to Ordnance for new parts. Next day, work commenced on a new gun position. A light railway ran behind the projected line of the guns, and by the evening of the 8th, two bridges had been built across a ditch from the railway, to plank platforms on spits of dry land between shell holes. Next day, orders were received to take a gun to Westhoek, using a team of horses. It was impossible to take the gun to the prepared position as the only access was by the light railway, so it was left on a plank siding off the road. A second gun was taken up and left in a similar position on the 10th, while a bridge was built to a spit of land large enough to accommodate two gun platforms. When these were finished, one gun was pulled into position by the evening of the 11th, and by the 12th, two guns were in position, and "properly prepared for action." Splinter-proof shelters were then built nearer the crest of the hill for the Battery Command post, wireless station, telephone exchange, and accommodation for gun detachments.

Another platform was laid on the 14th, and a gun in position twenty-four hours later. However, all this work had not gone unnoticed, and the position was heavily shelled, putting two guns out of action, one with a direct hit. Three days later, a new position was selected, and the first gun in place and firing by the 21st. The War Diary only gives the total number of casualties for the month, which include 23 men wounded. Albert was one of them, and died on 1st November 1917 in one of the hospitals in Boulogne. He is buried in Boulogne Eastern Cemetery.

HERBERT HANCOCK

Herbert Hancock was Albert's younger brother, born in 1889, and was working in one of the grocer's shops in the High Street by the time of the 1911 census. He and his mother were still living with his elder sister's family in Binfield Road. By the time he joined the Army, he had moved to Ware in Hertfordshire, attested in Bedford, and joined the 6th Battalion of the local regiment. As he was mobilised in February 1916, he was with the battalion for one of the last phases of the Battle of the Somme in November that year. The battalion were also involved in several battles in 1917, including the First Battle of Passchendaele. In March the following year, the battalion were in and out of the front trenches at Kruisstraatnoek, just to the southwest of Ypres. According to the War Diary, five men were wounded and eight gassed on the 20th. Herbert was one of the casualties, and is buried in Hooge Crater Cemetery. It should be noted the memorial inside Easthampstead Church has the regiments of Albert and Herbert transposed.

The late Pte. R. H. HANCOCKS, 1st Batt. Artists Rifles, Wokingham Road, Bracknell,—Killed in action.

RALPH HANCOCK

Ralph Henry Hancocks (the final 's' is missing from his surname on both memorials), was born at Sindlesham in 1893, and was the youngest of nine children. His father was a journeyman miller, the modern equivalent is a freelance worker, who would have been paid by the day. Although this meant he was not tied to an employer, it did mean the family had to move to where work was available, and Ralph's older siblings were born in Warwickshire and Worcestershire before the family moved to Berkshire. By 1901, they were living on Reed's Hill, Easthampstead, so presumably Ralph's father was working at the mill by Mill Pond. They subsequently moved to Wokingham Road, by which time Ralph had left school, and was working as an engine driver of a stationery engine in a corn mill (this again may have been at Mill Pond). He volunteered for service, going to London to attest, and went to France in January 1915, as a mechanic with the Army Service Corps. Later in the war, as casualties mounted, able-bodied men were moved into the infantry, their places being taken by less able men who were not deemed capable of fighting on the front line, and Ralph was transferred to the 1/28th Battalion, London Regiment, in late October 1916. In 1917, the battalion took part in the Battle of Messines, operations during the Third Battle of Ypres, and Cambrai Operations, as well as the two Battles of the Somme the following year. On 25th August, they were just to the southwest of Bapaume. An attack was held up by a machine gun, until it was cleared by the 189th Brigade, allowing them to cross the Amiens to Bapaume road, and capture La Barque. The enemy were seen to be massing, but were broken up by artillery fire. The whole Division was under heavy shelling, and a small enemy attack beaten off. An attack on Thilloy next day failed to materialise. The village was attacked again at 4am on the 27th. Again, they were under heavy enemy shelling, and held up by machine gun fire as well as sniping. At 5:15pm, a barrage was put on Thilloy, and the battalion attacked on both sides of the village, although still under heavy machine gun fire, which continued until they were relieved later in the evening. Ralph was killed in the fighting for Thilloy, and his body is buried in A.I.F. Burial Ground, Flers.

The late Pte. FRANCIS HARRIS, London Scottish, Easthampstead.—Killed in action. Aged 19.

F. W. FRANCIS HARRIS

Frederick William Francis Harris, known as Francis, was born in Easthampstead in 1897, and baptised in the local church on 25th April, along with his twin sister Emeline. His father was a clerk of works at a local estate (either South Hill Park or Easthampstead Park), supporting a family of four children. By the end of 1915, Francis had left school, was lodging at 16 Roberts Road, High Wycombe, and working as a bank clerk. He joined under the Derby Scheme, attesting at High Wycombe, and joined the 14th Battalion, London Regiment. He was described as being just over 5'6" tall and carried a scar on his left kneecap, but the rest of the physical description is missing from his Service Record. He was mobilised the following March, and after three months of training, sailed from Southampton to Le Havre on 21st June. The battalion had been sent to Ireland at the end of April for security reasons following the Irish rebellion a few days earlier, but it is not known whether Frederick, as a relatively new recruit, would have been involved, but in any case, they were there for barely a fortnight. While in France, the battalion were not involved in any major action, and would leave for Salonika in November. Before then, on 19th October, the battalion took its turn in the front line for six days, near Bray-sur-Somme, southeast of Albert. The War Diary entry for the next day blandly reads: "In the trenches, killed 3, wounded 7." Francis was one of the trio, and is buried in Maroeuil British Cemetery. It is fascinating to look at the list of personal effects which were returned to the next of kin after a soldier's death, as they often they give an insight into a man that no other record can portray. For Francis, the list comprised a disc (each man wore two identity discs, one of which was removed before burial), letters, photos, religious books, a cheque book, card case with hair (from a girlfriend?), two address books, keys, and a cigarette case.

The late Pte. FRANK HEADINGTON, 6th Batt. Royal Berks Regt. Killed in action. Aged 20.

FRANK HEADINGTON

Frank was born in Easthampstead in 1895, and baptised in the local church three days before Christmas the same year. He was one of a large family, having eight brothers and sisters. His father worked as a carter at Mill Farm (beside Mill Pond). Later, the family had moved to Skimped Hill Lane, and by 1911 Frank had left school and was working as a garden labourer at Easthampstead Park, a major local employer. He volunteered for service, attesting at Wokingham, and joined the 6th Battalion, Royal Berkshire Regiment. Training was done at Colchester and on Salisbury Plain until July 1915, when the battalion left for

Folkestone and sailed for Boulogne, arriving on the 26th. A week after their arrival, they were in trenches, receiving instruction on trench warfare, and although there were a few casualties in the next few days, it would be opposite Mametz on the 22nd when several men were killed by snipers. They stayed in the area until mid September before marching to Albert. Here there was a great deal of mining from both sides, and the battalion had over one hundred men, working four six-hours shifts every day on mining fatigues, removing and disposing of, over three thousand bags of chalk each day without the enemy being aware of what was happening. It was mid October before they went into billets at Buire and were able to enjoy such entertainments as a cinema. The rest of the autumn, winter and following spring followed a regular pattern of trenches and rest periods, although from March, training started in readiness for the coming Battle of the Somme. Five men were killed and 42 wounded during the four days' bombardment preceding the attack, largely due to the inadequacy of the dug-outs. The battalion moved into its assembly positions at 3am on 1st July, leaving the third trench empty after it was observed this was where the majority of the enemy's shells were falling. They were opposite Mine Trench, the most advanced of the enemy's defences, at the west end of which was Casino Point. A huge mine was exploded under this at 7:27am, and a few men of the battalion were hit by debris, and the crater from the explosion was forty feet deep and thirty yards across. Over sixty men from the battalion were killed on that day and almost 250 wounded. The next battle the Berkshires were involved in came on the 19th. The task was to clear the northern part of Delville Wood, after the 8th Norfolk had cleared the southern end. At just after 7am, the battalion moved off, but the Germans were shelling the road to the wood, and the delay of the Norfolks getting into it held them up, and they suffered many casualties. By the time they got into the wood, they found it had not been cleared as reported, and things became very confused before a line was eventually dug, and held with difficulty, by 5pm. Fighting continued for the next two days but Frank would play no part in it, having been killed; his body never recovered and is listed on the Thiepval Memorial.

ALBERT WILLIAM HEARNE

The late Rfn. A. W. HEARNE, Rifle Brigade, Binfield Rd., Bracknell.—Killed in action. Aged 19.

Albert William Hearne was born 2nd August 1899, and baptised on the 27th of the same month at Easthampstead Church. He was one of five children, with a sixth dying in infancy. The parent's address when Albert was baptised was recorded as Ramslade Cottages (in Broad Lane, by the Blue Lion pub), and as his father worked as a domestic coachman, it may have been for Lieutenant Colonel MacKenzie, the owner of nearby Ramslade House. But ten years later, Albert's father has made a career change, and was a licensed victualler, with the family living in Binfield Road. Albert was conscripted into the 2nd Battalion, Rifle Brigade, attesting at Reading. In 1918, the battalion were fighting in the Battles of the Somme, Aisne and Arras. Two weeks after the last of these, the battalion were just north of Gavrelle. On 13th September, 'D' Company took over the Outpost line, and attempted to establish a post at the junction of two trenches. However, the Germans held one of the trenches, and the attempt failed. Only one man was killed, but it was Albert, and he is buried in Roclincourt Military Cemetery.

The late Pte. BARTLETT W. HEATH, 2nd Batt. Royal Berks Regiment, The Square, Bracknell.—Killed in action. Aged 23.

BARTLETT W. HEATH

Bartlett William Heath was born 3rd May 1891, and baptised in Holy Trinity Church on 19th June. He was the third of nine surviving children, two others dying young, and the family lived in The Square, at the bottom of Bracknell High Street. His father worked mainly for the brewery, located opposite the current Columbia Centre on Station Road, but also had a spell at one of the local brickyards. In February 1910, Bartlett followed his brother Charles into the 2nd Battalion, Royal Berkshire Regiment, attesting at Reading, and was still based in England, in barracks at Dover in the census taken the following year. The battalion were in India when war was declared and sailed from there on 20th September, arriving at Liverpool just over a month later (there had been a delay at Gibraltar, due in part to news of an armed enemy raider which was duly captured by British destroyers). After two weeks at Winchester, they marched to Southampton, arrived in Le Havre on 5th November, and were in the front line trenches Fauquissart on the 14th. The British trenches were in low-lying ground and needed constant pumping to keep them more or less clear of water, but conditions were still miserable and the first cases of "trench foot" were seen. Of course, there was some relief on Christmas Day; the War Diary records, "Men got up on parapet and advanced half way towards German trenches and in some cases conversed with them. Orders given at 11am prohibiting men from going beyond parapet. Much work done in improving trenches during this day, the enemy protested against barb (sic) wire being repaired and we stopped enemy from repairing theirs." They continued in the trenches for the next two months. They had a week in billets and a couple of days of marching before arriving for the attack on Neuve Chapelle. They were ready, in position, by 7:30am on 10th March, with the advance due to start 35 minutes later. But the bombardment from the British artillery, preceding the advance, contained many "shorts," affecting the battalion badly (one shell alone buried more than a dozen men, killing or severely wounding several). The German front-line trenches and the first objective were taken with relatively little opposition, and the rest of the day was taken in consolidating the new position. Bartlett was probably one of the men killed by the 'friendly fire', and is buried in Neuve-Chapelle British Cemetery.

The late Sergt. CHARLES F. HEATH, 2nd Batt. Royal Berks Regiment, The Square, Bracknell.—Killed in action. Aged 28.

CHARLES F. HEATH

Charles Frederick Heath was Bartlett's older brother, born in 1886. He worked for a time as a building labourer after leaving school, before joining the 2nd Battalion, Royal Berkshire Regiment soon after his 18th birthday, attesting at Reading. In the 1911 census, he is listed with his colleagues at Meerut in India. He had already been promoted to the rank of Lance Corporal and would become a sergeant before his death. He had also transferred to the 1st Battalion before the outbreak of war, as he travelled with them from Southampton to Rouen, arriving on 13th August. They were in trenches on the 23rd and, although coming under heavy shelling for four hours, played no part in the attack that day. For the next two weeks, the British were in retreat, but the tables turned on 8th September, and they started to advance again. By the middle of the month, the advance was halted, and trench warfare on the Western Front began. The next major incident occurred on 24th October when the battalion, now northeast of Ypres, were ordered to drive some Germans out of the area around Westhoek. The attack began in mid- afternoon and, despite coming under heavy rifle and shell fire, was successful, and a ridge running from Zonnebeke to Bekelaere captured. The enemy attempted to deceive them by sounding the British "Retire" and representing themselves as Belgians, but "failed ignominiously." Another attack, three days later, gained five hundred yards of ground, but one on the 28th failed; twenty men were killed during the three attacks. A similar pattern followed until mid November, with successful attacks, failed attacks, general skirmishes, and mentions of heavy shelling in the War Diary. On the 15th, the battalion were relieved in the evening by the French and, having survived all the cold, rain and fighting of the past three weeks, Charles was killed during the day, possibly when a shell scored a direct hit on the section of trench he was in. His body was never recovered and he is listed on the Ypres (Menin Gate) Memorial.

The late Corpl T. HOLLINGS, South Hill Park, Bracknell.—Died of wounds.

THOMAS HOLLINGS

Edward Thomas F. Hollings, known by his second name, was born at Midgham, Berkshire, in 1898, and was the second of six children, a seventh dying in infancy. It is not clear whether Thomas actually ever lived in Easthampstead, as the family moved here between the 1901 and 1911 censuses, by which time he was working as a gamekeeper at Cuckoo Hall, Wendover, the same occupation as his father, who was employed at South Hill Park. At the outbreak of war, he joined the 2/4th Battalion, Berkshire Regiment, a Territorial Battalion, attesting at Reading. After training at Chelmsford and on Salisbury Plain, the battalion went to France, arriving at Le Havre at the end of May 1916. It is not clear precisely when Thomas joined up, but early in 1915, the battalion were guarding German prisoners-of-war at Holyport, the first to arrive in the UK. Having arrived in France, training continued for a few more days before they went into trenches for the first time on 8th June, with the first three men, all from Reading, being killed the next day. The first action of note occurred on 13th July, when a raid was planned to capture or kill Germans. This was not a great success as they had difficulty finding a hole in the enemy wire, and all five officers were killed or wounded, leaving a lack of leaders to co-ordinate the support when it was needed; six other men were also killed in the action. More casualties were sustained three days later when moving into trenches for an attack which was later cancelled, owing to mist which prevented artillery registration, and eight more men were wounded on returning from the attack positions. The attack actually took place on the 19th, with the artillery barrage commencing at 11am. It was due to start at 6pm, but even before then, forty men had been killed or wounded in the trenches by the enemy's artillery, and when they left the trenches, machine gun fire accounted for many more. The attack failed completely, and 123 men from the battalion were recorded as having been wounded that day. Thomas was probably one of them as he died of wounds the following day, and is buried in Merville Community Cemetery.

ALBERT HOLLY

Albert Holly was born in 1893, and baptised in the local church on 5th November by the curate. This was probably in St Andrew's Church as the family were living in Binfield Road at the time. He was the youngest of seven children, with another dying in infancy, and was almost twenty years younger than his oldest sister. His father did various labouring jobs. By the time Albert left school, the family had moved to Old Bracknell, and he worked as a carter lad for a local building contractor. Albert volunteered for service, attesting at Wokingham, and joined the 8th Battalion, Berkshire Regiment. This battalion contained men from London, Birmingham, Surrey and Wales, as well as local volunteers. Initial training took place in Reading before a move to Wiltshire for three months before they went to France, arriving on 8th August 1915. Their first time in the trenches occurred nine days later, but they were not involved in an attack until 25th September. This was against a German position east of Hulluch and, although successful, many casualties were incurred by a combination of gas, caused by leakages from the storage containers plus a change in wind direction blowing it back over the British lines, and machine gun fire, especially when there was a delay in getting through the wire which the artillery bombardment had failed to cut. They supported another attack the following day, but played no part in it, and were relieved on the 28th, by which time they were exhausted, having received no extra rations or water for three days after the ration parties had got lost. They were back in the front line a week later, and attacked a German front trench on the 13th. This started at 2pm, prior to which, chlorine gas and smoke bombs had been released, but machine gun fire from both the front and the flanks caused many casualties, and the attack failed. Albert was one of those killed; his body was never found and his name is recorded on the Loos Memorial.

The late Pte. FREDK. HOWARD, Nine Mile Ride, Crowthorne.—Killed in action.

FREDERICK HOWARD

Frederick Howard was born at the south lodge of Easthampstead Park in 1883, and baptised 10th February the following year at Easthampstead church. The lodge still stands, on the corner of Nine Mile Ride and South Road, the road leading to Easthampstead Park Crematorium. He was the second of eight children, and his father seems to have had several different jobs in the area, as some of Frederick's siblings were born at Wokingham, Sandhurst and Barkham. Frederick also had a variety of jobs, working in turn as a labourer, carter, and domestic gardener. He joined under the Derby scheme, attesting at Wokingham on 10th December 1915, and joined the 2nd Battalion, Berkshire Regiment. Parts of his service record survive, showing him to be 5'5" tall and weighing just under nine a half stone. It also notes he was 33 years of age, despite his protests that he was only 31; the younger age would only have delayed his mobilisation by a couple of weeks. He was also illiterate, signing his attestation form with a cross. He was mobilised on 25th March 1916, and went to France at the end of June, but within two months was transferred to the 17th Battalion, Manchester Regiment. He was soon in trouble in an incident with a superior officer, and faced a Court Martial on 27th September. The details of the incident are from a damaged section of the Service Record, but the word 'insubordinate' is clearly visible. He was sentenced to "5 to 6 days, Field Punishment Number 1." For this, he would have been tied to a post or a gun wheel for two hours per day, regardless of the weather. Almost all the men in the trenches were also affected by lice, further adding to the discomfort to the punishment. A few days later, the battalion were fighting in a phase of the Battle of the Somme, and cautiously advanced early the following year, as the Germans retreated to the Hindenburg Line. From March 27th to April 3rd, the Battalion were billeted in the tunnels at

Blairville, providing working parties under command of the Royal Engineers. They went into the front line on the 4th, remaining there until late on the 7th. Earlier that day, two officers and two men were killed while patrolling near Neuville Mill; one of these was Frederick. After the war, it was not uncommon for bodies to be exhumed from battlefield graves and small, local burial grounds, to be reburied in the official War Cemeteries. A letter was sent to Frederick's parents in June 1920, informing them of such a move. Although the records do not record his original grave site, he is now buried in Bucquoy Road Cemetery, Ficheux.

George Howard

George Howard was born in Easthampstead towards the end of 1892, and baptised on 11th December. He was one of five children, and a cousin to Frederick. His father, a labourer, died before George was eight years old, and his mother moved the family from Nine Mile Ride, where presumably they were living in a tied cottage for workers on the Easthampstead Park estate, to Binfield Road. Two years later, in 1902, she remarried, and the family moved again, to the Bagshot Road. After leaving school, George worked at Easthampstead Park, tending cows on one of the estate's farms. An indication of just how tight-knit the local communities were at this time, is that George was working alongside the brother of Frank Headington, whose name also appears on the Roll of Honour at Easthampstead church. Like his cousin, George attested at Wokingham, and joined the 2nd Battalion, Berkshire Regiment, albeit under the Derby Scheme. Although he did not go to France until 1916, he must have gone before Frederick, as he was involved in the Battle of the Somme on 1st July of that year. The battalion had the objective of capturing the village of Ovillers, north of La Boisselle. The Regimental History records the action that day: "After a night during which the trenches had been shelled by the Germans, at around 6:30am, the British barrage began. An hour later, the men climbed out of the trenches to start the attack, but immediately came under terrific rifle and machine gun fire from the German trenches in front of Ovillers, which prevented them from reaching the enemy line. A small group on the left did manage to get into the trench, but was eventually bombed out again. By 7:45am, the enemy fire on the parapet of the British trench made it impossible for any more men to leave it. In less than three hours after the attack started, over half the battalion had been killed, while the regiments to the left and right had lost an even higher proportion of men. With such losses, it was clearly impossible to mount another attack, and the Brigade remained in their trenches until dark, when it withdrew to bivouacs at Long Valley." George was one of those killed, and is buried in Ovillers Military Cemetery.

Sapper T. HUNT, Royal Engineers, Bracknell.

Thomas H. Hunt

Henry Thomas Cotterell (he seems to use the two forenames interchangeably) was born, illegitimately, in 1890. His mother was just seventeen years old when he was born. Although she married John Hunt three years later, and went on to have another ten children, Thomas, despite taking her husband's surname, appears to have been brought up by an aunt and uncle who had no children of their own. In 1901, the couple ran the Beehive Inn at Amen Corner, but by 1911, they had moved to Easthampstead Road, running what was described as a "general shop." By now, Thomas had left school and was working as a farm labourer, but later became a carpenter, working on the Easthampstead Park estate. He volunteered for service, attesting at Wokingham on 21st January 1915, and joined the 105th Field Company, Royal Engineers. He was just over 5'7" tall, and weighed a little over ten stones. Although his surviving service record is incomplete, it does state that he spent nine months training at various locations in Hampshire, before going to France in September; it also adds he objected to having an anti-typhoid inoculation, but it was still given. The Division was involved in phases of the Battle of the Somme in 1916, and fighting at Messines and Pilkem the following year. In January 1917, the unit was working on repairs and improvement of the trenches held by the 74th Infantry Brigade, including the construction of emplacements for Trench and Stokes Mortars, bomb and ammunition stores, and dug-outs. The War Diary also notes that work with concrete was hampered by the severe weather. It also states: "with exception of *a* heavy bombardment of our lines by enemy on 22nd, nothing out of ordinary has occurred." A couple of months later, another entry contains a list of men receiving awards, including 65025 Sapper T. Hunt, M.M. *(Military Medal)*. In mid July, Thomas's unit was at Hallebast, about four miles southwest of Ypres, making a road for wheeled traffic from bundles of brushwood, building huts, and general work around the camp. Five volunteers had gone to Ypres to take part in a raid, where their task was to blow up dug-outs in the enemy lines, but when they reported, they were informed their services were no longer required. The War Diary for the 17th also records, "65025, Sapper, Hunt T., killed in action," but adds no further information. He is buried in Dickebusch New Military Cemetery Extension. After his death, an official letter, dated August 1917, was received at the War Office, purporting to come from his widow, a Mrs Gertrude Ellen Hunt of Grazeley, near Reading, who submitted a claim for a pension, and provided details of her marriage at Holy Trinity Church, Grazeley on 26th June 1915. Enquiries were made as the marriage certificate listed him as Henry Thomas Hunt, while the Army records listed him as Thomas Hunt. The outcome is not recorded, but the civil registrations do show the marriage taking place. They also show she remarried in 1919 to a Frederick Brazier, with a new address in Mortimer.

JOHN HUTTON

John Hutton was born in the Partick area of Glasgow in 1880, and was one of eleven children. His father worked in one of the shipyards on the Clyde. After leaving school, John worked as a labourer, and married Louise Steel in London in 1907. It is not known when John moved to this area, but he was conscripted into the 1st Battalion, Worcestershire Regiment, attesting at Wokingham, and was mobilised at the end of May 1916. The battalion were involved in the Third Battle of Ypres the following year, and the Battles of The Somme and The Aisne in 1918. The Regimental History records the fighting at Albert towards the end of August: "On 16th August, the 1st Worcestershire, embussing at Mont St.-Eloy, were carried forward to the front line in the trenches facing Oppy. In front of them, the enemy had an elaborate system of defences, unaltered since the Arras battles of the previous year. Apart from gas shelling, which caused many casualties, the week which ensued was not marked by any great activity. From the 21st onwards, a continuous thunder of gun-fire to the southward told of the great attacks by which the enemy were being forced back from their prepared positions. For four days, the new offensive was at a distance, but by the 26th, the gun-fire came close to the 1st Worcestershire as the right flank of the First Army took up the battle, and drove the enemy from their positions in front of Arras. That evening orders came that the enemy in front of the 8th Division were probably retiring, and that efforts must be made to gain ground. The battalions in the front line were ordered to reconnoitre and to push forward where possible. In pursuance of these orders, the 1st Worcestershire advanced when darkness fell. 'A' Company led the way on the left flank, followed by 'D' Company. They came up against a strong force of the enemy in 'Severn Alley', and a sharp bombing fight ensued. Gallantly, the Worcestershire bombers forced back the enemy, but fresh German parties closed in on either flank and made a series of desperate counter-attacks. Amid a shower of bursting bombs, the Worcestershire lads held firm, inspired by the brave subaltern who, although wounded on the face, refused to leave his men until the position was secured. Further to the right, the bombers of 'B' Company were led with equal resolution. There also, an initial success was checked by violent counter-attacks, but after an obstinate fight, the enemy at length gave way and 'B' Company gained most of 'Z' trench. Next day, the fighting was resumed, and by nightfall, the whole system of trenches north of Oppy was in our hands. A series of counter-attacks from 'Albert Trench' were beaten off. Bombing and shooting went on around the Oppy trenches for the ensuing two or three days; then the enemy's efforts died away." Only two men were killed during the four days, but one of them was John, on the 27th. He is buried in La Targette British Cemetery, Neuville-St. Vaast.

ALFRED KEEN

The late Lce.-Corpl. ALFRED KEEN, Lewis Gun Section, Royal Berks Regt., Bracknell.—Killed in action.

Alfred Keen was born in Easthampstead in 1893, and baptised on 5th November in St Andrew's Church by the curate. He was one of fifteen children, three of whom died young. The family lived in a cottage on the Binfield Road, close to the brickworks where his father was employed. After leaving school, Alfred moved to Uxbridge, where he worked as a hairdresser. He volunteered for service, attesting at Uxbridge, and joined the 2nd Battalion, Royal Fusiliers. The battalion had left England in March 1915, and landed at Gallipoli the following month, where Alfred would join them on 15th December. But he was only there for three weeks, as the Division was evacuated early the following month, and returned to Egypt. They remained there for a couple of months, before sailing for Marseilles, and moved to the area east of Pont Remy, southeast of Abbeville, by the end of March. Beaumont Hamel was a fortress village, located just behind the German line on 1st July 1916, and commanded the valley over which the attacking troops had to cross. The War Diary tells of the action on that day: "From early dawn to 7:20am, bombardment was very fierce. The big mine opposite Hawthorn Redoubt was then exploded, and 'Z' Company rushed forward to occupy the crater, but were immediately met with heavy machine gun fire and artillery barrage. Five minutes later, at Zero hour, the general attack along whole front was launched. Very few of our men ever reached as far as enemy barbed wire, owing to our artillery persistently shelling 2nd and 3rd line of the enemy's first system. The Germans were able to freely use their own front line, and therefore resisted all attacks on it. This continued to about midday when the few remaining men in No Man's Land were forced to retire." Over fifty men from the battalion were killed, nearly three hundred wounded, and almost 150 were missing. Alfred was one of the latter; "Death presumed" is written in his medal card, and his name is listed on the Thiepval Memorial.

CHARLES LANGLEY

Charles Langley, known as Charlie was born in 1895, and baptised, probably in St Andrew's Church, on 2nd June the same year. He was one of ten children, with another another two dying in infancy. The family lived in Street Cottages, Binfield Road, close to where Charlie's father worked as a brickyard labourer, probably at the yard on the site now occupied by Arlington Square. After leaving school, Charlie worked as a barber's apprentice before volunteering for service, attesting at Wokingham, and joined the 2nd Battalion, Royal Scottish Fusiliers. After his initial training, he crossed the Channel in mid March 1915. At this time, each Infantry Battalion had four machine guns, but it soon became obvious that a single specialist Machine Gun Company per Infantry Brigade was required, replacing the guns and gun teams from the battalions; this was formed in October and Charles transferred to it. Charles was probably involved on the Battle of Loos in the autumn of 1915, the Battle of the Somme in the summer and autumn of 1916, and the Arras Offensive in spring of the following year. On 24th July, Charles's Machine Gun Company moved to Micmac Camp. The line was heavily shelled, with one gun and all the stores being blown up. Three men were killed, and another eight wounded. They remained in the line for the next two days, providing a barrage of nine guns on the 26th in support of a raiding party. During the course of this, the enemy shelled the battery for several minutes, but without inflicting any casualties. Charlie must have been one of the men wounded two days earlier, as he died of wounds on the 28th, and is buried in Dickebusch New Military Cemetery Extension. The photo shows Charlie (standing) with his elder brother William, who was wounded and lost an eye in the conflict, and died in 1963.

FRANK R. LOVEGROVE

Frank George Lovegrove (the middle initial is wrong on the memorial), was born in 1893 at Reading, and was one of ten children. The family were living in Friar Street when he was born, but had moved to Bracknell by 1901, and were living at the Blue Lion pub in Broad Lane. However, Frank's father was not a publican, but worked in the building trade, primarily as a plumber, but also as a gas fitter and house decorator. While living in Reading, he had also recorded bell-hanging in his list of occupations. Business must have been good as, despite having a large family to support, Frank's father could afford to move again, occupying a house called 'The Orchards' in Old Bracknell in 1911. After leaving school, Frank worked as a stationer's assistant, before joining the 2/4th Battalion, Royal Berkshire Regiment, a Territorial Battalion set up two months after the war started, attesting at Reading. This battalion was for Home Service, consisting of men who had not agreed to serve overseas, although later in the war this was changed, and all Territorial soldiers were eligible to serve on foreign soil. It is not known when Alfred joined the battalion, but training had started at Maidenhead in November 1914 with almost one thousand recruits. The first war duty they performed was providing guards for a Prisoner of War camp at The Philberds, a large house located between Holyport and the M4. The thirteen captured men there were among the first to arrive from France, and the camp later became one of the Officers' Prisoner-of-War Camps. The adjutant became suspicious when the inmates all suddenly took a keen interest in gardening, and a few weeks later, a well-constructed escape tunnel was discovered, almost ready for use. In February 1915, the battalion moved to Northampton to continue training, and two months later to Chelmsford, where their work involved digging trenches at Epping for the defence of London, and sentry duty around the roads of Essex. At the beginning of March the following year, they moved again to Salisbury Plain, and the Division was inspected by the King at Bulford on 5th May before setting off for France, landing at Le Havre towards the end of the month. The Berkshires were involved in the attack at Fromelles on 19th July 1916. This was designed as a subsidiary attack to the much larger offensive taking place further south on the Somme, but it was an unmitigated disaster with very heavy casualties and no significant gain; the Division was not used again, other than for holding trench lines until 1917, when it was involved in operations on the Ancre, the Battle of Langemarck, and at Cambrai late in the year when massed tanks were used for the first time in the conflict. In March 1918, the Germans began a great spring offensive, pushing the British back. Having been relieved two days earlier, the battalion were in the rear zone at Ugny on the 21st when the enemy were sweeping forward. By 8:30am, they were at Marteville, and were ordered to counter-attack on the high ground about Maissemy where the enemy had succeeded in penetrating into the battle area. This counter-attack was partially successful, but later all the ground recovered was lost again. The Germans had greatly superior numbers and their machine gun fire was recorded as being exceptionally heavy. There are no figures recorded in the War Diary for deaths on this day, but the phrase "heavy casualties" is ominous. Frank, by now a sergeant, was one of these; his body was never recovered, and his name is listed on the Pozieres Memorial.

The late Pte. SIDNEY C. LOVEGROVE, The Orchards, Old Bracknell.—Killed in action.

SIDNEY C. LOVEGROVE

Sidney Charles Lovegrove was an older brother of Frank's, born at Reading in 1891. Two of their brothers had joined their father in the plumbing and painting business, but Sidney worked as a bricklayer. He also played football for Bracknell Wanderers, who later became Bracknell Town Football Club, and was a member of the team that won the Ascot and District League Second Division title for the first time in 1914. He joined the 2/4th Battalion, Berkshire Regiment at the same time as Frank; they were given consecutive service numbers. The War Diary entry for 24th August 1916 refers to several men "who were conspicuous for gallantry in the Action for July 19th". This action was an assault on the German front and support trenches, commencing at 6pm. The artillery preparation started seven hours earlier, and the Berkshire suffered forty casualties from German artillery fire before the attack had even started. The attack failed completely due to heavy enemy machine gun fire. A few men managed to reach the wire, but finding it uncut, and with no support on either flank, were forced to retire. Among those listed was Sidney. "This N.C.O. was one of the leading wave of 'B' Company, and with a few companions managed to reach No Man's Land. Finding the assault checked, Lce.Cpl. Lovegrove returned for further instructions no less than three times, running the greatest risks on each occasion." In the early months of 1917, the Germans were falling back to the Hindenburg Line, with the British in cautious pursuit. At the end of March, the battalion advanced on Vermand. A patrol of two officers and twenty men were sent out to reconnoitre the cemetery, and by 6am on the 31st, the village had been taken. The following day, they were occupied in building defences, but opposition shell fire was heavy, and five men were killed and fifteen wounded.

Corporal Sidney Lovegrove was one of the quintet who lost their lives that day, and is buried in Vermand Communal Cemetery.

TERENCE F. MACKAY

Terence Faulkner Mackay was born in St John's Wood, London in 1898. His unmarried mother was Mary Faulkner, the daughter of a grocer from Sulhampstead, Berkshire, who was a student at a Teacher Training College in the King's Road, Chelsea, at the time of his birth. His father was William Mackay from the Marylebone area of London, who was to become a stage actor in the West End, and who also penned, with his wife, at least three plays still in print to this day. Terence was baptised at Warfield Parish Church on 3rd June 1898, with the parents recorded as William and a mysterious lady named Edith (this may have been his future wife Edith Bury; they married in 1907), the couple giving an address in the London Road as their place of residence. Terence's parents then seem to disappear from the picture as he is listed in the next two censuses, living with James Herrington, the Easthampstead parish clerk, and his family "near the church." Terence attended the newly opened Ranelagh School, which had moved to its present site in 1908, before continuing his education at Dauntsey's School, near Malmsbury, Wiltshire, moving there in February 1915. He was not entirely without family in Bracknell; two of his mother's brothers lived in the town, one running a shop, selling bread and groceries, the other a music teacher and organist at Holy Trinity Church, who lived in Larges Lane. Terence's father and his family must have been involved in his education, paying for his place at Dauntsey's School, after which, he gained a commission in the Kings Royal Rifle Corps, and was attached to the 4th Battalion. They had been in Greece from the end of 1915 until the middle of 1918, before returning to France. Here they joined the 50th (Northumbrian Division), which had suffered heavy casualties and were exhausted after taking part in three battles against the German Spring Offensive earlier that year. It was not until October that the Division was considered ready to face the enemy. On the 3rd, as part of the Battle of Cambrai, the battalion were ordered to clear villages of Gouy and Le Catelet, and control the high ground to the north of the latter. There was difficulty in moving the companies to the assembly positions as the ground was unfamiliar and no guides were available. Although it was carried out successfully, there were heavy losses, and units became scattered and disorganised. All troops on the west front of Le Catelet came under heavy machine gun fire from the road, and therefore stopped advancing and dug in. At about midday, the enemy tried to work their way to the outskirts of Gouy, and as the battalion were too weak to hold the position, they were forced to retire, and were relieved in the evening. At some point during the day, Terence was killed whilst leading his platoon, and is buried in Prospect Hill Cemetery, Gouy. His next-of-kin was listed as his father, Mr W. G. Mackay, of The Caledonian Club, St James Square, London.

GREVILLE E. MCCLELLAN

Greville Edward Gordon McClellan, known as George, was born on 21st January 1887 at Muttra, India. He was the youngest of seven children, two of whom had died by 1911. His father had been a Lieutenant Colonel in the Cavalry, serving in Ireland, as well as India. On returning to England, the family lived in Bristol, but moved had to an address in Easthampstead by 1911, where they employed three servants. In 1908, George obtained a commission with the 5th Battalion, Worcestershire Regiment, in the Special Reserve. This was a form of part-time soldiering, in some ways similar to the Territorial Force. Men would enlist into the Special Reserve for six years, with the possibility of being called up in the event of a general mobilisation. They would otherwise undertake all the same conditions as men of the Army Reserve. Their period as a Special Reservist started with six months of full-time training, with a further three to four weeks annual training for the rest of their service period. He also learnt to fly, obtaining his Royal Aero Club Aviator's Certificate at Brooklands, flying a Bristol Biplane on 20th May 1913; he was one of the first five hundred men to receive such a certificate in the country. With the outbreak of war, George was mobilised, and attached to the 2nd Battalion, Worcestershire Regiment who were already at Aldershot. They landed at Boulogne ten days after war was declared, and were involved in the Battles of Mons, the Marne, the Aisne and Ypres in 1914, and Festubert and Loos the following year. On 20th October 1915, he was shot through the heart by a sniper, while supervising his company at work in an exposed position. The Regimental History records, "His loss was much felt, for he had many times inspired all who saw him by his courage and contempt of danger." He is buried in the Cambrin Churchyard Extension.

Joseph H. Mills

Joseph Henry Mills was born in Bracknell in 1882, and baptised in Holy Trinity Church on 5th March. He was the youngest of three surviving children, two infant sisters having died within a few months of each other in 1880. The family lived in Searle Street, which ran on the north side of the pub opposite Bracknell station. His father had a variety of jobs, recorded in successive censuses as working in one of the local brickyards, as a coal porter, and then as a general labourer. Joseph married Elsie Gale in 1906, and a daughter was born two years later. They lived in Wokingham Road, with Joseph working at one of the butcher's shops in the High Street. He joined the 2/4th Battalion, Royal Berkshire Regiment, a Territorial Battalion set up two months after the war started, attesting at Wokingham. This battalion was for Home Service, consisting of men who had not agreed to serve overseas, although later in the war this was changed, and all Territorial soldiers were eligible to serve on foreign soil. It is not known when Alfred joined the battalion, but training had started at Maidenhead in November 1914 with almost one thousand recruits. The first war duty they performed was providing guards for a Prisoner of War camp at The Philberds, a large house located between Holyport and the M4. The thirteen captured men there were among the first to arrive from France, and the camp later became one of the Officers' Prisoner-of-War Camps. The adjutant became suspicious when the inmates all suddenly took a keen interest in gardening, and a few weeks later, a well-constructed escape tunnel was discovered, almost ready for use. In February 1915, the battalion moved to Northampton to continue training, and two months later to Chelmsford, where their work involved digging trenches at Epping for the defence of London, and sentry duty around the roads of Essex. At the beginning of March the following year, they moved again to Salisbury Plain, and the Division was inspected by the King at Bulford on 5th May before setting off for France, landing at Le Havre towards the end of the month. The Berkshires were involved in the attack at Fromelles on 19th July 1916. This was designed as a subsidiary attack to the much larger offensive taking place further south on the Somme, but it was an unmitigated disaster with very heavy casualties and no significant gain; the Division was not used again, other than for holding trench lines until 1917, when it was involved in operations on the Ancre, and the Battle of Langemarck. It was not known when Joseph returned to England, but he died at the Regimental Depot in Reading on 28th November 1917 from kidney disease, and is buried in Larges Lane Cemetery, Bracknell. His grave is at the far end of the graveyard, next to that of John Quick (see Bracknell men); his widow, Elsie, died 20th November 1975, aged 95, and is buried in the same grave.

STANDISH O'DONOGHUE

The late Pte. S. A. O'DONOGHUE, Royal Irish Fusiliers, Bagshot Road, Bracknell.—Killed in action.

Standish Hart (or Art) O'Donoghue was born in 1895 in Dublin, but appears to have been brought up by an aunt and uncle living on Bagshot Road, Bracknell. He had an older brother, who was also living with other relatives by 1901. His uncle worked as a domestic gardener, and Standish was doing a similar job after leaving school. As the junior, he would have started washing the clay flowerpots and sweeping paths, and gradually learning the skills of the job. He volunteered for service, attesting at Guildford, initially joining the Army Service Corps as a driver, but later, as the need for fit men increased, was transferred to the 2nd Battalion, Royal Irish Fusiliers, probably towards the end of 1916 or early the following year. The Fusiliers had been in Salonika since the end of 1915, but moved to Egypt in September 1917, for service in Palestine. The Ottoman Army held a line from Gaza to Beersheba, but the Egyptian Expeditionary Force began to drive them back at the Battle of Beersheba on the last day of October, followed by more success in the Third Battle of Gaza thirty-six hours later. Only Hariera, ten miles east of Beersheba, held out, and the Royal Irish Fusiliers were part of an attack on the 6th to capture it. They were in position by 9am, and the attack began three hours later. The War Diary gives no details of the fighting, but states "the battalion occupied enemy trenches by 4pm, and started consolidation. 10 prisoners captured and much war material." There were around fifty casualties, most of them wounded. At 6:30am the following morning, 'B' and 'C' Companies, along with a battalion from each of the Royal Irish Fusiliers and Inniskilling Fusiliers, attacked the Hareira Redoubt. As the gunnery horses were away being watered, the battalion's transport took the Howitzer battery into action for supporting fire. This was urgently required, as the attackers had to cross an open plain for three thousand yards under very heavy rifle and machine gun fire. By 4:30pm, they had occupied enemy trench system, and half an hour later, the Redoubt was captured as well. The battalion lost 21 men killed, with a further 36 missing. Standish was one of the former, and is buried in Gaza War Cemetery, probably one of the first to be interred there, as the city had only just fallen to the Allies.

PERCY A. PEARCE

Percy Arthur Pearce was born in 1886 at Thornbury, a few miles north of Bristol. He had an older sister, born before his parents married, and he was also conceived before they 'tied the knot'. Initially working as a corn merchant, Percy's father then got a job as a farm bailiff, and this brought him to Easthampstead at some time between the 1911 census, and his death in 1918. It is not clear whether Percy ever lived in the area, or when he joined the army. In 1911, he was living with his parents in Gloucestershire, but was unemployed, a rare occurrence for the period. He had joined the army early in the war, attesting at Bristol, and joined one of the Territorial Battalions of the Gloucestershire Regiment. As the war dragged on, these battalions were also sent overseas, and Percy crossed to France during 1916. It is not known when Percy was transferred to the 1/8th Battalion, Lancashire Fusiliers, but it may have been in November

1917 when the Lancashires were receiving new drafts. Percy's new battalion took part in both the First and Second Battles of the Somme in 1918. Trones Wood was one area keenly fought over during the course of the conflict. On 4th September, the Lancashires were ordered to attack the northern section of the wood. The Regimental History records the fighting: "They had been heavily shelled in Dublin Trench earlier in the day, but the leading company moved forward at 5:30pm. The rest of the battalion were greatly impeded by a relief moving up into Longueval Alley at the same time, but at 7pm, they assaulted the wood over a front of 750 yards. They were met by very heavy rifle, machine gun, and shell fire, and the advance was checked owing to no supporting troops being to hand. The enemy appeared to have suffered very little damage from the bombardment as he developed very heavy rifle fire, and also put a barrage on Longueval Alley. At 8:50pm, a message was received that the Northern Portion of Trones Wood would be re-bombarded, and that the attack was not to be pressed if success seemed unlikely. At 9pm, the remainder of the battalion reorganised for the defence of Longueval Alley. Just after midnight, instructions were received that the battalion might withdraw to the German old front line system if Longueval Alley was sufficiently held, and this was done a couple of hours later. But casualties had been heavy, with thirteen officers, and 216 other ranks killed or wounded." Percy's life was to end in Trones Wood, and he is buried in Lebucquiere Communal Cemetery Extension. As well as the War Memorial at Easthampstead, Percy's name is one of the five listed on the memorial in his home village.

STANLEY PRIOR

Pte. STANLEY PRIOR, "Bancroft," Bracknell.—Wounded in both arms and legs. One leg has been amputated.

Stanley Prior was born in Easthampstead in 1898, and baptised 6th February, probably in St Andrew's Church, as the family lived in Binfield Road. He had a younger brother, and by 1911, the family had moved to Wokingham Road. By this time, his father had changed from being a painter and decorator, to working as a letterpress printer, the main form of printing until well into the twentieth century. It is not clear how Stanley managed to get into the army when he did, as the records imply he did not go to France until 1916. However, he would still have been only eighteen years of age, twelve months short of being eligible. With the threat of the Derby Scheme and conscription looming, which would have enforced a wait of twelve months before he could join, a young man might decide to volunteer while he was still able to do so, adding one or two years to his age. Stanley attested at Reading, and joined the 2nd Battalion, Hampshire Regiment. Although the battalion initially fought at Gallipoli, they were in France by the time Stanley joined them, and he probably took part in the Battle of the Somme. On 12th October 1916, the battalion faced a very nasty proposition, when called on to tackle the German lines just beyond Gueudecourt, in the mud and wet, and suffered 150 casualties in three days. After two more days in support at Gueudecourt, when more heavy shelling caused another twenty casualties, the battalion moved up into Hilt Trench on the evening of October 17th for a fresh attack on Grease Trench. The Regimental History describes the fighting on that day: "'Zero' was at 3:40am the following morning, but before that the leading companies, 'Y' and 'Z', had formed up in No Man's Land. This drew the enemy's fire but it had little effect, and at 'Zero' the attackers went forward well and, despite heavy fire, both Hampshire and Worcestershire, keeping close to the barrage, were quickly into Grease Trench and overpowering its defenders, despite heavy fire from Stormy Trench and the heavy shelling.

Neither of these could shift the Hampshire, who held on stoutly, repulsing all attempts to dislodge them. But their endurance was severely taxed - the shelling was very heavy, the weather atrocious, with pelting rain, and to get supplies up to those in front required real energy and determination from the carrying parties." Four officers and 31 men were killed in the two days of the action. Again, according to the Regimental History, "October 18th ranks among the 2nd Hampshire's most notable achievements." Stanley had been badly wounded on the first day of the attack, was brought back to England for treatment, but died on 1st November 1916 at a hospital in the north of England, and is buried in Easthampstead churchyard. The Reading Mercury edition on 11th November briefly recorded his burial: "Pte Stan Prior (18), Hampshire Regiment, of 'Bancroft', Bracknell, succumbed to his severe injuries in hospital at Newcastle-upon-Tyne last week, and was interred at Easthampstead Churchyard on Saturday. The deceased was for ten years with the St. Andrew's Choir at Priestwood, and was an original member of the Easthampstead Troop of Baden Powell Scouts, the present members of which followed the coffin." Curiously, he has two graves, one with an official Commonwealth War Graves headstone, the other erected by his family, presumably at a later date. On both graves, he has been given the surname Lyford-Prior. His father appears to have been born with the surname Lyford, but brought up by an aunt and uncle with the surname Prior, who had no children of their own, and who later adopted him; both surnames appear at various times in the census entries for him.

The late Gnr. H. RIXON, Canadian Field Artillery, Station Road, Bracknell.—Killed by explosive shell.

HARRY RIXON

Harry James Rixon was born 14th February 1891 at Great Marlow, Buckinghamshire. He was one of six children, two of whom died in infancy; his eldest sister also died at the age of fifteen, by which time the family had moved to Bracknell. Initially, they lived on the Bagshot Road before moving to Station Road, closer to the town centre, where his father earned his living by looking after the horses belonging to a local coal merchant. After leaving school, Harry went into domestic service, working as a footman. But he was keen to make a better life for himself, and there were opportunities overseas in the British colonies for adventurous young men, especially in Canada which was actively encouraging them to move and build up the country. In March 1911, Harry boarded the vessel 'Southwark' at Liverpool, and crossed the Atlantic, reaching Halifax, Nova Scotia on 2nd April, and Maine, Portland, the following day. He stated Saskatchewan as his intended destination, working in a similar job to that which he had left. With higher wages and more opportunity for promotion, there were many chances of a better life than back in the socially rigid home country. But things were to change, and in November 1914, he was volunteering at Regina, Saskatchewan, to join the 5th Brigade, Canadian Field Artillery, part of the Canadian Expeditionary Force. By now he was working on the land, leading a team of horses; Canadian labourers could expect to earn enough money to purchase some land and set up their own farm within a few years. He was described as being 5'10" inches tall, with blue eyes, fair hair, and a ruddy complexion. Up to two thirds of the early volunteers from Canada were young men who had emigrated from the United Kingdom, and even by the end of the war, this figure was still more than fifty per cent. Harry started his training at McFadden Barracks, Winnipeg, in January the following year. The barracks were very overcrowded, and there were mild outbreaks of measles and influenza. The following month, they moved to Exhibition Grounds, Winnipeg, where various frame buildings had been improvised as barracks. A first draft of men was sent overseas, but it was noted that many of the new recruits to replace them were rejected as physically unfit. In May, there was an outbreak of cerebro-spinal meningitis at the camp, but prompt hospitalisation and precautions prevented any further infections. There are several references in the War Diary to insufficient toilet facilities, and the insanitary way garbage was dealt with. In June, the 5th Artillery Brigade transferred to Sewell Camp, an Army training camp west of Carberry, Manitoba; by the end of the war, over 38,000 men had been trained there. The camp, which started in 1909, was a city of tents and covered a large area. The name of the camp was changed in 1915 to Camp Hughes, in honour of Canada's Minister of Militia and Defence at the time. Extensive trench systems, grenade and rifle ranges, and military structures were built at Camp Hughes between 1915 and 1916, and there was also a variety of retail stores and entertainment complexes. On 5th August, Harry and his colleagues left on the Canadian Pacific Railway for Halifax, Nova Scotia, a journey that took four days. The following day, they left Canada on RMS 'Metagama', and arrived at Plymouth eight days later after an uneventful crossing, and were then moved to Otterpool Camp, near Shorncliffe, Kent. There were regular medical inspections, and one on the voyage revealed eight cases of gonorrhoea. The toilet facilities, lack of cleanliness, and poor supply of water at the new camp continued to cause complaints from the Medical Officer. At the end of the month, one thousand horses arrived for the unit, and on 2nd September, the troops were reviewed by the King. The next few weeks were filled by a routine of drills, training and marching. But the routine was interrupted on 13th October when the alarm was raised by the sight of a Zeppelin heading for the camp. Two lights had been left burning after 'lights out' (in the bath-house and kitchen), allowing it a target to drop four bombs in the vicinity, killing eleven men of the Canadian Artillery immediately, and wounding fourteen more. One bomb had struck the guard tent, and a second had fallen in the horse lines; almost forty horses were killed or had to be put down. Harry was one of those wounded, and died two days later. The Reading Mercury of 23rd October 1915 carried a brief report of his funeral: "The remains of Gunner H. Rixon, Canadian F. A., who was a victim of an explosive shell, dying in hospital at Shorncliffe, were interred at Easthampstead churchyard. The coffin was covered by the Union Jack, and was borne on a hand-bier drawn by a detachment of the Royal Berkshire Regiment, including a band, which played a funeral march as the cortege left Station Road (where his parents resided)." Harry is buried in Easthampstead Churchyard in a grave with an official Commonwealth War Graves headstone.

Bernard Sergeant

Bernard Theobald Sargeant was born on 18th July 1892 in Brixton, London, and had an elder brother. His father had been born in Easthampstead, the son of a wheelwright, but both he and an elder brother had become clerks in a solicitor's office, later qualifying as solicitors in their own right. Bernard's father moved to London, and his business was successful enough for him to employ a domestic servant at their home in Mervan Road, Brixton by 1911. Bernard worked as a clerk at the Sun Fire Insurance Office after leaving school. He joined the 5th Battalion, London Regiment, a Territorial Battalion, attesting on 24th April 1913. In June 1915, he was attached to 101st Provisional Battalion, a 'holding' unit for men who had not signed up to go overseas, and was posted to Southwold, Suffolk, where he completed a course in musketry in January 1916. In February, a new system of training for officers was introduced, after which temporary commissions could only be granted if a man had been through an Officer Cadet unit. Bernard joined the Inns of Court Officer Training Corps at Berkhampstead, Hertfordshire, gained his commission in January 1917, and joined the 8th Battalion, London Regiment. According to his application form, he was 5'6" tall, weighed nearly ten and a half stone, had been educated at Montrose College, Streatham Hill, an establishment that offered a practical education for young men preparing for commercial or professional careers, and was of "very good character." Although on the Roll of the 8th Battalion, Bernard was attached to the 3rd Battalion, who were in need of officers after fighting in the Battle of the Somme the previous year. At the beginning of April, the battalion moved into Brigade Support in front of Agny, and were ordered to dig an assembly trench overnight on the 2nd. It was a moonlit night and snow covered the ground, masking the tape laid out to mark the position of the trench; the men were also clearly visible on the skyline, making easy targets for the Germans. Four men were killed and seven wounded before attempts to start the digging were abandoned. They were involved in attack on the 8th, having taken over the trenches in front of Neuville Vitasse the previous evening. 'Zero' was at 5:30am, with the men leaving the assembly trenches a couple of hours later. All four companies took their objectives, meeting little opposition, though they encountered some machine gun fire from the left. Prisoners taken were sent back under escort of the walking wounded, and were also made to carry the wounded British soldiers. By nightfall the following evening, all the captured positions had been consolidated, although at a cost of around fifty casualties. On the 10th, they attacked again with a view to capturing Nepal Trench, but came under sniper fire plus machine gun fire from Hill 90. A bombing party was sent up to help, but all became casualties. There was more heavy fighting before the trench was finally taken on the 11th, at a cost of forty British lives. Bernard was one of eight officers killed during the three days of fighting, and is buried in London Cemetery, Neuville-Vitasse. His Commanding Officer wrote, "He fell on the 10th (sic) April at the head of his men, and he died instantaneously during one of the greatest victories of this war." And the Brigade Padre, "I am so very sorry to tell you of the death of your son Bernard, who was killed in the dreadful attack upon (censored) on Monday .... the other Padre in the Brigade, who buried him this afternoon in the cemetery under the hill, has handed me a pair of scissors and a button from his pocket .... I wish you could have been with me when the men brought down his body from the trenches. They were so tired and it was raining and cold, but they were coming out and they wanted to bring his body with them. They were such good chaps ..." His parents had moved back to Bracknell by the time Bernard was killed, and were living in Borough Green, an area on the Bagshot Road, just south of the Horse and Groom pub. Bernard had made a will, naming his mother as executrix and legatee, but by the time of his death, she was "of unsound mind," and his father took over the responsibilities of his son's estate, which had a value of almost £400. Bernard's medals came up for auction twice in the 1990s.

Cecil E. Sargeant

Cecil Edward Sargeant was born early in 1895, the second of five children, and baptised 3rd February, probably at St Andrews Church, as the family lived on Wokingham Road. His father was a bricklayer, but Cecil started his working life as an errand boy in a warehouse selling oil for lamps. However, by the time he joined the army under the Derby Scheme, he was working in domestic service as a footman. He attested at Ascot on 12th November 1915, when he was described as being 5'6" tall and just over eight stones in weight. He joined the

7th Battalion, King's Royal Rifle Corps, starting his training a week after signing his papers, and went to France in April the following year. Just before he left, Violet Arkwright, a 44 year-old spinster living at Firlands, a house on the Bagshot Road, gave him a book "The Happy Warrior," subtitled "Daily Thoughts, For All Who Are Serving Their Country, Whether on Land, or Sea, or in Air." Although he may have worked for her, it is more likely she knew him through Easthampsead Chuch, which they would both have attended. After just four months, Cecil was promoted to Lance Corporal, an appointment confirmed two months later with a pay rise. Although not involved on the first day of the Battle of the Somme, the battalion fought in two later phases, as well as in the Arras Offensive in the following year. They moved up to the front line at Simoncourt on 28th April. They were there for three days, improving the current trenches and digging new assembly ones, as well as providing working parties. There was much shelling at the time, and Cecil was killed by one of them on the 28th; his body was never recovered, and he is listed on the Arras Memorial. A list of personal effects returned to his family included his watch, identification disc, a handkerchief, letters, a photocase, and a wallet.

Frank F. Sargeant

Frank Frederick Sargeant was born in Easthampstead in 1886 and baptised in the church there on 9th May. He was the youngest of seven children and was only three years old when his father, who worked as a bricklayer, died. By now, his two eldest brothers were doing similar jobs, and the family continued to live near Easthampstead Church, but after they married and left home, Frank and his mother, who was now taking in washing, moved to Mill Lane. Frank also worked as a bricklayer after leaving school, marrying Maud Studd on 20th May 1912, with a daughter and a son being born by 1916. Although his service record still exists, it was damaged by fire and water when the building housing all the papers burnt down in 1940, making parts of it illegible. He joined up under the Derby Scheme, attesting at Wokingham on 7th December 1915, giving his address as London Road, and was mobilised in June the following year. He joined the 1/1st Battalion, Hertfordshire Regiment, a Territorial Battalion which initially stayed in England, but was posted on 2nd December, moved to Halton Camp near Wendover, Buckinghamshire, two days after Christmas, and left Folkestone for Calais on 2nd January 1917. At the end of July, the Hertfordshires took part in the Battle of Pilkem, part of the Battle of Ypres of that year. The attack started at 3:50am on July 31st, but his battalion were in reserve at the start and only left their bivouacs at 6am, and after moving several times, were ordered to be ready to attack at 5pm. This order was then cancelled and they moved back a couple of hundred yards, but came under heavy shell fire and moved into adjacent trenches. Frank was killed during the shelling and his body not found; his name is listed on the Ypres (Menin Gate) Memorial. Although he lived in Bracknell, his mother still lived in the parish of Easthampstead, and he is listed on the Roll of Honour in both churches.

Harold Sargeant

Harold William Sargeant was born in Brixton in 1885, and was Bernard's elder brother. After leaving school, he worked as a wallpaper salesman, and married Rose Wickes in 1914, around the time of the outbreak of war. He signed up under the Derby Scheme, attesting on 9th December 1915 at Lambeth, and joined the 18th Battalion, London Regiment, now giving his profession as commercial clerk, and citing four years previous experience with the King's Royal Rifle Corps Cadet Battalion. He was mobilised three months later, but stayed in England for twelve months, by which time he had been promoted to Lance Sergeant. Harold then applied for a commission, which was granted in June. It is not known when Harold went to France, but the battalion were involved in phases of the Third Battle of Ypres in August and September, and the Cambrai Operations in October and November of 1917. They also faced the German Spring Offensive of 1918. Unfortunately, the War Diary for this period at the end of March, as the Germans advanced on Amiens, is missing, but Regimental Sergeant Major Harry Tyers, wrote this compelling narrative of a series of chaotic rearguard actions against fearful odds: "This is an account of the 1918 retirement, and I can claim to know a great deal about this as I was the senior bloke, apart from the Quartermaster, to come through the whole business from start to finish. The Battalion had been in the neighbourhood of Ytres (south west of Cambrai) for some time prior to 21st March, and we had a good idea that Jerry anticipated making his breakthrough. I was RSM at the time, and in that capacity, went up to Welsh Ridge in the afternoon to take over from the Fusiliers. Then, before dawn, about 3am on the 21st, the enemy bombarded all along the line, and runners came through to HQ to say that 'A' Company were being smashed up. Gas shells and big stuff was raining down close to Battalion HQ, which, however, was fairly secure. As soon as dawn broke, Colonel Neeley called me and said that we should try and get through to the front line. He went with one party of battalion HQ staff, and I with another small crowd. My party slid over the ravine and endeavoured to reach the front line, but was stopped by intense gunfire, but eventually reached an isolated party from 'A' Company who informed us that Jerry was in a portion of the line. On returning to battalion HQ, I told the CO that 'A' and 'B' Companies were withdrawing as soon as dusk fell. I loaded up all the ammunition and bombs, and punctured all the water tins and destroyed all the rations. It was a calm night, but with Verey lights going up on our flank, it looked as though Fritz had got right through. The remnants of 'A' and 'B' Companies came to Battalion HQ. The amusing incident, to my mind, was the fact that CSM 'A' Company, one Tommy Cave, had paid his initial visit to the line, and I asked him how he liked real war. Poor Tommy, who was sweating blood, shook his head disconsolately, and enquired if there was any rum about! Tommy was taken prisoner shortly afterwards. Colonel Neeley withdrew his front line companies to avoid further losses. Shortly afterwards, the Brigade withdrew to new defensive positions. They were then attacked by enemy infantry in large numbers from the direction of Villers-Plouich. Rapid fire from the battalion's rifles and Lewis Guns repelled the attack. However, the withdrawal of the 9th Division left 47th Division's flank exposed, so they were compelled to fall back to Rocquigny. At dawn on 22nd March, Jerry came over again. Our boys however, were 'real hot', having last night's smashing in mind, and mowed down the oncoming Germans like ninepins. At Villers-Plouich, which was actually on the ridge - just a few old bricks - we even counter-attacked, and gave the Boche a real hiding. We could have held on indefinitely, but orders came through that we were to vacate the position in the night, as we should be entirely cut off. Again we slid out, by this time sadly decimated, and were told we were to take over the last line of defence. Eventually *we* found it, but it wasn't a trench... but a shallow depression in the ground, about three feet deep and ten feet wide. We packed down, and shortly afterwards, the enemy appeared in thousands. They came on in extended order, line after line, and we fired until our rifle barrels were hot. It was here that I was able to do a little bit, being instrumental in putting a Jerry machine gun (which was hammering our right flank) out of action with a few bombs, and for which I was given the DCM. The enemy was too much for us, and we were told to prepare to retire, and the Welsh Fusiliers (our Pioneer Battalion) would cover our retirement. After this things became very confused. I woke up out of a trance, I think, and saw the Welsh Fusiliers legging it past me, and Jerry following closely. Needless to say, I legged it too, but had to rest every few hundred yards until leaving this enforced rest too long, was nabbed by a Jerry, but got away." The fighting withdrawal continued through Neuville and Ytres until, on 25th March, they found themselves once again at High Wood. The remnants of 141 Brigade took up positions on the high ground at Contalmaison, and held them until the Division was ordered to withdraw across the River Ancre at Aveluy. Harry Tyers goes onto say, "…returned to Lechelle. There was a glorious scrap in the wood between Jerry and 142nd Brigade HQ; the Brigadier and staff were taken prisoner. On 24th March, reached Ytres, went to EFC Canteen, it was being cleared of stores, no water but plenty of whisky. I refrained. At Rocquigny, the brigade was formed into a composite battalion - not many Irish left – under command of Captain Charlie Watson, Colonel Neeley having been wounded and evacuated. …. the Composite Battalion were not even up to Battalion strength. Jerry came on again on the rise, in close formation even bringing up field guns, and firing at us over open sights. It was a debacle. Captain Watson saw I was all in, as was he, and advised me to get away. I legged it through Bus, too weary to worry about the aeroplanes bombing and machine gunning the roads. Reported to the Transport Officer, Captain Slattery, at Contalmaison, and fainted. Later, watched our transport being blitzed by the Red Baron's Squadron. Arrived in Albert at dead of night on 26th March, moved on to Bouzincourt, arrived 29th March. Lieutenant McKenzie Smith was in command of the Battalion. Later, investigating the ruins of the Cure's house with my batman, found in the cellar dusty bottles that looked like wine, smelled like wine and tasted like wine! We also found cigars, cognac, champagne and curacao. Foraging, we shot a stray pig and on returning to our billets, found that Jerry had stopped at Albert." Harold was wounded at some point during the retreat, and died in No. 46 Casualty Clearing Station on 4th April. He is buried in Picquigny British Cemetery. His Service Record ends with a list of personal effects returned to his widow, and includes his wrist watch, a gold ring, match box and cigarette cases, cheque book, Officer's Advance book, letters, a diary, and a mutilated ten Franc note.

ONE OF FOUR SOLDIER SONS.

ROBERT SARGEANT

Robert Emeny Sargeant, known as Robin or Bob, was born in 1891. He was one of fourteen children, and a cousin of Bernard and Harold. As well as being a solicitor, his father was a Superintendent Registrar (recording local births, death and marriages), and a preacher at the Congregational Chapel in Bracknell High Street (located on the site now occupied by the National Westminster Bank). The family lived at Holly Bank, a large house on the south side of Church Road, with two tennis courts in the garden (these courts were used by Bracknell Lawn Tennis Club when it formed in 1948), before moving to Wokingham. Victor, one of Robert's elder brothers, had gone to Canada but returned to visit the family in 1909; when he returned three months later, Robert travelled with him, bound for Saskatchewan. But he soon returned and, on the outbreak of war, volunteered for the Army, attesting at Reading on 21st August 1914. He was described as just over 5'10" in height, weighing almost ten stones, with light brown hair, hazel eyes, and a fresh complexion. It was not just Victor who had gone to Canada, as Robert's Service Record lists two more brothers residing there. He was posted to the 9th Heavy Battery, Royal Garrison Artillery, and appointed to the rank of Acting Bombardier in January the following year, while training at Woolwich. In February, he moved to Odiham, Hampshire, but just two weeks later, he was admitted to hospital, suffering from cerebro-spinal meningitis, and died two weeks afterwards in Tring Isolation Hospital. He is buried in Easthampstead Churchyard in a family grave; only the base remains, although the inscription is still clearly visible. The Reading Standard newspaper reported his death: "Only three months after joining the Army, Robert Sargeant, of the Royal Garrison Artillery, fell a victim to the dreaded 'spotted fever' and his death at the age of 23 aroused intense sympathy in Wokingham, his home. He was a keen footballer and cricketer and a general favourite. He was one of four brothers who had answered the nation's call to arms and whose Christmas Day visit to the Poor Law Institution *(Church Hill House, then the Easthampstead Parish Workhouse, opposite Easthampstead Church),* where they sang the National Anthem in the wards, is still affectionately recalled by the inmates." The Reading Mercury of 6th March also carried a report on the funeral: "An imposing spectacle was presented on Thursday when the body of Pte R. E. Sargeant, R.G.A., was interred at Easthampstead churchyard ....it was borne on a gun carriage by 8 horses and an escort of about 30 men to Easthampstead. The coffin was covered by a Union Jack and the whole surmounted by a large cross, consisting of daffodils and white narcissus .... The bugler sounded The 'Last Post,' the notes of which were interspersed with three volleys by a party of 12 men .... 'Robin', as he was affectionately known, was the youngest but one of the 5 boys. He unfortunately contracted an illness which developed into cerebral-spinal meningitis, of which he died."

VICTOR SARGEANT

Pte. VICTOR SARGEANT, Holly Bank, Bracknell.—Wounded.

Victor Sargeant was born on 1st September 1887, an older brother of Robert. He first sailed for Canada in 1905, aged just seventeen, arriving at Halifax, Nova Scotia on 1st April, bound for Prince Albert, Saskatchewan, and soon found work helping on a farm. He returned to visit the family in 1909, but returned three months later, and within two years, was living in Moosejaw, Saskatchewan, with three men working for him. He paid a final visit to England in 1913. The Canadian Expeditionary Force was formed in August the following year, but recruiting in Saskatchewan did not start until the start of July 1915. Victor volunteered on 7th April 1916 at Prince Albert, giving his address as Red Deer Hill, a farming settlement south of the city, and joined the 46th Battalion, Canadian Infantry (Saskatchewan Regiment). He was 5'10" tall, large-chested, with brown hair, grey eyes, and a ruddy complexion. A fascinating series of letters from another recruit in the same regiment give an idea of what the men experienced. Although they are not Victor's experiences, they give an insight into what men of the time went through. They had been training at Camp Hughes in Manitoba until late October, before starting their journey to Europe. It took two days to reach Ottawa by train, where they paraded through the city and were inspected, before entraining again at midday for Montreal; the Officer in charge arranged for them to sit on leather seats, rather than wooden slats, for which they were all very grateful! They reached Halifax after five days, and were on board a converted Belgian tramp steamer and sailing within five hours. Conditions for the ranks were very crowded, and food was eaten in the alleyways beside their beds. Lifebelts were worn continually, and there were daily fire drills and practise at getting away the lifeboats. At night, no light was allowed on deck, not even a lighted cigarette. They arrived at Liverpool after eleven days at sea, the last two days being escorted by a destroyer. Then there was another train journey, in very crowded conditions, to Seaford on the south coast. His impressions of the home country were not very flattering, "Everything here is so old and out-of-date." He also complained about the cost of buying anything, the unfriendliness of the British people, the narrow streets. And it snowed to remind him of home! Many of the men were confined to barracks due to an outbreak of measles, making extra work for the rest, but it did help to pass the time, for there was not a lot to do apart from marching, training and fatigues. At the end of the month, he had a few days of leave and visited London which impressed him, especially St Paul's Cathedral, the zoological gardens, and "the wonderful waxworks." They stayed in accommodation donated by the Royal Family and subsidised by the Canadian Government, but the rich, old men supplied as tour guides were so slow, they left them and went their own way round the city sights. Several men were taken from the battalion to train as officers, but after being asked about his education, he was turned down. He started training on machine guns and hoped to make the grade. Then someone found out he was a foreman on the railroad back home and used to dealing with men, so suddenly he was taken off the machine gunnery course and started the Officer training. The Germans were offering peace and declaring the war to be "a draw," but he thought the British politicians would not accept that; anyway he wanted to see some action having come all this way. Measles were still a problem, and they stopped doing training when it rained; all his hut were in quarantine. His bridge playing improved. The British didn't celebrate New Year's Day like the Canadians did, so they improvised a game of football in the afternoon between the men of two huts. He oscillated between wanting to get to France to see some action, and being homesick and wanting to get back to Canada. He thought Lloyd George, the British Prime Minister, was a great man. The old man, teaching them how to fire a rifle, had taken a week so far. He was kicked off the O.T.C. and then reinstated. They were going out at night, with loaded rifles, on picket duty to protect the roads against air raids. A battalion from Winnipeg arrived as reinforcements, but they were a very drunken bunch, even their paymaster and Regimental Sergeant Major. The O.T.C. had been scrapped; the new policy being that experienced men make the best officers, not the ones who can pass exams (despite his getting 96% on map reading, his weakest subject). He was due to go France the following week, but had now been told he can't go because his glasses have not arrived – he had been waiting for them for a month. If wasn't raining, it was foggy; if it wasn't foggy, it was raining. At the end of February, he finally moved to Bramshott, near Liphook in Hampshire, reached by marching, which he enjoyed, as it gave him the chance to see the country. and break the boredom of training, study and inactivity at Seaford. He did not think much of the British Officers he had come into contact with; they were waited on hand and foot, but were petty about regulations. Another draft went to France at the end of March, but he missed out again. There were rumours about a German invasion on the east coast. In mid April, he expected to go to France any day. Two weeks later and he was in France. They marched fifteen miles, and had another fifteen to go. Apart from a few ruined buildings, the French have 'made good' everything the Germans destroyed after driving them back, filling in the trenches, and carrying on work as normal, although it is mostly women doing it. He noticed the rats and 'the other friends' (lice) which were 'very numerous.' The weather now was too hot (it was mid May). He mentioned the Germans were pressing for peace again, but the British and French will have none of it. There were references to people he knows getting wounded or killed, and the noise of the weaponry. His letters were now weekly, rather than every couple of days. On 5th June, an official letter, telling the recipient their son has been admitted to hospital with wounds to his right arm, hand, and both legs, and 'getting on as well as can be expected.' Four days later: 'A severe gunshot wound in his leg .... on the seriously ill list.' This news was repeated three days later. A few days later, the man himself wrote – the medical care was excellent, but the food was awful. In the next letter, he told the family his leg has been saved, but he would need another operation to remove shrapnel from his ankle. After a couple more letters recording his progress, there is a gap of a month and then a letter written from a hospital in Ipswich. The hospital in France was full of banter and good cheer, but the one back in Britain has a bad atmosphere, and the reality of his injury is beginning to sink in. There are a couple more letters and then he is sent back to Canada. Victor must have had a similar start, as he left Canada in November 1916. After arriving in France, he was severely wounded at Vimy Ridge, returning to England to recover at Bearwood, south of Wokingham (now a College). This was used as a Canadian Convalescent Home during the war, with up to nine hundred soldiers at a time recovering there. The Canadians played many football matches against local sides, including one against the Portsmouth Ladies; the Ladies won 8-5, but the men were playing with one arm tied behind their backs! Victor returned to France in 1918. As they were barely involved in the German offensive in the spring of that year, the Canadians were ordered to spearhead the campaigns in the last three months of the War. Victor was one of the Grenade Section, and during the advance on Aulnoy on the morning of 1st November 1918, he was struck by shrapnel in the left arm, right hip, right side and face. He was attended to and immediately carried out, but succumbed to his wounds at No. 1 Canadian Casualty Clearing Station the following day, and is buried at Auberchicourt British Cemetery; he is also listed on the family grave in Easthampstead Churchyard. During his time in the fighting, he was awarded the Military Medal; unfortunately there are no citations for this medal, so his actions in earning it are unrecorded.

FAR FROM THE ROAR OF BATTLE.

STEPHEN SHARP

Stephen Sharp was born in 1895 at Worplesdon near Guildford. He was one of nine children born in a family that moved several times; his two eldest siblings were born in Warfield, two more in Willesden Green, Middlesex, one in Wokingham, and his youngest sister in Easthampstead, by which time the family were living in Easthampstead Road. His father was a brick burner, responsible for maintaining the firing temperature in a brick kiln. After leaving school, Stephen worked as a shop lad in a greengrocers, before joining the 3rd Battalion, Berkshire Regiment, a Reserve Battalion, about nine months before the declaration of war. He would have been mobilised when war broke out, but did not go to France with the first draft, as it would have taken time for him to report to Brock Barracks, be transferred to Aldershot, get kitted out and generally organised, but he crossed the Channel on 12th September 1914. Without a surviving service record, it is not possible to know when Stephen was wounded, but it may have occurred during the Battle of Ypres towards the end of October. His wounds were serious enough for him to be brought back to England, where he died in London on 3rd December. He is buried in Easthampstead Churchyard in a grave with an official Commonwealth War Grave headstone.

FRANK R. SHEAF

Frank Richard Sheaf was born in 1874 at Alcester, Warwickshire, and had a younger sister. His father was almost forty when he married, and had worked in the brewing trade, making and selling malts, and was able to retire in his fifties, move to Streatham, and maintain a household employing one or two servants. Frank, aged sixteen, was still at school in the 1901 census at a time when the school leaving age was fourteen, and ten years later listed his occupation as portrait painter. He married Hilda Furtado in 1905, had a daughter the following year, and moved to Twickenham, supporting the family with a private income, supplemented by painting portraits. It is not known when he moved to Easthampstead, but he was conscripted into the army, attesting in Wokingham, and joined the Royal Field Artillery in the latter half of 1916. At the time of his death, he was with 'C' Battery, 186th Brigade, part of the 62nd Division. The Division had been involved in Arras Offensive and Cambrai operations in 1917, as well as the First Battle of the Somme and Second Battle of Arras the following year. At the beginning of September 1918, Frank's battery was at Englebelmer, northwest of Albert, supporting an infantry attack on the 2nd, firing continuously for over eight hours. Frank was killed during the action, and is buried in Valley Cemetery, Vis-en-Artois.

ERNEST G. TAPPING

Ernest George Tapping was born in 1899 in Warfield. He was the son of a dairy farmer, living at Honeywood Farm (on the Ascot Road), and had a younger sister. He was conscripted into the Hampshire Regiment, attesting at Reading, but later transferred to the Royal West Kent Regiment, and then attached to the 1/20th Battalion, London Regiment. These moves make it difficult to trace Ernest's war experience, but the Londons were taking part in the Battle of Bapaume, part of the Second Battle of Ypres at the end of the summer in 1918. On 1st September, the battalion began an attack at 5:30am behind a creeping barrage, with the aim of capturing a trench system west of Moslains Wood. Although they were successful, the War Diary coldly reported "casualties very heavy due to stiff resistance of a machine gun nest." They then took over front line until evening, when they were withdrawn to Reserve. Ernest was killed during the attack; his body was never found, and his name is listed on the Vis-en-Artois Memorial. His parents were living in Mill Lane, Easthampstead, when the memorial was being erected, so his name is listed in the parish as well as on the Roll of Honour inside Warfield Church.

The late Sgt. VERNON H. TAYLOR, 1/4th Royal Berks Regt., Station House, Bracknell.—Died of wounds.

VERNON H. TAYLOR

Vernon Howard Taylor was born in Bracknell in 1892, the youngest of seven children. His father was Bracknell's station master for over twenty years, before retiring to Pangbourne. After leaving school, Vernon became an apprentice mining engineer, and joined 1/4th Battalion, Royal Berkshire Regiment, a Territorial Battalion, having attested at Reading. They had started their annual training at Marlow two days before war broke out, but immediately brought back to Reading. All the men were invited to volunteer for foreign service, with the majority heeding the call. Much of the training took place in and around Chelmsford, before they arrived in France at the end of March 1915, where they spent their first night on a hill overlooking Boulogne, shivering under a thin blanket and awoke to driving snow. A week later, they received their first instructions in trench warfare and shared the trenches with other, more experienced battalions, and on the 15th manned the front line themselves for two days, albeit in a sector that was totally quiet. All through the spring and summer, they took their turns in the front line and in reserve, digging trenches, improving defences, carrying supplies, and generally keeping busy without being involved in any major operations, and a projected attack in late September never materialised. Patrols went out from time to time to spy out the enemy positions, with a Corporal Taylor being mentioned in four of them, but it is not clear whether this refers to Vernon. In another patrol, an officer was killed and three other men wounded when they were ambushed in a sunken road between the lines; soon after the British got revenge by shooting two Germans, with Corporal Vernon H. Taylor despatching one of them (this may have been the incident in which he earned the Military Medal). The winter was cold with snow, frost and rain; the conditions took a higher toll than the enemy. Everywhere was water and liquid mud, and cases of trench foot were seen until new thigh boots arrived. But there was some light relief at Christmas when each man received two plum puddings, a tin of cigarettes, a packet of cigars, chocolate, socks, a shirt and muffler. A football tournament was organised, two travelling variety entertainments visited along with a cinematograph. As winter turned to spring, activity began to increase again. New constructions and defences were dug, new drafts arrived, and heavy shelling bombardments started. On 16th May, they faced their first serious test when an intense bombardment was followed by a German attack; it was eventually beaten off, but at the cost of almost one hundred killed, wounded or missing. The following day they were withdrawn into reserve and spent the next two weeks in billets. They then moved to a training area near Abbeville where they spent the mornings training, the afternoons playing football or cricket, and the evenings enjoying civilian life in the nearby villages. All around were preparations for the Somme battle on 1st July, but Vernon's battalion were not involved on that day, spending it in Corps Reserve. On the 2nd came orders that they would attack the next day, but this was cancelled just as they started filing into the trenches that night. They had to wait until the 23rd to be involved in an attack. The objective was the enemy front line and a strong point which could enfilade No Man's Land. The Oxfordshire and Buckinghamshire Light Infantry led the attack, but the support of the Berkshires was crucial as they arrived at a critical moment and turned an uneasy situation into a resounding success and, despite heavy shelling the next day, held the position until relieved the following night. Just over one hundred men were wounded; this may have included Vernon, now a sergeant, who died of wounds on 18th August 1916 and was buried in Boulogne Eastern Cemetery, which was used for the mortalities in all the hospitals in the town. His parents erected a brass plaque in his memory in St James the Less Church, Pangbourne, and he is also mentioned on his mother's grave in the churchyard.

LEONARD TODD

Leonard Arthur Todd was born at Wokingham in 1880. He was the eldest of four siblings, but after his mother died in 1889, his father remarried the following year, and another four children were born. Leonard's father worked as a house painter and moved the family to Easthampstead Road between 1907 and 1911. Leonard, by now, had left school, but was still living at home, and working as a bricklayer. He volunteered for service, attesting at Wokingham, joined the Royal Engineers, and went to France a few days before Christmas 1915. The Royal Engineers Training Centre, which carried out basic recruit and field works training, was in the grounds of Coddington Hall, just to the east of Newark, Nottinghamshire. At its height, it housed around three thousand men, but there is now no trace of this establishment or the Hall. Field Companies were attached to the fighting portions of the Divisions, and often saw action and took part in the fighting. Each Company was composed of 217 men, including 186 other ranks, representing many kinds of trades required by the army in the field. On 20th November 1917, Leonard's unit, the 155th Field Company, was working near Boiry-Becquerelle when the enemy put down a severe barrage on the area. The War Diary records that thirty men were wounded during the day. Leonard was probably one of these, as he died in Reading on 16th December, probably in the War Hospital (now the Royal Berks). He is buried in Easthampstead (SS Michael and Mary Magdalene) churchyard in a grave with a Commonwealth War Graves headstone. Leonard's father had died a few months earlier, his brother Ralph in 1915, and another brother, Edwin, also in 1917 (although he does not appear to have served).

The late Pte. RALPH TODD, East-hampstead Road, Bracknell.—Killed in action.

RALPH TODD

Ralph Todd was a younger brother of Leonard, born at Wokingham in 1894. He worked as a labourer after leaving school, and volunteered almost as soon as war was declared, attesting at Reading. He joined the 2nd Battalion, Berkshire Regiment, and arrived in France two days after Christmas 1914, with the War Diary recording a draft of twenty men joining on 3rd January. The winter was very cold, and for a time the fire trenches became unusable as they filled with water. During this period, the battalion were taking turns with the 2nd Battalion, Rifle Brigade in the front trenches at Fauquissart, a hamlet near Laventie. The War Diary continues to record the occasional casualty, and men going to, or returning from, hospital. The entry for 4th February 1915 records just one man having been killed, the battalion having taken over the front line the previous day. This was Ralph, and he is buried in Fauquissart Military Cemetery, Laventie.

The late Pte. A. TURNER, Gordon Highlanders, Bracknell.—Killed by a sniper while acting as stretcher-bearer. Aged 23.

AUGUSTUS TURNER

Augustus Turner was born at Wraysbury, between Windsor and Staines, in 1894. He was one of five children, with his two youngest brothers being born in Bracknell. His father worked as a gardener nurseryman with his own business, and Augustus worked alongside him on leaving school. He was conscripted into the 5th Battalion, Gordon Highlanders, enlisting at Northampton, so may have moved away from the area for another job after the 1911 census. The battalion took part in two phases of the Battle of the Somme in 1916, and were involved in the capture and defence of the village of Roeux in May 1917, part of the Battle of Arras. Roeux was one of the fortified villages that formed part of the German defences behind the German front line. The area posed many difficulties for the British, including the Arras to Douai railway line which ran through a cutting and on an embankment, and the River Scarpe with its surrounding marshland. Earlier assaults on the village in April had failed, due in part to the poor state of the ground preventing the artillery being placed to provide an effective bombardment. A new assault was made at the end of the month, but this too was unsuccessful. On 11th May, Augustus's battalion assisted in another attack, and over the course of the next two days, the village was taken. But the Germans were not going to give up without a fight, and on the 17th, they launched a counter-attack from the north which gained much of the lost ground. The Gordons were ordered to counter-attack, and regain the Chemical Works, astride the railway. This they achieved, shooting down many Germans as they streamed back. A fierce barrage threatened to push them back again, but they went forward again as soon as the fire slackened. North of the railway, the British front line (Cupid Trench) remained in German hands. The Gordons were ordered to retake it, with only a few minutes' notice, in conjunction with a battalion of the 17th Division on their left. Unhappily, the other battalion were too far away when the orders reached it, and never got to the scene. This left the left flank of the Gordons open, and they abandoned Cupid Trench. The losses were very high with eleven officers and more than two hundred other ranks killed, wounded or missing. Augustus, who was awarded the Military Medal, appears to have been a stretcher-bearer during the action, but disappeared during the fighting, and his name appeared in the Red Cross Missing lists. His body was never found, and he is listed on the Arras Memorial.

HARRY WHARTON

The late Pte. H. WHARTON, Royal Warwick Regt., Easthampstead Road, Bracknell.—Died of pneumonia.

Henry William Edward Wharton, known as Harry, was born in Binfield in 1900, and baptised 26th August. As his parents lived at Amen Corner, this may well have been St Mark's Church rather than All Saint's. His parents had married no more than a couple of months before he was born, and he had ten younger siblings, three of whom died in infancy. Soon after Harry was born, the family moved to Easthampstead Road, although his father continued to work excavating clay at the local brickworks. Harry was conscripted into the 51st Battalion, Warwickshire Regiment, a Training Reserve battalion, based at Henham Park, near Southwold, Suffolk. This would have happened a month after his 18th birthday. While he was there, the camp was hit by the Spanish influenza, which claimed many victims, including Harry on 23rd October 1918. He is buried in Easthampstead Churchyard in a grave with an official Commonwealth War Graves headstone. The Reading Mercury of 2nd November 1918 contained a report of his burial: "Private Wharton, Royal Warwickshire Regiment, of Easthampstead Road, Bracknell, had been in the Army ten weeks when he was taken ill with influenza, and died in hospital at Norwich on Thursday the 24th, age 18 years. The body was brought home and buried in Easthampstead Church on Tuesday. A sergeant, six men, and a bugler came over from Reading, and the 'Last Post' was sounded."

ARTHUR WILSON

Pte. A. WILSON, Rose Hill, Binfield.—Missing since Sept. 25th, 1915, believed killed.

Arthur James Wilson was born in 1897 at High Callerton, Ponteland, about ten miles northwest of Newcastle-upon-Tyne. His father worked in domestic service as a coachman, in several parts of the country, before finally coming to Binfield. Arthur had six siblings (a seventh died in infancy), as well as six half-siblings from his father's first marriage. The family were living in Rose Hill by the time of the 1911 census. Arthur volunteered almost as soon as war was declared, attesting at Wokingham, and joined the 2nd Battalion, Berkshire Regiment, and arrived in France two days after Christmas 1914, with the War Diary recording a draft of twenty men joining on 3rd January. The battalion were involved in the Battles of Neuve Chapelle, Aubers and Festubert in the first half of 1915, losing over 150 men. On 24th September, they went into trenches near Bois Grenier for an attack at 4:30am the following day. The attack had been preceded by three days of bombardment from the British artillery, so the German wire was cut in most places. 'B' Company in the centre reached the German trenches without too much trouble, and 'C' Company on the left were similarly successful, although a machine gun caused heavy casualties on the extreme left platoon. But 'A' Company on the right had a bad time, facing inadequately cut enemy wire, and a German searchlight exposing their movements; consequently their losses were heavy and there were too few men left to hold the trench once they reached it. 'D' Company, in reserve, also suffered badly from shelling. The struggle for the German first trench developed into a series of bombing attacks, but eventually the Germans fought off the Berkshires, who withdrew to their starting positions. 130 men from the battalion were killed in the attack, two hundred wounded, and a further sixty men were missing. Arthur was one of the latter; his body was never found, and his name is listed on the Ploegsteert Memorial. He is also listed on the Binfield War Memorial.

Bert Wood

It has not been possible to positively identify this man. His first name could be an abbreviation for Bertram, Bertie, Albert, Cuthbert, Herbert, or Hubert (or even, it has been suggested, Robert). The most likely candidate is Herbert Wood, living in Warfield at the outbreak of war, although he does not appear, from the records, to have served with the Army Service Corps, the unit recorded against his name on the Roll of Honour inside Easthampstead Church. Herbert Wood was born in 1885 at Oxted, Surrey. He was the youngest survivor of six children, although a younger brother died at the age of five. His father worked in domestic service, working his way up from coachman to butler, a job which entailed being away from home for long periods. He later worked as a hotel waiter, before being able to retire. Herbert worked as a hall boy after leaving school, possibly in the same house where his father worked, before turning his hand to gardening, and appears at Rockshaw Gardens, Merstham, Surrey, in the 1911 census. He married Ellen Knight in 1913, and soon moved to Warfield. His mother had been born in Winkfield and lived in the area until her marriage, so Herbert may have heard of a job opportunity from a local family member. He joined under the Derby Scheme, attesting at Wokingham on 30th May 1916, and joined the 3rd Battalion, Royal Berkshire Regiment, a training battalion, before a posting to France. It is not possible to fully document Herbert's war experience as at some point, he was transferred to the 2nd Battalion, Oxfordshire and Buckinghamshire Light Infantry. On the 13th November 1916, they attacked the German front line system at 5:45am, which came, according to the War Diary, as a complete surprise to the enemy who offered little, if any, resistance. The Diary continues, "Some havoc was caused by a party of about forty Germans who remained for nearly two days, 'un-mopped up' in the German front line, possibly because they happened to be at the point of junction between the attacking brigades, and neither troop felt directly responsible for the task. The battalion sustained a certain number of casualties from our own artillery, due to an attempt to follow too closely our own barrage, but otherwise the casualties west of the German line were inconsiderable. There was considerable bombing of German dugouts west of the Green Line, one soldier being seen by an officer to throw 21 bombs in succession down the steps of a German 'Regimental Command Post' in Munich Trench. In the Yellow Line, no British troops could be found right or left, although on our right, elements of 17th Royal Fusiliers had also entered it, but these failed to get in touch on either flank and withdrew. Considerable fighting ensued on the Yellow Line, in Munich Trench and in Lager Alley, our forward parties being at one time all but surrounded. After some difficulty and numerous casualties, a withdrawal, covered very well by bombers and Lewis gunners, was effected to the Green Line, which was consolidated." The casualty figures recorded cover the period from the 13th to the 17th, when 24 men were killed, and almost 150 were missing. Herbert was one of the latter, and his name is listed on the Thiepval Memorial. By the time of his death, his widow had left Warfield and returned to live with the rest of her family near Hayward's Heath, Sussex. He is also recorded on the Roll of Honour inside Warfield Church.

OTHER GRAVES

There is one other war casualty buried at Easthampstead
who is not listed on the memorials.

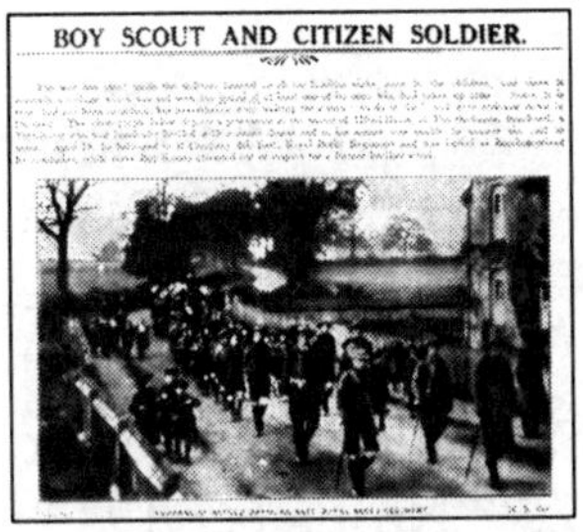
BOY SCOUT AND CITIZEN SOLDIER.

ALFRED HENRY DAVIS

Alfred Henry Davis was born in 1896, the younger brother of Edwin Thomas Davis who is listed on the Easthampstead memorials. The family lived in Binfield Road before moving to Wokingham Road by the time of the 1911 census. His father worked in the building trade and is variously described as a builder, plumber and house decorator. While his eldest son worked with him, Alfred worked as a printer's assistant after leaving school. He was a member of the Territorial Army and a former boy scout, who died "with a dread illness" (possibly cerebral meningitis, then known as 'spotted fever', which claimed the lives of many men during the conflict), while still in training with the 4th Battalion, Berkshire Regiment, prior to deployment overseas. A photo of his funeral procession appeared in the Reading Mercury, on its way to Easthampstead Churchyard on 14th November 1914. The procession was accompanied "by comrades, while forty Boy Scouts attended out of respect for a former brother scout." Alfred was buried in an unmarked grave, and it has not been possible to find its location in the churchyard.

OTHER MEMORIALS

One memorial inside Easthampstead Church records a casualty from the conflict.

CHARLES WILLIAM MAXWELL

Charles William Maxwell was born in India on 12th February 1889, and arrived back in England in June the following year with his mother and three siblings. His father was a Lieutenant Colonel in the Indian Army, whose sister was to married Herbert Salway, the vicar of Easthampstead Church. Charles attended Lambrook School, Winkfield Row, and Wellington College, Crowthorne. He was commissioned Second Lieutenant, 8th Gurkha Rifles, Indian Army, in 1909, and promoted to Lieutenant two years later. On 23rd November 1914, the battalion was diverted from the route of its march to assist in the recapture of a section of trench near Le Plautin. This was partially successful, but at a cost of more than sixty casualties. Initially reported missing, his body was later found and buried in Guards Cemetery, Windy Corner, Cuinchy.

POSTSCRIPT

The Armistice, when it came, was a surprise to many soldiers on the ground. While it was a relief and a cause for celebration, it left many at a loss. They had survived, but what of the future? When could they go home, and what would they find? Their whole life, for up to four years, had been one of fighting in the mud and trenches, and they could not conceive of a different one. Younger men had gone straight from school to military training and then the trenches – 'normal' working life was something they had never experienced. Others had unfinished apprenticeships or degree courses, now useless and forgotten. An entry in an autograph book kept by a nurse at one of the many hospitals in France treating the wounded, sums up the attitude of the time: "We held them on the Marne, we beat them on the Aisne, we gave them equal at Neuve Chapelle, and here we go again." Many questioned what they had been fighting for, and what had been achieved. There were hopes a more equal society; had not all classes fought together, suffering the same hardships and privations? Did the humble farm labourer not deserve the same future as the monied landowner? The street sweeper and the solicitor? But the world was a different place, and the country to which they returned had changed. Women had replaced absent men in the workplace (and there were almost two million more women than men), the country was almost bankrupt (Britain incurred debts during the war equivalent to 136% of its gross national product), and the swathes of unskilled, many with physical or mental scars, returning from the front, found no jobs, no money, and sometimes no waiting families. Rationing had been imposed in early 1918, limited to meat, sugar, and butter, but not bread. Inflation doubled between 1914 and 1920; income tax rose from 6% before the war, to 60% for the richest. The value of the pound sterling fell by more than 60%.

The end of the fighting was not followed by an immediate return home by every man overseas. Surrendering Germans had to be guarded and escorted, their captured and abandoned equipment and ammunition destroyed, dismantled or otherwise dealt with. British equipment also had to be returned to home shores in an orderly and organised fashion. The land and infrastructure had to be returned to returning civilian populations, and the inevitable looting and 'souvenir hunters' discouraged or imprisoned. After four long years of chaos, order was not something that could be reinstated overnight. The territories of Germany and her allies needed occupying forces until such time as the politics had been sorted out. The Naval Blockade on Germany would be maintained for several months until the Peace Treaty was signed at Versailles at the end of June 1919.

Illness was still prevalent, and soon a flu pandemic, originating in America, but known as the Spanish Flu, would sweep the world, striking down many who had survived the fighting. However ordered the return, many felt they were being treated unfairly. Young conscripts, still being trained at home, were the first to be discharged. Why were those who had sacrificed years serving their country not the first? Next to return were those in jobs considered 'essential' to the recovering country. Were miners more necessary than shopkeepers; were farm workers or clerks more important? Should those with injuries gain preferential treatment? But within twelve months, the British army of 3.8 million men had been reduced to less than one million, and by 1922, only 230,000 remained in the country's fighting force.

Lloyd George, who had been Prime Minister since 1916 in a coalition government, won the General Election of 1919 with the promise of "a country fit for heroes to live in." For the soldiers who came back from the trenches, there was the thanks of a grateful country, a suit of civilian clothes, a pair of medals, and a small cash payment. A private was given the equivalent of a few weeks' wages, an officer got rather more, and Sir Douglas Haig, who commanded the British Expeditionary Force from 1915, was given an earldom and £100,000, and eventually was the subject of the last equestrian statue in London. Most returning men were successfully re-integrated into the British economy, although their War Bonus was spent on new clothes, the army diet having caused them to grow and put on weight. But the ambitious wartime program of 'reconstruction' was abandoned during the economic slump of 1921, and many men found themselves with no job, reduced to selling matches, cards and war mementoes on street corners, and visiting soup kitchens and food distribution centres. The economic impacts of the war were huge as industry had been completely focussed on providing materials and resources for the armed forces, producing everything from ships to uniforms. Britain's pre-war economy had been built on exports and the four core industries of coal, ship-building, textiles and iron. During the war, Britain's previous markets had developed their own industries, and, after an initial post-war boom, a balance of payments crisis ensued. By 1922, one and half million men were unemployed. Despite an ambitious post-war building program, housing facilities were woefully short, none having been built during the war years. The seriously wounded were often denied their pensions as medical tribunals discharged their rights. Local newspapers of the time reported cases of domestic abuse or abandonment as men struggled to adapt, many having married in haste before going off to fight. Some returned to find their wives living with other men.

The British Legion was set up to help those who fought, and many Comrades of the Great War Clubs were formed, with men keen to consolidate and foster the comradeship of the trenches (Bracknell's Comrades had their own clubhouse in Park Road). It very quickly began to dawn on large numbers of demobilised soldiers, whatever their wartime rank, the dream of coming home to the secure job, which they believed was their right, was not going to come true. A letter from an ex-Officer was published in The Times in February 1920: "During the War, all those who put on the King's uniform had a great access of friends. We were heroes in those days. Our relations, too, even our rich relatives, took a new interest in us. On leave from the Front we were welcome and honoured guests - especially as we gained promotion: 'My Cousin the Major' ... when at last we came home, were demobilised and doffed our uniforms, we realised how much our welcome had depended on the glamour of our clothes, with all that they implied. In mufti, we were no longer heroes, we were simply 'unemployed', an unpleasant problem. Many businessmen think they did their part in the war at home, just as much as those on active service, and that no obligation rests on them to help ex-officers. I know that many of them worked long hours, even overworked in their country's cause, but they got a reward in experience, in an increase of income, and in good positions. And although the strain of long hours is great, their offices did not admit poison gas, mud, and shells, with the ever present threat of sudden death. There is a large balance outstanding to the credit of the ex-officer. Are you going to withhold payment until it is too late?" There were thinkers among the rank and files too, among them a Private from the Machine Gun Corps: "One universal question which I have never seen answered: two or three million pounds a day for the 1914-18 war, yet no monies were forthcoming to put industry on its feet on our return from that war. Many's the time I've gone to bed, after a day of 'tramp, tramp' looking for work, on a cup of cocoa and a pennyworth of chips between us; I would lay puzzling why, why, after all we had gone through in the service of our country, we have to suffer such poverty, willing to work at anything but no work to be had. I only had two Christmases at work between 1919 and 1939." Another ex-soldier, who fell on hard times, recounts a couple of experiences from 1923. "I had a walk round and eventually sat on a seat on the Embankment. I must have dozed off because it was dark as I woke up, so I decided to stay put till morning. I woke as the dawn was breaking and what a sight it was. All the seats were full of old soldiers in all sorts of dress - mostly khaki - and a lot more were lying on the steps, some wrapped up in old newspapers. Men who had fought in the trenches, now unwanted and left to starve were all huddled together .... Later I met a man crying in a doorway. He had on an army greatcoat and a turban and a tray round his neck with lucky charms on it. Another, unwanted, after three years in the trenches. He and his wife were penniless when some crook offered a chance to earn easy money for five shillings He pawned his wife's wedding ring to get it, and in return he got a tray, a turban and a dozen-or-so lucky charms to sell at 6d each. Now, after a day without anything to eat or drink, he was broken-hearted at the thought of going home to his wife without a penny. He was an ex-CSM *(Company Sergeant Major)*." In later life, Jim Hooley, who grew up in a poor area in Stockport in the years after the war, remembered the frequent sight of people, unable to pay their rent, being evicted by bailiffs: "The furniture would be taken out of the house and left on the pavement. The father would stay to watch it, while neighbours looked after his wife and children. One case always stood out in my memory. On my way to school I had to pass an old disused public house. A family had taken up residence in this building. I knew the boy who lived there: his mother and father were quite respectable. However, one morning on my way to school I saw a crowd of people round the old building. Making my way to the front of the crowd I could see the old familiar scene - another eviction. Next morning, on my way to school, I again saw a crowd round the old pub. On looking at the scene, I saw three First World War medals placed on an old sideboard which the bailiffs had taken out of the house the day before. A lady in the crowd told me that the father had got back into the building during the night and hanged himself." The writer and broadcaster J. B. Priestly wrote an account of a reunion of his old battalion in 1934: "Several of us had arranged with the secretary to see that original members of the battalion, to whom the price of the dinner was prohibitive, were provided with free tickets. But this, he told me, had not worked very well; and my old platoon comrades confirmed this, too, when I asked about one or two men. They were so poor, these fellows, that they said they could not attend the dinner, even if provided with free tickets, because they felt that their clothes were not good enough."

Despite the economic problems, the post-war administration established a genuine mass-democracy in Britain. The Representation of the People Act of 1918 enfranchised all males over the age of 21, and all women over the age of 30, and abolished the pre-war property qualifications. The 1920s, and perhaps the following decade, was one of the brief interludes when a three-party democracy existed in British politics. However, the post-war period wrought one important change: the Labour Party replaced the Liberals as the principle opposition to the Conservatives. In conjunction with coming to terms with mass-democracy, Britain also experienced fraught industrial relations. From 1914 to 1918, trade union membership had doubled, to a little over eight million. Work stoppages and strikes became frequent in 1917–1918 as the unions expressed grievances regarding prices, alcohol control, pay disputes, fatigue from overtime and working on Sundays, and inadequate housing. A notable clash took place in Glasgow in 1919, where protestors battled with the police, and eventually the army, over shorter working hours. The most potent symbol of the industrial malcontent fostered after the First World War was the general strike of 1926. In a similar fashion to democracy, the welfare provision began to develop. The school leaving age was increased to fourteen, and the Unemployment Insurance Act of 1920, extending National Insurance provision to eleven million more workers.

The aftermath years were a time of paradox; the men who returned from the horrors of the trenches wanted to forget, and where those who had stayed behind, and had lost husbands and brothers, and sons and fathers were equally determined never to forget. It was a world where questioning whether the war had been right was attacked as a slur on the memory of the dead. The last living link with the war was broken when Harry Patch, the last veteran who served in the trenches, died on 25th July 2009, aged 111. The Head Teacher at Crowthorne Church of England School summed up the mood of the time at the unveiling of their Roll of Honour: "We hope in all the years to come, the families and scholars of every generation will never fail to give honour to the memory of these 'old boys' who made the supreme sacrifice for England. They are very dear to us of today, and we ask all who succeed to us that their names and records shall not be forgotten. We transmit this as a precious heritage."

Many returned with scars, both physical, and more damagingly, mental, from which they would never recover. The ones who survived are often the forgotten ones; those who died are remembered annually. As one veteran, who had obviously given some thought to what would happen when the War finally ended, summed up to a younger companion in the days after the Armistice, "Peace is going to bring one glorious mess, an unequal fight against a public who will soon forget our sacrifices, and new generations who will know nothing of the war and what it meant to those who served."

It is hoped this book will go some way to redressing some of the mess.

ACKNOWLEDGEMENTS

I would like to thank the following people and organisations for their help in compiling the three volumes of Bracknell's Great War Fallen.

BRACKNELL
Bracknell (Holy Trinity) Church for allowing me access to see the Roll of Honour
Ranelagh School for also allowing me access to see their Roll of Honour
Vera Bain for showing me the Roll of Honour at Bracknell Bowling and Social Club

EASTHAMPSTEAD
Easthampstead (St Michael and St Mary Magdelene) Church for allowing me access to see the Roll of Honour, and details of the burial of Alfred Henry Davis

Fred Reece for access to his research on the men buried in the churchyard

Diane Collins for background information on the parish

Ruth Timbrell for alerting me to the Roll of Honour from Bracknell Working Men's Club, and sharing her knowledge of the area and background information on some of the men in both Winkfield and Bracknell

Staff at The National Archives, Kew, Berkshire Record Office, Reading, and Reading Central Library for their help during my visits for research

The staff at Bracknell and Harmanswater Libraries for obtaining books through inter-library loans to assist my research

John Chapman for assistance with men in the Royal Berkshire Regiment

Andrew French, Assistant Honorary Curator at the Berkshire Yeomanry Museum, Windsor, for information on the men from that regiment

The relatives of men who supplied information for inclusion in these biographies

All those organisations and individuals who made a contribution to the costs of publishing these volumes

Cath Murray for turning my ideas for the book covers into reality

The staff at Grosvenor Publishing for dealing with my queries over the publication of these volumes

BIBLIOGRAPHY

History of the Royal Regiment of Artillery: Western Front 1914-1918
General Sir Martin Farndale

The Royal Berkshire Regiment 1914-1918
F. Loraine Petre

The 2nd Battalion Royal Berkshire Regiment in World War One
Ian Cull

Coldstream Guards 1914-1918
Ross of Bladensburg

Devonshire Regiment 1914-1918
C. T. Atkinson

Faithful; The Story of The Durham Light Infantry
S. G. P. Ward

A Contemptible Little Flying Corps
I McInnes and J. V. Webb

Gloucestershire Regiment in the War 1914-1918
Everard Wyrall

The Grenadier Guards in The Great War 1914-1918
Sir Frederick Ponsonby

Regimental History, The Royal Hampshire Regiment
C. T. Atkinson

From Trench and Turret, Royal Marine's Letters and Diaries 1914-18
S. M. Holloway

Annals of The King's Royal Rifle Corps: Vol 5: "The Great War"
Major-Gen. Sir Steuart Hare

Die-Hards in The Great War (Middlesex Regiment)
Everard Wyrall

History of The Rifle Brigade in the War of 1914-1918
Capt. Reginald Berkley and Brig. Gen. William W. Seymour

Britain's Sea Soldiers: A Record of the Royal Marines during the War 1914-1919
General Sir H. E. Blumberg

History of the Somerset Light Infantry 1914-1918
Everard Wyrall

The Queen's Own Royal West Regiment
C. T. Atkinson

Worcestershire Regiment in The Great War
Capt. M. Fitzm. Stacke

King's Own Yorkshire Light Infantry in The Great War 1914-1918
R. C. Bond

The Zeebrugge Raid 1918
Paul Kendall

The Goodchilds of Grundisburgh: Four Brothers in the First World War
Henry Finch

Old Soldiers Never Die
Frank Richards

Indian Corps in France
Merewether Merewether and Sir Frederick Smith

Bloody Red Tabs: General Officer Casualties of the Great War, 1914 1920
Frank Davies and Graham Maddocks

Boy Soldiers of the Great War
Richard van Emden

First Day on the Somme
Martin Middlebrook

APPENDIX I

BATTLES

MAJOR BATTLES ON THE WESTERN FRONT

1914

Battle of Mons	23rd to 24th August
Battle of Cateau	26th August to 1st September
Battle of the Marne	7th to 10th September
Battle of the Aisne	12th to 15th September
Defence of Antwerp	4th to 10th October
Battle of La Bassee	10th October to 2nd November
Battle of Messines	12th October to 2nd November
Battle of Armentieres	13th October to 2nd November
First Battle of Ypres	19th October to 22nd November

1915

Battle of Neuve Chapelle	10th March to 22nd April
Second Battle of Ypres	22nd April to 25th May
Battle of Aubers	9th to 10th May
Battle of Festubert	15th to 25th May
Battle of Loos	25th September to 18th October

1916

Battle of the Somme	1st July to 18th November
Battle of Albert	1st to 13th July
Battle of Bazentin	14th to 17th July
Battle of Delville Wood	15th July to 3rd September
Attack at Fromelles	19th July
Attacks on High Wood	20th to 25th July
Battle of Pozieres	23rd July to 3rd September
Battle of Guillemont	3rd to 6th September
Battle of Ginchy	9th September
Battle of Flers-Courcelette	15th to 22nd September
Battle of Morval	25th to 28th September
Battle of Thiepval	26th to 28th September

Battle of Le Transloy	1st to 18th October
Battle of Ancre Heights	1st October to 11th November
Battle of Ancre	13th to 18th November

1917

Operations on the Ancre	11th January to 13th March
German Retreat to the Hindenburg Line	14th March to 5th April
Arras Offensive	9th April to 16th June
Battle of Vimy	9th to 14th April
First Battle of the Scarpe	9th to 14th April
Second Battle of the Scarpe	23rd to 24th April
Battle of Arleux	28th to 29th April
Third Battle of the Scarpe	3rd to 4th May
Battle of Messines	7th June to 14th June
Battle of Langemarck	16th to 18th August
Third Battle of Ypres	31st July to 10th November
Battle of Pilkem	31st July to 2nd August
Battle of Langemarck	16th to 18th August
Battle of the Menin Road	20th to 25th September
Battle of Polygon Wood	26th September to 3rd October
Battle of Broodseinde	4th October
Battle of Poelcapelle	9th October
First Battle of Passchendaele	12th October
Second Battle of Passchendaele	26th October to 10th November
Cambrai Operations	20th November to 30th December

1918

First Battles of the Somme 1918 (the German Spring Offensive)

	21st March to 4th July
Battle of St Quentin	21st March to 23rd March
First Battle of Bapaume	24th to 25th March
Battle of Rosieres	26th to 27th March
First Battle of Arras	28th March
Battle of Avre	4th April
Battle of the Ancre	5th April
Battles of the Lys	9th to 29th April
Battle of Estaires	9th to 11th April
Battle of Messines	10th to 11th April
Battle of Hazebrouck	12th to 15th April
Battle of Bailleul	13th to 15th April
First Battle of Kemmel	17th to 19th April
Battle of Bethune	18th April
Second Battle of Kemmel	25th to 26th April
Battle of Scherpenberg	29th April
Battle of the Aisne	27th May to 6th June
Battles of the Marne	20th July to 2nd August

Battle of Amiens	8th to 11th August
Second Battles of the Somme 1918	21st August to 3rd September
Battle of Albert	21st to 23rd August
Second Battle of Bapaume	31st August to 3rd September
Advance in Flanders	18th August to 6th September
Second Battles of Arras	26th August to 3rd September
Battles of the Hindenberg Line	12th September to 12th October
Battle of Havrincourt	12th September
Battle of Epehy	18th September
Battle of the Canal du Nord	27th September to 1st October
Battle of the St Quentin Canal	29th September to 2nd October
Battle of Beaurevoir	3rd to 5th October
Battle of Cambrai	8th to 9th October
Final Advance in Flanders	28th September to 11th November
Battle of Ypres	28th September to 2nd October
Battle of Coutrai	14th to 19th October
Final Advance in Artois	2nd October to 11th November
Final Advance in Picardy	17th October to 11th November
Battle of the Selle	17th to 25th October
Battle of Valenciennes	1st to 2nd November
Battle of the Sambre	4th November
Germany signs Armistice	11th November

THE MESOPOTAMIA CAMPAIGN

1914

Capture of Basra	5th to 21st November
Capture of Qurna	3rd to 19th December

1915

Capture of Nasiriyeh	27th June to 24th July
First Advance on Baghdad (including capture of Kut-al-Amara)	12th September to 7th October
Battle of Clesiphon	22nd to 24th November
Retreat to Kut-al-Amara	25th November to 3rd December

1916

Siege of Kut-al-Amara	7th December 1915 to 29th April
Efforts to relieve Kut-al-Amara	
Battle of Sheik Sa'ad	7th January
Battle of the Wadi	13th January
Battle of the Hanna	21st January
Attack on the Dujaila Redoubt	7th to 9th March
Battles of the Hanna and Fallahiyeh	5th to 8th April
Battles of Bait Alsa and Sannaiyat	7th to 22nd April
Surrender of the Kut-al-Amara Garrison	29th April

1917

Battle of Mohammed Abdul Hussan	9th January
Battles of the Hal Salient, Dahra Bend, and the Shumran Peninsula	11th January to 24th February
Capture of Baghdad	11th March
Battle of Istanbulat	21st April
Battle of 'The Boot' at Band-i-Adhaim	30th April
Battle of Tikrit	5th November

1918

Action of Khan Badghdadi	26th March
Turkey signs Armistice	1st October

THE GALLIPOLI CAMPAIGN

1915

Naval bombardment of the Straights Forts	9th February to 16th March
Naval attempt to force the Straights	18th March
Landings at Cape Helles and Anzac Cove	25th April
First Battle of Krithia	28th April
Second Battle of Krithia	6th May
The Third Battle of Krithia	4th June
Battle of Gully Ravine	28th June
Landings at Suvla Bay and the ANZAC attack on Chunuk Bair	6th to 9th August
Battle of Scimitar Hill and attack on Hill 60	21st August
Evacuation of ANZAC bridgehead and Suvla Bay	10th to 19th December
Evacuation of Cape Helles bridgehead	10th December to 9th January 1916

THE CAMPAIGN IN EGYPT AND PALESTINE

1915

Defence of the Suez Canal	26th January to 12th August
Operations in the Sinai Peninsula	15th November to 9th January 1917
Operations against the Senussi in the Western Desert	23rd November to 8th February 1917

1916

Operations against the Sultan of Darfur	1st March to 31st December
Arab revolt in the Hejuz	6th June to 22nd September
Battle of Romani	4th to 5th August

1917

First Battle of Gaza	26th to 27th March
Second Battle of Gaza	17th to 19th April
Third Battle of Gaza	27th October to 7th November

Affair of Huj, Action of El Mughar, and Capture of Junction Station	8th to 14th November
Battle of Nabi Samweil	20th to 24th November
Capture of Jerusalem	7th to 9th December
Battle of Jaffa	21st to 22nd December

1918

Operations in the Jordan Valley	19th February to 4th May
Battles of Megiddo, Sharon and Nablus	19th to 25th September
Final Offensive beyond the Jordan	to 26th October
Armistice	31st October 1918

The Campaign In Salonika

1915

Landing at Salonika	21st October

1916

Occupation of Mazirko	2nd October
Capture of Karajakois	30th September to 2nd October
Capture of Yenikoi	3rd to 4th October
Battle of Tumbitza Farm	17th November to 7th December

1917

First Battle of Doiran	22nd April to 8th May
Capture of Ferdie and Essex Trenches	15th May
Capture of Bairakli and Kumli	16th May
Capture of Homonodos	14th October

1918

Capture of the Roche Noir Salient	1st to 2nd September
Second Battle of Doiran	18th to 19th September
Passage of the Vardar and the Pursuit to the Strumica Valley	20th to 30th September
Armistice	30th September

The Campaign In Italy

1917

First troops arrive	5th November

1918

Battle of the Piave River	15th to 23rd June
Battle of Vittorio Veneto	24th October to 3rd November
Armistice	3rd November

NAVAL BATTLES

1914

Battle of Heligoland Bight	28th August
Battle of Coronel	1st November
Battle of the Falkland Islands	8th December
Raid on Scarborough and Hartlepool	16th December

1915

Battle of Dogger Bank	24th January

1916

Battle of Jutland	31st May to 1st June

1917

Battle of Otranto Straights	14th to 15th May

1918

Zeebrugge Raid	23rd April

APPENDIX II

CEMETERIES AND MEMORIALS

The following list of cemeteries and memorials contain at least one man from Bracknell Forest Borough.

ABBEVILLE COMMUNAL CEMETERY EXTENSION

The town of Abbeville is on the main road from Paris to Boulogne (N1), about 80 kms south of Boulogne.

For much of the First World War, Abbeville was headquarters of the Commonwealth lines of communication and various hospitals were stationed there from October 1914 to January 1920. The communal cemetery was used for burials from November 1914 to September 1916, the earliest being made among the French military graves. The extension was begun in September 1916.

A.I.F. BURIAL GROUND, FLERS

A.I.F. BURIAL GROUND is 2 kms north of the village of Flers, in the Department of the Somme.

Flers was captured on 15 September 1916, in the Battle of Flers-Courcelette, when it was entered by the New Zealand and 41st Divisions behind tanks, the innovative new weapons that were used here for the first time. The village was lost during the German advance of March 1918 and retaken at the end of the following August.

The cemetery was begun by Australian medical units, posted in the neighbouring caves, in November 1916 to February 1917. It was very greatly enlarged after the Armistice when almost 4,000 Commonwealth and French graves were brought in from the battlefields of the Somme, and later from a wider area.

AIRE COMMUNAL CEMETERY

Aire is a town about 14 kms south-south-east of St. Omer.

From March 1915 to February 1918, Aire was a busy but peaceful centre used by Commonwealth Forces as Corps Headquarters. The Highland Casualty Clearing Station was based there as was the 39th Stationary Hospital (from May 1917). It was used again when the 54th Casualty Clearing Station came to Aire and the town was, for a while, within 13 kms of the German lines.

AIX-NOULETTE COMMUNAL CEMETERY EXTENSION

Aix-Noulette is a village in the Department of the Pas-de-Calais, about 13 kms south of Bethune.

The Cemetery Extension was begun by French troops early in 1915, and the two French plots are next to the Communal Cemetery. It was taken over by the 1st and 2nd Divisions in February,

1916, and used by fighting units and Field Ambulances until October, 1918. It was increased after the Armistice by the concentration of graves from the battlefields to the east.

ALBERT COMMUNAL CEMETERY EXTENSION

Albert is a town 28 kms north-east of Amiens.

It was held by French forces against the German advance on the Somme in September 1914. It passed into British hands in the summer of 1915; and the first fighting in July 1916, is known as the Battle of Albert, 1916. It was captured by the Germans on 26th April 1918, and before its recapture on the following 22nd August (in the Battle of Albert, 1918), it had been completely destroyed by artillery fire.

The Extension was used by fighting units and Field Ambulances from August 1915 to November 1916, and more particularly in and after September 1916, when Field Ambulances were concentrated at Albert. From November 1916, the 5th Casualty Clearing Station used it for two months. From March 1917, it was not used (except for four burials in March 1918) until the end of August 1918, when Plot II was made by the 18th Division.

ALLONVILLE COMMUNITY CEMETERY

Allonville is a village in the Department of the Somme, 8 kms north-east of Amiens.

The communal cemetery was used from August 1916 to February 1917 by the 39th Casualty Clearing Station then posted at Allonville, and from April to July 1918, by Australian fighting units.

AMARA WAR CEMETERY

Amara is a town on the left bank of the Tigris some 520 kms from the sea.

Amara was occupied by the Mesopotamian Expeditionary Force on 3rd June 1915 and it immediately became a hospital centre. The accommodation for medical units on both banks of the Tigris was greatly increased during 1916 and in April 1917, seven general hospitals and some smaller units were stationed there.

NOTE: Whilst the current climate of political instability persists it is not possible for the Commission to manage or maintain its cemeteries and memorials located within Iraq. Alternative arrangements for commemoration have therefore been implemented and a two volume Roll of Honour listing all casualties buried and commemorated in Iraq has been produced. These volumes are on display at the Commission's Head Office in Maidenhead and are available for the public to view.

ANCRE BRITISH CEMETERY, BEAUMONT-HAMEL

ANCRE BRITISH CEMETERY is about 2 kms south of the village of Beaumont-Hamel.

The village of Beaumont-Hamel was attacked on 1st July 1916 but without success. On 3rd September a further attack was delivered between Hamel and Beaumont-Hamel and on 13th and 14th November, the Allies finally succeeded in capturing it. Following the German withdrawal to the Hindenburg Line in the spring of 1917, V Corps cleared this battlefield and created a number of cemeteries, of which ANCRE BRITISH CEMETERY (then called Ancre River No.1 British Cemetery) was one. There were originally 517 burials almost all of the 63rd (Naval) and 36th Divisions, but after the Armistice the cemetery was greatly enlarged when many more graves from the same battlefields and smaller burial grounds.

ARNEKE BRITISH CEMETERY

The village of Arneke is approximately 50 kms south-east of Calais and about 8 kms north-west of the town of Cassel.

The cemetery was begun by the 13th Casualty Clearing Station which moved to Arneke from the Proven area in October 1917. It was joined by two further Clearing Stations in April 1918. The cemetery was used by these hospitals until the end of May, and again from July to September 1918. In November it was used for a short time by the 4th and 10th Stationary Hospitals. A few French soldiers were buried from clearing stations in April 1918 and French units buried at the north-west end of the cemetery, mainly in May and June 1918.

ARRAS MEMORIAL AND ARRAS FLYING SERVICES MEMORIAL

The two memorials will be found in the FAUBOURG-D'AMIENS CEMETERY, which is in the Boulevard du General de Gaulle in the western part of the town of Arras.

The ARRAS MEMORIAL commemorates almost 35,000 servicemen from the United Kingdom, South Africa and New Zealand who died in the Arras sector between the spring of 1916 and 7 August 1918, the eve of the Advance to Victory, and have no known grave.

The ARRAS FLYING SERVICES MEMORIAL commemorates almost 1,000 airmen of the Royal Naval Air Service, the Royal Flying Corps, and the Royal Air Force, either by attachment from other arms of the forces of the Commonwealth or by original enlistment, who were killed on the whole Western Front and who have no known grave.

ASCOT (ALL SAINTS) CHURCHYARD EXTENSION

This cemetery is located off Priory Road, Chavey Down, and contains seven WWI burials.

ATH COMMUNAL CEMETERY

The town of Ath is located east of the town of Tournai on the N7.

The 38 Commonwealth burials of the First World War in ATH COMMUNAL CEMETERY date from November 1918 to March 1919, and are mainly those of men who died at No. 2 Australian Casualty Clearing Station.

AUBERCHICOURT BRITISH CEMETERY

Auberchicourt is a village 11.5 kms east of Douai on the road to Valenciennes.

The village was occupied by Commonwealth troops in October 1918. The cemetery was begun at the end of that month and used until February 1919 while three Canadian Casualty Clearing Stations were in the neighbourhood. These original graves are in Plot I, but the cemetery was enlarged after the Armistice when graves (mainly of 1918-19, but also of August 1914) were brought in from the surrounding battlefields and from the following smaller burial grounds.

AUCHONVILLERS MILITARY CEMETERY

Auchonvillers is approximately 20 kms south of Arras.

From the outbreak of the war to the summer of 1915, this part of the front was held by French troops, who began the military cemetery in June 1915. It continued to be used by Commonwealth field ambulances and fighting units, but burials practically ceased with the German withdrawal in February 1917.

AWOINGT BRITISH CEMETERY

Awoingt is a village some 3 kms east-south-east of Cambrai.

AWOINGT BRITISH CEMETERY was begun in the latter half of October 1918 and used until the middle of December; the village had been captured on 9/10th October. By 28th October, three Casualty Clearing Stations were posted in the neighbourhood, and the great majority of the burials were made from those hospitals.

BAILLEUL COMMUNAL CEMETERY EXTENSION (NORD)

Bailleul is a large town in France, near the Belgian border, 14.5 kms south-west of Ieper.

Bailleul was occupied on 14th October 1914 and became an important railhead, air depot and hospital centre, with several Casualty Clearing Stations quartered in it for considerable periods. It was a Corps headquarters until July 1917, when it was severely bombed and shelled, and after the Battle of Bailleul (13-15th April 1918), it fell into German hands and was not retaken until 30th August 1918. The earliest Commonwealth burials at Bailleul were made at the east end of the communal cemetery and in April 1915, when the space available had been filled, the extension was opened on the east side of the cemetery. The extension was used until April 1918, and again in September, and after the Armistice graves were brought in from the neighbouring battlefields and other burial grounds.

BAILLEUL ROAD EAST CEMETERY, ST LAURENT-BLANGY

St. Laurent-Blangy is a village adjoining the north-east side of Arras.

A greater part of the village was included in the front taken over by British troops in March, 1916, and the remainder fell into British hands on the first day of the Battles of Arras, the 9th April, 1917. BAILLEUL ROAD EAST CEMETERY was begun in April, 1917, and carried on by fighting units until the following November. After the Armistice isolated graves from a very wide area north, east and south of Arras were brought in.

BARD COTTAGE CEMETERY

The Cemetery is located near Ieper, on the Diksmuidseweg road (N369) in the direction of Boezinge (BARD COTTAGE CEMETERY is the first cemetery on the left, the second being TALANA FARM CEMETERY).

For much of the First World War, the village of Boesinghe (now Boezinge) directly faced the German line across the Yser canal. Bard Cottage was a house a little set back from the line, close to a bridge called Bard's Causeway, and the cemetery was made nearby in a sheltered position under a high bank. Burials were made between June 1915 and October 1918; after the Armistice, 46 graves were brought in from the immediate area.

BARLIN COMMUNAL CEMETERY EXTENSION

Barlin is a village about 11 kms south-west of Bethune on the D188.

The extension was begun by French troops in October 1914 and when they moved south in March 1916 to be replaced by Commonwealth Forces, it was used for burials by the 6th Casualty Clearing Station. In November 1917, Barlin began to be shelled and the hospital was moved back to Ruitz, but the extension was used again in March and April 1918 during the German advance on this front.

BASRA MEMORIAL

Until 1997, the Basra Memorial was located on the main quay of the naval dockyard at Maqil, on the west bank of the Shatt-al-Arab, about 8 kms north of Basra. Because of the sensitivity of the site, the Memorial was moved by presidential decree. The move, carried out by the authorities in Iraq, involved a considerable amount of manpower, transport costs and sheer engineering on their part, and the Memorial has been re-erected in its entirety. The Basra Memorial is now located 32 kms along the road to Nasiriyah, in the middle of what was a major battleground during the first Gulf War. The Basra Memorial commemorates more than 40,500 members of the Commonwealth forces who died in the operations in Mesopotamia from the autumn of 1914 to the end of August 1921 and whose graves are not known.

NOTE: Whilst the current climate of political instability persists it is not possible for the Commission to manage or maintain its cemeteries and memorials located within Iraq. Alternative arrangements for commemoration have therefore been implemented and a two volume Roll of Honour listing all casualties buried and commemorated in Iraq has been produced. These volumes are on display at the Commission's Head Office in Maidenhead and are available for the public to view.

BASRA WAR CEMETERY

Basra is a town on the west bank of the Shatt-al-Arab, 90 kms from its mouth in the Persian Gulf. The cemetery now contains 2,551 burials of the First World War, 74 of them unidentified. The headstones marking these graves were removed in 1935 when it was discovered that salts in the soil were causing them to deteriorate. The names of those buried in the graves affected are now recorded on a screen wall.

The cemetery also contains the BASRA (TANOOMA CHINESE) MEMORIAL, commemorating 227 unidentified casualties of the Chinese Labour Corps who were attached to the Inland Water Transport during the First World War. A panel in their memory was added to the screen wall when it became evident that their graves in TANOOMA CHINESE CEMETERY could no longer be maintained.

NOTE: Whilst the current climate of political instability persists it is not possible for the Commission to manage or maintain its cemeteries and memorials located within Iraq. Alternative arrangements for commemoration have therefore been implemented and a two volume Roll of Honour listing all casualties buried and commemorated in Iraq has been produced. These volumes are on display at the Commission's Head Office in Maidenhead and are available for the public to view.

BAVINCOURT COMMUNAL CEMETERY

Bavincourt is a village and commune in the Department of the Pas-de-Calais, a little north of the main road from Doullens to Arras. Five soldiers from the United Kingdom, who fell in May 1916, and March 1917, are buried in two groups in the Communal Cemetery, near the entrance.

BAZENTIN-LE-PETIT COMMUNAL CEMETERY AND BAZENTIN-LE-PETIT COMMUNAL CEMETERY EXTENSION

Bazentin is a village in the Department of the Somme, to the north-east of Albert, containing the villages of Bazentin-le-Grand and Bazentin-le-Petit.

Bazentin was in German hands until 14th July 1916, when the 3rd and 7th Divisions captured the two villages (and the communal cemetery) and held them against counter-attacks. The ground was lost in April 1918 during the great German advance but recaptured on the following 25th August.

The COMMUNAL CEMETERY contains two Commonwealth burials dating from August 1916. The COMMUNAL CEMETERY EXTENSION was begun immediately after the capture of the village and used until December 1916 as a front-line cemetery. It was enlarged after the Armistice when 50 graves were brought in from the battlefields of Bazentin and Contalmaison.

BEAURAIN BRITISH CEMETERY

Beaurain (not to be confused with Beaurains near Arras) is a village in the Department of the Nord 19 kms south of Valenciennes and 4 kms from Solesmes railway station.

It was captured on 23rd October, 1918; the British Cemetery was made in the fortnight after the capture of the village.

BEAURAINS ROAD CEMETERY, BEAURAINS

Beaurains is a village on the southern outskirts of Arras.

The cemetery was begun a few days before Beaurains was captured by Commonwealth forces on 18th March 1917. It was a month before the Battle of Arras began, and the Germans were still in nearby Tilloy-les-Mofflaines. The cemetery was used (sometimes under the name of Ronville Forward Cemetery) until the beginning of June, and later for a short time in August and September 1918, in the Second Battle of Arras. It contained, at the date of the Armistice, the graves of 129 British soldiers, 15 French soldiers and four German prisoners. It was enlarged after the armistice when graves were brought in from the surrounding battlefields and cemeteries.

BEERSHEBA WAR CEMETERY

Beersheba is a southern town on the edge of the Negev Desert, 75 kms south-west of Jerusalem. The cemetery was made immediately on the fall of the town, remaining in use until July 1918, by which time 139 burials had been made It was greatly increased after the Armistice when burials were brought in from a number of scattered sites and small burial grounds.

BERLIN SOUTH-WESTERN CEMETERY

The cemetery is located in the village of Stahnsdorf, lying approx 22 kms south-west of Berlin and approx 14 kms to the east of Potsdam.

In 1922-23 it was decided that the graves of Commonwealth servicemen who had died all over Germany should be brought together into four permanent cemeteries. Berlin South-Western was one of those chosen and in 1924-25, graves were brought into the cemetery from 146 burial grounds in eastern Germany.

BERNAFAY WOOD BRITISH CEMETERY, MONTAUBAN

BERNAFAY WOOD BRITISH CEMETERY is 10 kms east of Albert and 2 kms south of Longueval.

The Bois De Bernafay is a pear-shaped wood close to the east end of Montauban village. It was taken on 3rd and 4th July 1916, lost on 25th March 1918, in the retreat to the Ancre, but finally regained 27th August.

The cemetery was begun by a dressing station in August 1916 and used as a front-line cemetery until the following April. It contained at the Armistice 284 burials but was then increased when graves were brought in from Bernafay Wood North Cemetery and from the battlefields immediately east of the wood.

BEAUMONT-HAMEL BRITISH CEMETERY

Beaumont-Hamel is a village 10 kms north of Albert. It was attacked and reached on 1st July 1916, but it could not be held. It was attacked again, and this time taken, on 13th November 1916, and the British cemetery (originally titled as 'V Corps Cemetery No.23') was made by units taking part in that and subsequent operations until February 1917. It was increased after the Armistice when graves were brought in from the surrounding battlefields.

BEAURAIN BRITISH CEMETERY

Beaurain (not to be confused with Beaurains near Arras) is a village in the Department of the Nord 19 kms south of Valenciennes and 4 kms from Solesmes railway station. It was captured by the 5th Division on 23rd October, 1918; the British Cemetery was made in the fortnight after the capture of the village.

BETHUNE TOWN CEMETERY

Bethune is a town 29 kms north of Arras.

For much of the First World War, Bethune was comparatively free from bombardment and remained an important railway and hospital centre, as well as a corps and divisional head-quarters. The 33rd Casualty Clearing Station was in the town until December 1917. Early in 1918, Bethune began to suffer from constant shell fire and in April 1918, German forces reached Locon, five kms to the north. The bombardment of 21st May did great damage to the town and it was not till October that pressure from the Germans was relaxed.

BINFIELD CEMETERY

The cemetery is situated in Church Lane, to the east of All Saints Church. There are two WWI graves in the cemetery.

BLEUET FARM CEMETERY

The cemetery is located to the northwest of the town of Ieper near a village called Elverdinge. Bleuet Farm was used as a dressing station during the 1917 Allied offensive on this front. The cemetery was begun in a corner of the farm and was in use from June to December 1917, though a few of the burials are of later date. Two graves were brought into the cemetery after the Armistice from isolated positions close by.

BOULOGNE EASTERN CEMETERY

Boulogne Eastern Cemetery, one of the town cemeteries, lies in the district of St Martin Boulogne, just beyond the eastern (Chateau) corner of the Citadel (Haute-Ville).

Boulogne was one of the three base ports most extensively used by the Commonwealth armies on the Western Front throughout the First World War. It was closed and cleared on 27th August 1914 when the Allies were forced to fall back ahead of the German advance, but was opened again in October, and from that month to the end of the war, Boulogne and Wimereux formed one of the chief hospital areas. Until June 1918, the dead from the hospitals at Boulogne itself were buried in the CIMETIERE DE L'EST, one of the town cemeteries, the Commonwealth graves forming a long, narrow strip along the right hand edge of the cemetery. In the spring of 1918, it was found that space was running short in the Eastern Cemetery in spite of repeated extensions to the south, and the site of the new cemetery at Terlincthun was chosen.

BOUZINCOURT RIDGE CEMETERY, ALBERT

Bouzincourt is a village 3 kms north-west of Albert on the D938 road to Doullens.

The village remained partly in German hands after the battles of March 1918. It was attacked at the end of June 1918, and cleared in the latter half of August. In the first week of September, nearby the battlefields were cleared and after the Armistice, 500 further graves were brought in from the immediate neighbourhood.

BOVES EAST COMMUNAL CEMETERY

Boves is a village in the Department of the Somme, 9.7 kms from Villers-Bretonneux.

Boves has two communal cemeteries, on either side of the river. The 49th Casualty Clearing Station was at Boves from 23rd April to the end of August 1918 and the 1st Canadian and 4th Canadian during August 1918. The burials in the two communal cemeteries and the extension to the West cemetery are mainly those of soldiers who died in the three hospitals.

BOVES EAST COMMUNAL CEMETERY contains 15 Commonwealth burials of the First World War.

BOVES WEST COMMUNAL CEMETERY contains 51 Commonwealth burials of the First World War and 12 French graves. BOVES WEST COMMUNAL CEMETERY EXTENSION was made in August 1918 and after the Armistice, 32 graves were brought into it from Boves Military Cemetery.

BRACKNELL (LARGES LANE) CEMETERY

Larges Lane runs behind the Bracknell and Wokingham College and is accessed from the westbound carriageway of London Road, just east of the Met Office roundabout. The cemetery lies to the left on the bend just past Bracknell Football Club.

BRANDHOEK NEW MILITARY CEMETERY

Brandhoek New Military Cemetery is located 6.5 km west of Ieper town centre, on the Zevekotestraat.

During the First World War, Brandhoek was within the area comparatively safe from shell fire, which extended beyond Vlamertinghe Church. Field ambulances were posted there continuously. Until July 1917 burials had been made in the Military Cemetery, but the arrival of three Casualty Clearing Stations in preparation for the new Allied offensive launched that month made it necessary to open the New Military Cemetery, followed in August by the New Military Cemetery No 3.

BRAY MILITARY CEMETERY

Bray-sur-Somme is a village about 9 kms south-east of Albert.

The cemetery was begun in April 1916 by fighting units and field ambulances. In September 1916, the front line having been pushed further east, it was used by the XIV Corps Main Dressing Station and in 1917, three Casualty Clearing Stations came forward and used it. In March 1918, the village and the cemetery fell into German hands, but were retaken by the 40th Australian Battalion on 24th August, and during the next few days the cemetery was used again. After the Armistice graves were brought in from the battlefields immediately north and south of the village and in 1924, further isolated graves were brought in.

BROOKWOOD MILITARY CEMETERY

The main entrance to BROOKWOOD MILITARY CEMETERY is on the A324 from the village of Pirbright, Surrey.

BROOKWOOD MILITARY CEMETERY is owned by the Commission and is the largest Commonwealth war cemetery in the United Kingdom, covering approximately 37 acres.

In 1917, an area of land in Brookwood Cemetery (The London Necropolis) was set aside for the burial of men and women of the forces of the Commonwealth and Americans, who had died, many of battle wounds, in the London district.

BUCQUOY ROAD CEMETERY, FICHEUX

BUCQUOY ROAD CEMETERY is situated on the D919 heading south from Arras to Ayette.

In November 1916, the village of Ficheux was behind the German front line, but by April 1917, the German withdrawal had taken the line considerably east of the village and in April and May, the VII Corps Main Dressing Station was posted near for the Battles of Arras. It was followed by the 20th and 43rd Casualty Clearing Stations, which remained at Boisleux-au-Mont until March 1918, and continued to use the BUCQUOY ROAD CEMETERY begun by the field ambulances. From early April to early August 1918 the cemetery was not used but in September and October, the 22nd, 30th, and 33rd Casualty Clearing Stations came to Boisleux-au-Mont and extended it. By the date of the Armistice, it contained 1,166 burials but was greatly increased when graves were brought in from the surrounding battlefields and from small cemeteries in the neighbourhood.

BUSIGNY COMMUNAL CEMETERY EXTENSION

Busigny is a village about 10 kms south-west of Le Cateau and 24 kms north-east of St. Quentin. It was captured by the 30th American Division and British cavalry on 9th October 1918, in the Battle of Cambrai, and in the course of the next two months three Casualty Clearing Stations came successively to the village. The majority of the burials were made from these three hospitals. The cemetery extension was begun in October 1918, and used until February 1919. After the Armistice it was enlarged when graves were brought in from a wide area between Cambrai and Guise.

BUZANCY MILITARY CEMETERY

Buzancy is a village in the Department of the Aisne, 7 kms south of Soissons and 50 kms west of Reims, Northern France.

Buzancy was reached (though not held) by the 1st American Division on 21st July, 1918, after an advance begun on the 18th. It was attacked on the 23rd July, and taken on the 28th.

The Military Cemetery was made beside a French Military Cemetery from which the graves have been removed to Ambleny; and the original graves contain 96 burials. After the Armistice, graves were brought in from the surrounding battlefields.

CABARET-ROUGE BRITISH CEMETERY, SOUCHEZ

Souchez is a village 3.5 kms north of Arras on the main road to Bethune.

Caberet Rouge was a small, red-bricked, red-tiled café that stood close to this site in the early days of the First World War. The café was destroyed by shellfire in March 1915, but it gave its unusual name to this sector and to a communication trench that led troops up the front-line. Commonwealth soldiers began burying their fallen comrades here in March 1916. It was greatly enlarged in the years after the war when as many as 7,000 graves were concentrated here from over one hundred other cemeteries in the area. For much of the twentieth century, Cabaret Rouge served as one of a small number of 'open cemeteries' at which the remains of fallen servicemen newly discovered in the region were buried. Today the cemetery contains over 7,650 burials of the First World War, over half of which remain unidentified.

CAIX BRITISH CEMETERY

The village of Caix is situated about 28 kms south-east of Amiens.

Caix was occupied by Commonwealth troops in March 1917, lost during the German advance in March 1918, and recaptured on 8th August 1918 by the Canadian Corps.

CAIX BRITISH CEMETERY (called at first Caix New British Cemetery) was made after the Armistice when graves (mainly of March and August 1918) were brought in from the battlefields and from other smaller cemeteries.

CAMBRAI EAST MILITARY CEMETERY

Cambrai is a town about 32 kms south-east of Arras on the main straight road to Le Cateau.

It was occupied by German forces on 26th August 1914, and it remained in German hands until 9th October 1918. The Battle of Cambrai in 1917 left the Allied line still five miles from the city on the southwest side, and the German offensive of March 1918, drove it far to the west, but the Battle of Cambrai in 1918, the last of the Battles of the Hindenburg Line, delivered the very badly hit city into the hands of Commonwealth forces. Two Casualty Clearing Stations were later posted to the town. CAMBRAI EAST MILITARY CEMETERY was made by the Germans during their occupation and laid out with the greatest care, with monuments erected in it to the French, Commonwealth and German dead. On 11th August 1918, as an inscription in the cemetery records, the Bavarian Commandant handed over to the city the care and maintenance of the cemetery.

The graves have now been regrouped, including those brought from the battlefields east and south of the city, as well as graves of Commonwealth prisoners.

CAMBRAI MEMORIAL, LOUVERVAL

The small village of Louverval is on the north side of the D930, Bapaume to Cambrai road.

The Memorial stands on a terrace in LOUVERVAL MILITARY CEMETERY, and commemorates more than 7,000 servicemen of the United Kingdom and South Africa who died in the Battle of Cambrai in November and December 1917 and whose graves are not known.

CAMBRIN CHURCHYARD EXTENSION

Cambrin is a village about 24 kms north of Arras and about 8 kms east of Bethune, on the road to La Bassee.

At one time, the village of Cambrin housed Brigade Headquarters, but until the end of the First World War, it was only about 800 metres from the front line trenches. The village contains two cemeteries used for Commonwealth burials; the churchyard extension, taken over from French troops in May 1915, and the Military Cemetery "behind the Mayor's House."

The churchyard extension was used for front line burials until February 1917 when it was closed, but there are three graves of 1918 in the back rows. The extension is remarkable for the very large numbers of graves grouped by battalion, all dating from 25th September 1915, the first day of the Battle of Loos.

CANADIAN CEMETERY NO 2, NEUVILLE-ST, VAAST

Neuville-St. Vaast is a village about 6 kms north of Arras and 1 kilometre east of the main road from Arras to Bethune.

The cemetery was established by the Canadian Corps after the successful storming of Vimy Ridge on 9th April, 1917, and some of those buried in the cemetery fell in that battle or died of wounds received there, though the majority of the graves were made later for the burial of the dead recovered from surrounding battlefields and from isolated graves which were transferred into the cemetery over a period of years after the Armistice.

CHATBY MEMORIAL

Chatby is a district on the eastern side of the city of Alexandria. The CHATBY MEMORIAL is situated within CHATBY WAR MEMORIAL CEMETERY which is located centrally within the main Alexandria cemetery complex.

In March 1915, the base of the Mediterranean Expeditionary Force was transferred to Alexandria from Mudros, and the city became a camp and hospital centre for Commonwealth and French troops. After the Gallipoli campaign of 1915, Alexandria remained an important hospital centre during later operations in Egypt and Palestine, and the port was much used by hospital ships and troop transports bringing reinforcements and carrying the sick and wounded out of the theatres of war.

The CHATBY MEMORIAL stands at the eastern end of the ALEXANDRIA (CHATBY) WAR MEMORIAL CEMETERY and commemorates almost 1,000 Commonwealth servicemen who died during the First World War and have no other grave but the sea. Many of them were lost when hospital ships or transports were sunk in the Mediterranean, sailing to or from Alexandria. Others died of wounds or sickness while aboard such vessels and were buried at sea.

More than 700 of those commemorated on the memorial died when their vessels were topedoed or mined. Officers and men of the merchant services lost in these incidents are commemorated on appropriate memorials elsewhere.

CHATHAM NAVAL MEMORIAL

The Memorial overlooks the town of Chatham and is approached by a steep path from the Town Hall Gardens. After the First World War, an appropriate way had to be found of commemorating those members of the Royal Navy who had no known grave, the majority of deaths having occurred at sea where no permanent memorial could be provided.

An Admiralty committee recommended that the three manning ports in Great Britain - Chatham, Plymouth and Portsmouth - should each have an identical memorial of unmistakable naval form, an obelisk, which would serve as a leading mark for shipping. The Chatham Naval Memorial was unveiled by the Prince of Wales (the future King Edward VIII) on 26th April 1924.

CHAUNY COMMUNAL CEMETERY BRITISH EXTENSION

Chauny is a commune 35 kms west of Laon. The Cemetery Extension was made after the Armistice for the burial of remains brought in from the battlefields of the Aisne and from the smaller cemeteries in the surrounding countryside; the majority of them having died in 1918 and most of the rest in September 1914.

CHESTER FARM CEMETERY

Chester Farm Cemetery is located 5 kms south of Ieper town centre, on the Vaartstraat.

Chester Farm was the name given to a farm about 1 km south of Blauwepoort Farm, on the road from Zillebeke to Voormezeele. The cemetery was begun in March 1915 and was used by front line troops until November 1917.

CHOCQUES MILITARY CEMETERY

Chocques is 4 kms north-west of Bethune on the road to Lillers.

Chocques was occupied by Commonwealth forces from the late autumn of 1914 to the end of the war. The village was at one time the headquarters of I Corps and from January 1915 to April 1918, No.1 Casualty Clearing Station was posted there. Most of the burials from this period are of casualties who died at the clearing station from wounds received at the Bethune front. From April to September 1918, during the German advance on this front, the burials were carried out by field ambulances, divisions and fighting units.

After the Armistice it was found necessary to concentrate into this Cemetery a large number of isolated graves plus some small graveyards from the country between Chocques and Bethune.

COJEUL BRITISH CEMETERY, ST MARTIN-SUR-COJEUL

St. Martin-sur-Cojeul is a village about 8 kms south-south-east of Arras on the D33.

The village of St. Martin-sur-Cojeul was taken by the 30th Division on 9th April 1917, lost in March 1918, and retaken in the following August.

COJEUL BRITISH CEMETERY was begun in April 1917, and used by fighting units until the following October. It was very severely damaged in later fighting.

COLCHESTER CEMETERY

Colchester Cemetery was opened in 1856 and now belongs to the Corporation. There are 266 Commonwealth burials of the 1914-1918 war. After the war a Cross of Sacrifice was erected on a site overlooking both the plot and the group of war graves, in honour of all the servicemen buried here.

COLOGNE SOUTHERN CEMETERY

The city of Cologne lies in the west of Germany, approx 30kms to the north of Bonn. More than 1,000 Allied prisoners and dozens of German servicemen were buried in COLOGNE SOUTHERN CEMETERY during the First World War. Commonwealth forces entered Cologne on 6th December 1918, less than a month after the Armistice, and the city was occupied under the terms of the Treaty of Versailles until January 1926. During this period the cemetery was used by the occupying garrison. In 1922, it was decided that the graves of Commonwealth servicemen who had died all over Germany should be brought together into four permanent cemeteries at Kassel, Berlin, Hamburg and Cologne. Over the course of the following year, graves were transferred to Cologne Southern Cemetery from over 180 different burial grounds in Hanover, Hessen, the Rhine and Westphalia.

COMBLES COMMUNITY CEMETERY EXTENSION

The large village of Combles is 16 kms east of Albert and 13 kms south of Bapaume.

It was entered on 26th August 1916, and remained in Allied occupation until the 24th March 1918, when the place was captured by the Germans. It was retaken on the 29th August 1918. The cemetery was begun in October 1916, by French troops, but the 94 French graves made in 1916 have been removed to another cemetery. The first British burials took place in December, 1916. From March 1917, to the end of May 1918, the Extension was not used. During the next three months, 194 German soldiers were buried but these graves, too, have been removed; and in August and September further burials were made by the 18th Division. After the Armistice almost one thousand graves from the battlefields in the neighbourhood were brought in.

CORBIE COMMUNAL CEMETERY EXTENSION

Corbie is a small town 15 kms east of Amiens.

Corbie was about 20 kms behind the front when Commonwealth forces took over the line from Berles-au-Bois southward to the Somme in July 1915. The town immediately became a medical centre, with Nos 5 and 21 Casualty Clearing Stations based at La Neuville until October 1916 and April 1917 respectively. In November 1916, the front moved east, but the German advance in the Spring of 1918 came within 10 kms of the town, and brought with it field ambulances of the 47th Division and the 12th Australian Field Ambulance.

The communal cemetery was used for burials until May 1916, when the plot set aside was filled and the extension opened. The majority of the graves in the extension are of officers and men who died of wounds in the 1916 Battle of the Somme. The remainder relate to the fighting of 1918.

COUIN NEW BRITISH CEMETERY

Couin is a village 15 kms east of Doullens.

Couin Chateau was used as a divisional headquarters from 1915 to 1918. The BRITISH CEMETERY was begun in May 1916 by the field ambulances of the 48th (South Midland) Division, and was used by units and field ambulances during the Battle of the Somme in 1916. It was closed at the end of January 1917 because further extension was not possible.

The NEW BRITISH CEMETERY was opened across the road and was used by field ambulances from January 1917 (with a long interval in 1917-18) to the end of the war.

COURCELETTE BRITISH CEMETERY

Courcelette is a village some 10 kms north-east of the town of Albert, just off the D929 road to Bapaume.

The commune and the village of Courcelette were the scene of very heavy fighting and taken on 15th September 1916. It was destroyed by German artillery after its capture and remained very close to the front line until the German retreat in the following spring.

The cemetery was begun in November 1916 (as Mouquet Road or Sunken Road Cemetery), and used until March 1917. The original 74 burials are now parts of Plot I, Rows A to F. On 25th March 1918, Courcelette passed into German hands, but was retaken on 24th August. The cemetery was greatly enlarged after the Armistice when almost 2,000 graves were brought in, mostly those of men who died around Courcelette and Pozieres in 1916.

COXYDE MILITARY CEMETERY

Coxyde Military Cemetery is located approximately 500 metres beyond the village of Koksijde.

In June 1917, Commonwealth forces relieved French forces on 6 kms of front line from the sea to a point south of Nieuport (now Nieuwpoort), and held this sector for six months. Coxyde (now Koksijde) was about 10 kms behind the front line. The village was used for rest billets and was occasionally shelled, but the cemetery, which had been started by French troops, was found to be reasonably safe. It became the most important of the Commonwealth cemeteries on the Belgian coast and was used at night for the burial of the dead brought back from the front line. The French returned to the sector in December 1917 and continued to use the cemetery, and during 1918, Commonwealth naval casualties from bases in Dunkirk (now Dunkerque) were buried there. After the Armistice, the remains of 44 British soldiers were brought into the cemetery. Ten of them had been buried in isolated graves.

CRANBOURNE (ST PETER) CHURCHYARD

The churchyard surrounds the church in Hatchet Lane. There are five WWI graves.

CROISILLES BRITISH CEMETERY

Croisilles is a village about 13 kms south-east of Arras.

Croisilles was taken on 2nd April 1917, lost on 21st March 1918 and recaptured on the following 28th August, after heavy fighting.

Plots I and II of the cemetery, were made between April 1917 and March 1918, and the rest was formed after the Armistice when graves were brought in from the neighbouring battlefields and from some smaller burial grounds.

CROUY-VAUXROT FRENCH NATIONAL CEMETERY, CROUY

Crouy is a village in the Department of the Aisne, 4 kms north-east of Soissons on the road to Laon.

There are now fifty WWI war casualties commemorated in this site. Of these, nearly half are unidentified, and special memorials are erected to ten soldiers who are believed to be among them. All were brought in after the Armistice and fell in September and October, 1914.

CROWTHORNE (ST JOHN THE BAPTIST) CHURCHYARD

The churchyard surrounds the church which is situated in Church Road, Crowthorne.

DANTZIG ALLEY BRITISH CEMETERY, MAMETZ

Mametz is a village about 8 kms east of the town of Albert.

It was carried by the 7th Division on 1st July 1916, the first day of the Battle of the Somme, after very hard fighting at Dantzig Alley (a German trench) and other points. The cemetery was begun later in the same month and was used by field ambulances and fighting units until the following November. The ground was lost during the great German advance in March 1918, but regained in August, and a few graves were added to the cemetery in August and September 1918. At the Armistice, the cemetery consisted of 183 graves, but it was then very greatly increased by graves (almost all of 1916) brought in from the battlefields north and east of Mametz and from other smaller burial grounds,

DELHI WAR CEMETERY AND DELHI 1914-18 MEMORIAL

DELHI WAR CEMETERY was created in 1951 when graves from many cemeteries in northern India were moved into the site to ensure their permanent maintenance. Among them are graves from cantonment cemeteries in Allahabad, Cawnpore, Dehra Dun and Lucknow. It also contains the DELHI 1914-18 MEMORIAL, commemorating 153 casualties buried in Meerut Cantonment Cemetery, where their graves could no longer be maintained.

DELSAUX FARM CEMETERY, BEUGNY

This cemetery is near the village of Beugny, 19 kms south-west of Cambrai on the Bapaume-Cambrai road (RN30).

Delsaux Farm was a point on the German defensive system known as the Beugny-Ytres line, which was reached by Commonwealth troops on 18th March 1917, and passed on the following day. The farm was lost on 23rd March 1918, but it was retaken on 2nd September 1918, and on the next day the same division occupied Beugny village.

After their advance in March 1918, the Germans made a cemetery (Beugny Military Cemetery No.18) at the cross-roads, and in it buried 103 Commonwealth and 82 German dead. The site was extended in October - November 1918 by two Casualty Clearing Stations, which came to Delsaux Farm and made the present cemetery. A little later, the German graves of March 1918 were removed and the 103 Commonwealth dead reburied. The rest of the cemetery was made when graves were later brought in from the battlefield.

DELVILLE WOOD CEMETERY, LONGUEVAL

The cemetery is on the east side of Longueval, a village 11 kms east of Albert.

Delville Wood was a tract of woodland, nearly 1 kilometre square, the western edge of which touched the village. On 14th July 1916, the greater part of Longueval was taken, and most of Delville Wood on the following day. The wood now formed a salient in the line, with Waterlot Farm and Mons Wood on the south flank still in German hands, and, owing to the height of the trees, no close artillery support was possible for defence. Battles for control ebbed and flowed until the beginning of August, but it was then held until the end of April 1918 when it was lost during the German advance, but retaken on the following 28th August. DELVILLE WOOD CEMETERY was made after the Armistice, when graves were brought in from a few small cemeteries and isolated sites, and from the battlefields. Almost all of the burials date from July, August and September 1916.

DERNANCOURT COMMUNAL CEMETERY EXTENSION

Dernancourt is a village 3 kms south of Albert.

Field ambulances used the Communal Cemetery for Commonwealth burials from September 1915 to August 1916, and again during the German advance of March 1918. It contains 127 Commonwealth burials of the First World War. The XV Corps Main Dressing Station was formed at Dernancourt in August 1916, when the adjoining EXTENSION was opened. Five further Casualty Clearing Stations came over the next two years, but on 26th March 1918, Dernancourt was evacuated ahead of the German advance, and the extension remained in their hands until the village was recaptured on 9th August 1918. In September it was again used by Casualty Clearing Stations under the name of "Edgehill", due to the rising ground on the north-west. At the Armistice, the Extension contained more than 1,700 burials; it was then enlarged when graves were brought in from isolated positions in the immediate neighbourhood and other small cemeteries.

DICKEBUSCH NEW MILITARY CEMETERY EXTENSION

From Ieper town centre the Dikkebusseweg (N375), is reached via Elverdingsestraat.

The New Military Cemetery was begun in February 1915, and was used until May 1917 by fighting units and field ambulances, with a few further burials taking place in March and April 1918. The Extension was used from May 1917 to January 1918.

DOIRAN MILITARY CEMETERY AND DOIRAN MEMORIAL

THE DOIRAN MEMORIAL stands near DOIRAN MILITARY CEMETERY, which is situated in the north of Greece close to the Yugoslav frontier and near the south-east shore of Lake Doiran.

The DOIRAN MEMORIAL stands roughly in the centre of the line occupied for two years by the Allies in Macedonia, but close to the western end, which was held by Commonwealth forces. It marks the scene of the fierce fighting of 1917-1918, which caused the majority of the Commonwealth battle casualties. From October 1915 to the end of November 1918, the British Salonika Force suffered some 2,800 deaths in action, 1,400 from wounds and 4,200 from sickness. The campaign afforded few successes for the Allies, and none of any importance until the last two months. The action of the Commonwealth force was hampered throughout by widespread and unavoidable sickness, and by continual diplomatic and personal differences with neutrals or Allies. On one front there was a wide malarial river valley and on the other, difficult mountain ranges, and many of the roads and railways it required had to be specially constructed. The memorial serves the dual purpose of Battle Memorial of the British Salonika Force (for which a large sum of money was subscribed by the officers and men of that force), and place of commemoration for more than 2,000 Commonwealth servicemen who died in Macedonia and whose graves are not known.

The memorial stands near DOIRAN MILITARY CEMETERY. The cemetery (originally known as Colonial Hill Cemetery No.2) was formed at the end of 1916 as a cemetery for the Doiran front. The graves largely reflect the fighting of April and May 1917 (the attacks on the Petit-Couronne), and 18-19th September 1918 (the attacks on Pip Ridge and the Grand-Couronne). In October and November 1918, after the final advance, a few burials were added by the 25th Casualty Clearing Station.

After the Armistice, graves were brought into the cemetery from the battlefields and from some small burial grounds nearby.

DON COMMUNAL CEMETERY, ANNOEULLIN

Don is a town and commune in the Department of the Nord, 12 kms south-west of Lille.

Annoeullin was held by the Germans from an early date in the War until shortly before the Armistice. No.15 Casualty Clearing Station came to Don on the 25th October 1918, and remained until the 19th January 1919, and No. 32 came at the end of November and left at the end of December. From these two hospitals, soldiers were buried in Don Communal Cemetery, and later a number of bodies were brought in from the neighbouring fields.

DOVER (ST. JAMES'S) CEMETERY

During the First World War, Dover was a port of embarkation for troops bound for the Western Front and between August 1914 and August 1919, some 1,300,000 Commonwealth sick and wounded were landed there. The port was bombed in 1915 and again in August 1916.

There are 373 identified burials of the 1914-1918 war here. In addition there are 19 unidentified burials, 9 of whom can be named as victims of the Zeebrugge Raid, and these 9 are inscribed on a Special Memorial on the Cross of Sacrifice in the Zeebrugge Plot.

DOULLENS COMMUNAL CEMETERY EXTENSION NO 1

Doullens is a town in the Department of the Somme, approximately 30 kms north of Amiens on the N25 road to Arras.

Doullens was Marshal Foch's headquarters early in the First World War, and the scene of the conference in March 1918, after which he assumed command of the Allied armies on the Western Front. From the summer of 1915 to March 1916, the town was a junction between the French Tenth Army on the Arras front and the Commonwealth Third Army on the Somme. The citadel, overlooking the town from the south, was a French military hospital, and the railhead was used by both armies. In March 1916, Commonwealth forces succeeded the French on the Arras front, and five Casualty Clearing Stations came to Doullens at various times during the remainder of the War. From February 1916 to April 1918, these medical units continued to bury in the French extension (No 1) of the communal cemetery. In March and April 1918, the German advance and the desperate fighting on this front threw a severe strain on the Canadian Stationary Hospital in the town. The extension was filled, and a second extension begun on the opposite side of the communal cemetery.

DOZINGHEM MILITARY CEMETERY

The cemetery is located to the north-west of Poperinge near Krombeke.

Westvleteren was outside the front held by Commonwealth forces in Belgium during the First World War, but in July 1917, in readiness for the forthcoming offensive, groups of casualty clearing stations were placed at three positions, called by the troops Mendinghem, Dozinghem and Bandaghem.

Three Casualty Clearing Stations were posted at Dozinghem and the military cemetery was used by them until early in 1918.

DUD CORNER CEMETERY, LOOS

Loos-en-Gohelle is a village 5 kms north-west of Lens.

The name "Dud Corner" is believed to be due to the large number of unexploded enemy shells found in the neighbourhood after the Armistice. Only burials were made here during hostilities, the remainder of the graves were brought in later from isolated positions near Loos and to the North, and other small cemeteries.

DUHALLOW A.D.S. CEMETERY

The Cemetery is located on the Diksmuidseweg, N369 road, in the direction of Boezinge. Duhallow Advanced Dressing Station, believed to have been named after a southern Irish hunt, was a medical post 1.6 kms north of Ypres (now Ieper). The cemetery was begun in July 1917 and in October and November 1918, it was used by the 11th, 36th, and 44th Casualty Clearing Stations.

The cemetery contains many graves of the artillery and engineers and 41 men of the 13th Company Labour Corps, killed when a German aircraft dropped a bomb on an ammunition truck in January 1918. After the Armistice, the cemetery was enlarged when graves were brought into this cemetery from isolated sites and a number of small cemeteries on the battle-fields around Ypres. Special memorials commemorate a number of casualties known to have been buried in two of these cemeteries, whose graves were destroyed by shellfire.

DUISANS BRITISH CEMETARY, ETRUN

Duisans and Etrun are villages in the Department of the Pas-de-Calais, about 9 kms west of Arras.

The area around Duisans was occupied by Commonwealth forces from March 1916, but it was not until February 1917 that the site of this cemetery was selected for the 8th Casualty Clearing Station. The first burials took place in March and from the beginning of April the cemetery grew very quickly. Most of the graves relate to the Battles of Arras in 1917, and the trench warfare that followed. From May to August 1918, the cemetery was used by divisions and smaller fighting units for burials from the front line. In the autumn of 1918, three Clearing Stations remained at Duisans for two months, while a fourth was there from November 1918 to November 1920.

DURY CRUCIFIX CEMETERY

Dury is a village about 17 kms east-south-east of Arras. The cemetery was begun by Canadian units immediately after the capture of the village, and contained 72 graves at the Armistice. It was then enlarged by the concentration of graves from the battlefields of April and May 1917, and March, August and September 1918, north and west of Dury.

EASTHAMPSTEAD (SS MICHAEL AND MARY MAGDALENE) CHURCHYARD

The churchyard surrounds the church which is located on the north side of Crowthorne Road, opposite Church Hill House. Most of the War graves are on the north side of the church, with the exception of one to the west.

EAST MUDROS MILITARY CEMETERY

The Cemetery is on the Greek island of Limnos (Lemnos) in the northeast Aegean Sea.

Because of its position, the island of Lemnos played an important part in the campaigns against Turkey during the First World War. It was occupied by a force of marines on

23rd February 1915 in preparation for the military attack on Gallipoli, and Mudros became a considerable Allied camp. The 1st and 3rd Canadian Stationary Hospitals, the 3rd Australian General Hospital, and other medical units were stationed on both sides of Mudros Bay, and a considerable Egyptian Labour Corps detachment was employed. After the evacuation of Gallipoli, a garrison remained on the island and the 1st Royal Naval Brigade was on Lemnos, Imbros and Tenedos for the first few months of 1916. On 30th October 1918, the Armistice between the Entente Powers and Turkey was signed at Mudros.

EAST MUDROS MILITARY CEMETERY was begun in April 1915 and used until September 1919.

EBBLINGHEM MILITARY CEMETERY

Ebblinghem is a village halfway between St. Omer and Hazebrouck.

The cemetery was begun by the 2nd and 15th Casualty Clearing Stations, who came to Ebblinghem in April 1918 at the beginning of the German offensive, and used the cemetery until July. Further graves were added after the war from nearby cemeteries.

EPEHY WOOD FARM CEMETERY, EPEHY

Epehy is a village between Cambrai and Peronne about 18 kms north-east of Peronne.

The village was captured at the beginning of April 1917. It was lost on 22nd March 1918 and retaken (in the Battle of Epehy) on 18th September 1918. The cemetery takes its name from the Ferme du Bois, a little to the east. Graves mainly date from the capture of the village in September 1918 and also after the Armistice when graves were brought in from the battlefields surrounding Epehy and smaller nearby cemeteries.

ERQUELINNES COMMUNAL CEMETERY

Erquelinnes is located 21 kms south east of Mons.

ERQUELINNES COMMUNAL CEMETERY contains 67 Commonwealth burials of the First World War, all of which were made by the Germans in October and November 1918.

ESQUELBECQ MILITARY CEMETERY

Esquelbecq is a village near the Belgian frontier, 24 kms north of Hazebrouck, and the same distance south of Dunkirk.

The cemetery was opened in April 1918 during the early stages of the German offensive in Flanders, when the 2nd Canadian and 3rd Australian Casualty Clearing Stations came to Esquelbecq. It was closed in September 1918.

ESSEX FARM CEMETERY

Boezinge is a village in the province of West Flanders, north of Ieper on the Diksmuidseweg road (N369).

The land south of Essex Farm was used as a dressing station cemetery from April 1915 to August 1917. The burials were made without definite plan, and some of the divisions which occupied this sector may be traced in almost every part of the cemetery.

ETAPLES MILITARY CEMETERY

Etaples is a town about 27 kms south of Boulogne.

During the First World War, the area around Etaples was the scene of immense concentrations of Commonwealth reinforcement camps and hospitals. It was remote from attack, except from aircraft, and accessible by railway from both the northern and the southern battlefields. In 1917, 100,000 troops were camped among the sand dunes and the hospitals, which included eleven general, one stationary, four Red Cross hospitals, and a convalescent depot, could deal with 22,000 wounded or sick. In September 1919, ten months after the Armistice, three hospitals and the Q.M.A.A.C. convalescent depot remained.

The cemetery is the largest in France under the Commission.

EUSTON ROAD CEMETERY, COLINCAMPS

Colincamps is a village 11 kms north of Albert. Colincamps and "Euston", a road junction a little east of the village, were within the Allied lines before the Somme offensive of July 1916. The cemetery was started as a front line burial ground during and after the unsuccessful attack on Serre on 1st July, but after the German withdrawal to the Hindenburg Line in March 1917, it was scarcely used. It was briefly in German hands towards the end of March 1918, when it marked the limit of the German advance, but the line was held and pushed forward by the New Zealand Division allowing the cemetery to be used again for burials in April and May 1918. The cemetery is particularly associated with three dates and engagements; the attack on Serre on 1st July 1916; the capture of Beaumont-Hamel on 13th November 1916; and the German attack on the 3rd New Zealand (Rifle) Brigade trenches before Colincamps on 5th April 1918. After the Armistice, more than 750 graves were brought in from small cemeteries in the neighbouring communes and the battlefields.

FAUBOURG D'AMIENS CEMETERY, ARRAS

Faubourg-d'Amiens Cemetery is in the western part of the town of Arras in the Boulevard du General de Gaulle, near the Citadel.

The French handed over Arras to Commonwealth forces in the spring of 1916, and the system of tunnels upon which the town is built were used and developed in preparation for the major offensive planned for April 1917. The Commonwealth section of the FAUBOURG D'AMIENS CEMETERY was begun in March 1916, behind the French military cemetery established earlier. It continued to be used by field ambulances and fighting units until November 1918. The cemetery was enlarged after the Armistice when graves were brought in from the battlefields and from two smaller cemeteries in the vicinity.

FAUQUISSART MILITARY CEMETERY, LAVENTIE

Fauquissart and Fleurbaix are hamlets of Laventie, a town near Armentieres in the Pas de Calais.

FAUQUISSART MILITARY CEMETERY was begun in November 1914 by the 2nd Royal Berks and the 2nd Rifle Brigade, and used until June 1915.

FERME BUTERNE MILITARY CEMETERY, HOUPLINES

Ferme Buterne Military Cemetery will be found 1 kilometre south-east of the village of Houplines.

Houplines was in Allied hands (but near the front line) from 17th October 1914, when it was taken by the 4th Division. It fell into German hands in April 1918 during their great advance, but was recovered in September. The village contained four Commonwealth cemeteries in addition to plots in the communal cemetery, but the graves were regrouped after the war and only two cemeteries remain.

FIFTEEN RAVINE BRITISH CEMETERY, VILLERS-PLOUICH

Villers-Plouich is a village about 13 kms south-west of Cambrai.

"Fifteen Ravine" was the name given by the Army to the shallow ravine, once bordered by fifteen trees, which ran at right angles to the railway about 800 metres south of the village of Villers-Plouich, but the cemetery is in fact in "Farm Ravine," on the east side of the railway line, nearer to the village. The cemetery, sometimes called FARM RAVINE CEMETERY, was begun in April 1917, a few days after the capture of the ravine. It continued in use during the Battle of Cambrai (November 1917) and until March 1918, when the ravine formed the boundary between the Third and Fifth Armies. On 22nd March, the second day of the great German offensive, the ground passed into their hands after severe fighting, and it was not regained until the end of the following September.

In March 1918, the cemetery contained 107 graves, but it was greatly enlarged after the Armistice when graves were brought in from the battlefields south-west of Cambrai and other cemeteries.

FINS NEW BRITISH CEMETERY, SOREL-LE-GRAND

Fins is a village on the road between Cambrai and Peronne.

Fins and Sorel were occupied at the beginning of April 1917, in the German Retreat to the Hindenburg Line. They were lost on the 23rd March 1918, and regained in the following September.

The first British burials at Fins were carried out in the CHURCHYARD and the CHURCHYARD EXTENSION, and the NEW BRITISH CEMETERY was not begun until July 1917. It was used until March 1918, when it comprised about 590 graves; it was then used by the Germans, who added 255 burials, including 26 British. In September and October 1918, about 73 British soldiers were buried and the cemetery completed, by the concentration of 591 graves after Armistice from the surrounding battlefields and from other smaller cemeteries.

FLATIRON COPSE CEMETERY, MAMETZ

The cemetery is on the right hand side of D929, Amiens-Albert-Bapaume, 10 kms east of Albert.
Flatiron Copse was the name given by the army to a small plantation a little to the east of Mametz Wood. The ground was taken on 14th July 1916, and an advanced dressing station was established at the copse. The cemetery was begun later that month, and it remained in use until April 1917. Two further burials were made in August 1918, and after the Armistice, more than 1,100 graves were brought in from the neighbouring battlefields and smaller cemeteries

FORT WILLIAM (ST. ANDREW) EPISCOPALIAN CHURCHYARD

This site is on the end of a pedestrian-only High Street.

The two WWI graves are west of the church.

FRETOY COMMUNAL CEMETERY

FRETOY COMMUNAL CEMETERY contains three Commonwealth burials from the First World War.

GAZA WAR CEMETERY

Gaza is 3 kms inland from the Mediterranean coast, 65 kms southwest of Tel Aviv.

Gaza was bombarded by French warships in April 1915. At the end of March 1917, it was attacked and surrounded by the Egyptian Expeditionary Force in the First Battle of Gaza, but the attack was broken off when Turkish reinforcements appeared. The Second Battle of Gaza, 17-19th April, left the Turks in possession, and the Third Battle of Gaza, begun on 27th October, ended with the capture of the ruined and deserted city on 7th November 1917. Casualty Clearing Stations arrived later that month, and General and Stationary hospitals in 1918.

Some of the earliest burials were made by the troops that captured the city. About two-thirds of the total were brought into the cemetery from the battlefields after the Armistice. The remainder were made by medical units after the Third Battle of Gaza, or, in some cases, represent reburials from the battlefields by the troops who captured the city.

GEZAINCOURT COMMUNAL CEMETERY EXTENSION

Gezaincourt is a village a little south-west of the town of Doullens.

The COMMUNAL CEMETERY at Gezaincourt contains nine Commonwealth burials of the First World War, made between October 1915 and March 1916. The adjoining EXTENSION was opened in March 1916 and used until March 1917, and again from March to October 1918. In most cases, the burials were carried out from casualty clearing stations and, in June to August 1918, from the 3rd Canadian Stationary Hospital.

GIAVERA BRITISH CEMETERY, ARCADE

Giavera is 12 kms east of Montebelluna and 20 kms west of Conegliano on the S248, the road that joins the two towns.

The Italians entered the war on the Allied side, declaring war on Austria, in May 1915. Commonwealth forces were at the Italian front between November 1917 and November 1918. On 4th December 1917, the XIth and XIVth British Corps relieved the Italians on the Montello sector of the Piave front. The Commonwealth troops on the sector were not involved in any large operations, but they carried out continuous patrol work across the River Piave, as well as much successful counter-battery work. In January 1918, an additional sector of the defence on the right was taken over by the Commonwealth troops. Between December and March, the Royal Flying Corps carried out a large number of successful raids on enemy aerodromes, railway junctions, and other objectives. Sixty-four hostile aeroplanes and nine balloons were destroyed during this period against British losses of twelve machines and three balloons. In March 1918, the Commonwealth troops on the Montello sector were relieved. On 4th November, the Armistice came into effect, and active hostilities ceased.

Men who died in defending the Piave from December 1917 to March 1918, and those who fell on the west of the river during the Passage of the Piave, are buried in this cemetery.

GLYMPTON CHURCHYARD, GLYMPTON, OXFORDSHIRE

Although one of the men listed on the Binfield War Memorial is buried in GLYMPTON CHURCHYARD, he did not die until 1923 and is therefore not classed as a War Grave.

GOMIECOURT SOUTH CEMETERY

Gomiecourt is a village in the Department of the Pas-de-Calais, 16 kms south of Arras and 6 kms north-west of Bapaume. It was captured on 23rd August 1918, and the cemetery made at the end of August 1918. Gomiecourt South Cemetery contains around two hundred Commonwealth burials of the First World War; 27 German burials form a separate plot on the south-west side.

GOMMECOURT BRITISH CEMETERY NO 2, HEBUTERNE

Gommecourt is a village 19 kms south-west of Arras.

Hebuterne village remained in Allied hands from March 1915 to the Armistice, although during the German advances of the summer of 1918, it was practically on the front line. Gommecourt and Gommecourt Wood were attacked on 1st July 1916, with only temporary success, but the village was occupied on the night of 27-28th February 1917, remaining in Allied hands until the Armistice. Gommecourt was later "adopted" by the County Borough of Wolverhampton. GOMMECOURT BRITISH CEMETERIES NO. 1, NO. 2, NO. 3 and NO. 4 were made in 1917 when the battlefields were cleared.

GONNEHEM BRITISH CEMETERY

Gonnehem is a village about 7 kms north-west of Bethune and 7 kms east of Lillers.

The cemetery was begun in the middle of April 1918, when the German front line came within 3.2 kms of the village. It was used until September. After the Armistice graves were brought in from the battlefields east of Gonnehem.

GOUZEAUCOURT NEW BRITISH CEMETERY

Gouzeaucourt is a large village 15 kms southwest of Cambrai and 15 kms northeast of Peronne.

The village was captured on the night of 12-13th April 1917. It was lost on 30th November 1917 in the German counterattack at the end of the Battle of Cambrai, and recaptured the same day. It was lost again on 22nd March 1918, and finally retaken by the 21st Division on 8th October. The cemetery was begun in November 1917, taken over by the Germans in 1918, and used again by Commonwealth forces in September and October 1918, but the original burials are only 55 in number. It was enlarged after the Armistice when graves were brought in from other cemeteries and from the battlefield of Cambrai.

GRANGEGORMAN MILITARY CEMETERY, DUBLIN

The cemetery is situated on Blackhorse Avenue, off Navan Rd, facing the wall of the Phoenix Park, and just up the road from McKee Barracks.

The cemetery was opened in 1876, and was used for the burial of British service personnel and their near relatives. It contains war graves from both World Wars. Some of the graves were re-located to this site at a later date. A Screen Wall Memorial of a simple design standing nearly two metres high and fifteen metres long has been built of Irish limestone to commemorate the names of those war casualties whose graves lie elsewhere in Ireland and can no longer be maintained. Arranged before this memorial are the headstones of the war dead, buried in Cork Military Cemetery, but now commemorated here.

GREEN HILL CEMETERY

Heading North from Anzac, you will encounter the cemetery after 17.6 kms on the right, adjacent to the track.

The eight month campaign in Gallipoli was fought by Commonwealth and French forces in an attempt to force Turkey out of the war, to relieve the deadlock of the Western Front in France and Belgium, and to open a supply route to Russia through the Dardanelles and the Black Sea.

The Allies landed on the peninsula on 25-26th April 1915; the 29th Division at Cape Helles in the south, and the Australian and New Zealand Corps north of Gaba Tepe on the west coast, an area soon known as Anzac. On 6th August, further troops were put ashore at Suvla, just north of Anzac, and the climax of the campaign came in early August when simultaneous assaults were launched on all three fronts. Green Hill and Chocolate Hill (which form together Yilghin Burnu), rise from the eastern shore of the salt lake. They were captured on 7th August 1915, but once taken, no further advance was then made. GREEN HILL CEMETERY was made after the Armistice when isolated graves were brought in from the battlefields of August 1915, and from small burial grounds in the surrounding area.

GREVILLERS BRITISH CEMETERY

Grevillers is a village in the Department of the Pas de Calais, 3 kms west of Bapaume.

The village was occupied by Commonwealth troops on 14th March 1917, and in April and May, three Casualty Clearing Stations were posted nearby. They began the cemetery and continued to use it until March 1918, when Grevillers was lost to the Germans during their great advance. On the following 24th August, the New Zealand Division recaptured Grevillers, and in September, another three Casualty Clearing Stations came to the village and used the cemetery again. After the Armistice, two hundred graves were brought in from the battlefields to the south of the village.

GROVE TOWN CEMETERY, MEAULTE

Meaulte is a village just south of Albert.

In September 1916, the 34th and 2/2nd London Casualty Clearing Stations were established at this point, known to the troops as Grove Town, to deal with casualties from the Somme battlefields. They were moved in April 1917 and, except for a few burials in August and September 1918, the cemetery was closed.

GUARDS CEMETERY, WINDY CORNER, CUINCHY

Cuinchy is a village about 7 kms east of the town of Bethune and north of the N41 which runs between Bethune and La Bassee.

A little west of the crossroads known to the army as 'Windy Corner', was a house used as a battalion headquarters and dressing station. The cemetery grew up beside this house. The original cemetery was begun in January 1915, and used extensively in and after February. It was closed at the end of May 1916, when it contained 681 graves. After the Armistice it was increased when more than 2,700 graves were brought in from the neighbouring battlefields - in particular the battlefields of Neuve-Chapelle, the Aubers Ridge and Festubert - and from certain smaller cemeteries.

HAIDAR PASHA CEMETERY AND HAIDAR PASHA MEMORIAL

Haidar Pasha is a suburb of Istanbul between Scutari (Uskudar) and Kadikoy on the Asiatic side of the Bosphorous.

The HAIDAR PASHA MEMORIAL stands within the war graves plot of HAIDAR PASHA CEMETERY, and commemorates more than thirty Commonwealth servicemen of the First World War who died fighting in South Russia, Georgia and Azerbaijan, and in post-Armistice operations in Russia and Transcaucasia, whose graves are not known. An Addenda panel was later added to commemorate over 170 Commonwealth casualties who are buried in cemeteries in South Russia and Transcaucasia whose graves can longer be maintained. The war graves plot also contains the HAIDAR PASHA CREMATION MEMORIAL, which commemorates 122 soldiers of the Indian Army who died in 1919 and 1920, who were originally commemorated at Mashiak and Osmanieh Cemeteries. In 1961, when these cemeteries could no longer be maintained, the ashes of the Hindus, whose remains were cremated in accordance with their faith, were scattered near this memorial, while the remains of their comrades of the Muslim faith were brought here and re-interred.

HAIDAR PASHA CEMETERY was first established for Crimean war burials and was used during the First World War by the Turks for the burial of Commonwealth prisoners of war. After the Armistice, when Istanbul was occupied, further burials were made mainly from No. 82 General Hospital, and graves were brought in from other civil cemeteries in the area.

HAM BRITISH CEMETERY, MUILLE-VILLETTE

Ham is a small town about 20 kms south west of St. Quentin.

In January, February, and March 1918, the 61st (South Midland) Casualty Clearing Station was posted at Ham, but on 23rd March the Germans, in their advance towards Amiens, crossed the Somme at Ham, and the town remained in German hands until the French First Army re-entered it on the following 6th September.

Ham British Cemetery was begun in January-March 1918 as an extension of MUILLE-VILLETTE GERMAN CEMETERY, made by the Casualty Clearing Station. In 1919, these graves were regrouped and others were added from the German cemetery and from other cemetreies.

HASLAR ROYAL NAVAL CEMETERY

During both wars, Gosport was a significant sea port and Naval depot, with many government factories and installations based there, as well as the Haslar Naval Hospital. HASLAR ROYAL NAVAL CEMETERY, which was attached to the Naval Hospital of 2,000 beds, contains 763 First World War graves, two of which are unidentified, scattered throughout the cemetery.

HAWTHORN RIDGE CEMETERY NO. 2, AUCHONVILLERS

Auchonvillers is approximately 20 kms south of Arras.

HAWTHORN RIDGE CEMETERY NO.1 was made by the V Corps, who cleared the Ancre battlefields in the spring of 1917; HAWTHORN RIDGE CEMETERY NO. 2 is 460 metres south of NO. 1. It was made in the spring of 1917, and seven isolated graves were brought in after the Armistice.

HAZEBROUCK COMMUNAL CEMETERY

Hazebrouck is a town lying about 56 kms south-east of Calais.

From October 1914 to September 1917, casualty clearing stations were posted at Hazebrouck. The Germans shelled and bombed the town between September 1917 and September 1918, making it unsafe for hospitals, but in September and October 1918, No. 9 British Red Cross Hospital was stationed there. Commonwealth burials began in the communal cemetery in October 1914 and continued until July 1918. At first, they were made among the civilian graves, but after the Armistice these earlier burials were moved into the main Commonwealth enclosure.

HEBUTERNE MILITARY CEMETERY

Hebuterne is a village 15 kms north of Albert (Somme) and 20 kms south-west of Arras. HEBUTERNE MILITARY CEMETERY was begun in August 1915, and used by fighting units and Field Ambulances until the spring of 1917; it was reopened in 1918.

HEDAUVILLE COMMUNAL CEMETERY EXTENSION

Hedauville is approximately 5 kms northwest of Albert, on the road to Doullens.

The extension was begun at the end of March 1918, when the front line was consolidated a short distance east of the village following the German offensive. It was used by field ambulances and fighting units until the following August. The extension contained 95 graves at the Armistice, but was later increased when graves were brought in from the surrounding battlefields of March-August 1918.

HEILLY STATION CEMETERY, MERICOURT-L'ABBE

Mericourt-l'Abbe is a village approximately 19 kms northeast of Amiens and 10 kms southwest of Albert.

The 36th Casualty Clearing Station was at Heilly from April 1916. It was joined in May by the 38th, and in July by the 2/2nd London, but these hospitals had all moved on by early June 1917. The cemetery was begun in May 1916, and was used by the three medical units until April 1917. From March to May 1918, it was used by Australian units, and in the early autumn for further hospital burials, when the 20th Casualty Clearing Station was there briefly in August and September 1918. The last burial was made in May 1919.

HELLES MEMORIAL

The Anzac and Suvla cemeteries are first signposted from the left hand junction of the Eceabat-Bigali Road. The HELLES MEMORIAL stands on the tip of the Gallipoli Peninsula. It takes the form of an obelisk over 30 metres high that can be seen by ships passing through the Dardanelles.

The eight month campaign in Gallipoli was fought by Commonwealth and French forces in an attempt to force Turkey out of the war, to relieve the deadlock of the Western Front in France and Belgium, and to open a supply route to Russia through the Dardanelles and the Black Sea.

The Allies landed on the peninsula on 25-26th April 1915; the 29th Division at Cape Helles in the south, and the Australian and New Zealand Corps north of Gaba Tepe on the west coast, an area soon known as Anzac. On 6th August, further landings were made at Suvla, just north of Anzac, and the climax of the campaign came in early August when simultaneous assaults were launched on all three fronts. However, the difficult terrain and stiff Turkish resistance soon led to the stalemate of trench warfare. From the end of August, no further serious action was fought and the lines remained unchanged. The peninsula was successfully evacuated in December and early January 1916. The HELLES MEMORIAL serves the dual function of Commonwealth battle memorial for the whole Gallipoli campaign, and place of commemoration for many of those Commonwealth servicemen who died there and have no known grave. The United Kingdom and Indian forces named on the memorial died in operations throughout the peninsula, the Australians at Helles. There are also panels for those who died or were buried at sea in Gallipoli waters. The memorial bears more than 21,000 names.

HENINEL COMMUNAL CEMETERY EXTENSION

Heninel is a village some 10 kms south-east of Arras on the D33.

Heninel village was captured in a snowstorm on 12th April 1917. The extension was begun in April 1917 and was used by fighting units until the following November.

HENINEL-CROISILLES ROAD CEMETERY

Heninel and Croisilles are villages approximately 5 kms and 8 kms southeast of Arras.

Heninel was captured on 12th April 1917, the attack continuing eastwards on the two following days. In April 1918, this ground was lost, and the eleven German graves were made when the cemetery was in German hands. After the Armistice, graves were brought in from a wide area round Heninel.

HOLLYBROOK MEMORIAL, SOUTHAMPTON

The Hollybrook Memorial is situated in SOUTHAMPTON (HOLLYBROOK) Cemetery behind the plot of First World War graves near the main entrance.

The Hollybrook Memorial commemorates by name almost 1,900 servicemen and women of the Commonwealth land and air forces whose graves are not known, many of whom were lost in transports or other vessels torpedoed or mined in home waters. The memorial also bears the names of those who were lost or buried at sea, or who died at home but whose bodies could not be recovered for burial.

HONNECHY BRITISH CEMETERY

Honnechy is a village in the Department of the Nord, 8 kms south-west of Le Cateau.

The village was part of the battlefield of Le Cateau in August 1914, and from that time it remained in German hands until the 9th October 1918. It had been a German Hospital centre, and from its capture until the end of October, it was a British Field Ambulance centre. The village was inhabited by civilians during the whole of the War.

The cemetery stands on the site of a German Cemetery, begun in the Battle of Cambrai 1917, and used by German troops and then by British until the 24th October 1918. The 300 German graves were removed to another burial ground, leaving 44 British graves; and the cemetery was re-made in 1922 and 1923 by the concentration of British graves, almost entirely from German Cemeteries.

HOOGE CRATER CEMETERY

HOOGE CRATER CEMETERY is 4 kms east of Ieper town centre on the Meenseweg (N8), connecting Ieper to Menen.

Hooge Chateau and its stables were the scene of very fierce fighting throughout the First World War. On 31st October 1914, the staff of the 1st and 2nd Divisions were wiped out when the chateau was shelled; from 24th May to 3rd June 1915, the chateau was defended against German attacks, and in July 1915, the crater was made by a mine sprung by the 3rd Division. It changed hands several times in the course of the conflict, and was retaken for the final time on 28th September 1918. The cemetery was begun early in October 1917. It contained originally 76 graves, but was greatly increased after the Armistice when graves were brought in from the battlefields of Zillebeke, Zantvoorde and Gheluvelt and the other smaller cemeteries.

ISLINGTON CEMETERY AND CREMATORIUM

The cemetery is located on High Road, East Finchley, London.

ISLINGTON CEMETERY contains almost 350 First World War graves, scattered throughout the cemetery. A screen wall in the western part bears the names of those whose graves could not be marked individually.

JERUSALEM WAR CEMETERY AND JERUSALEM MEMORIAL

The JERUSALEM MEMORIAL stands in JERUSALEM WAR CEMETERY, 4.5 kms north of the walled city, and is situated on the neck of land at the north end of the Mount of Olives, to the west of Mount Scopus.

At the outbreak of the First World War, Palestine (now Israel) was part of the Turkish Empire, and it was not entered by Allied forces until December 1916. The advance to Jerusalem took a further year, but from 1914 to December 1917, about 250 Commonwealth prisoners of war were buried in the German and Anglo-German cemeteries of the city. By 21st November 1917, the Egyptian Expeditionary Force had gained a line about five kms west of Jerusalem, but the city was deliberately spared bombardment and direct attack. Very severe fighting followed, lasting until the evening of 8th December, when all the city's prepared defences were captured. Turkish forces left Jerusalem throughout that night and in the morning of 9th December, the Mayor came to the Allied lines with the Turkish Governor's letter of surrender. Jerusalem was occupied that day and on 11th December, General Allenby formally entered the city, followed by representatives of France and Italy. JERUSALEM WAR CEMETERY was begun after the occupation of the city, with 270 burials. It was later enlarged to take graves from the battlefields and smaller cemeteries in the neighbourhood.

KANTARA WAR MEMORIAL CEMETERY

Kantara War Memorial Cemetery is situated at Kantara East on the eastern side of the Suez Canal, 160 kms northeast of Cairo and 50 kms south of Port Said.

In the early part of the First World War, Kantara was an important point in the defence of Suez against Turkish attacks, and marked the starting point of the new railway east towards

Sinai and Palestine, begun in January 1916. Kantara developed into a major base and hospital centre, and the cemetery was begun in February 1916 for burials from the various hospitals, continuing in use until late 1920. After the Armistice, the cemetery was more than doubled in size when graves were brought in from other cemeteries and desert battlefields, notably those at Rumani, Qatia, El Arish and Rafa.

Near the entrance to the cemetery is the KANTARA MEMORIAL, bearing the names of 16 New Zealand servicemen of the First World War who died in actions at Rumani and Rafa, and who have no known grave.

KARASOULI MILITARY CEMETERY

Karasouli Military Cemetery is on the edge of the town of Polikastro (formerly Karasouli) which lies some 56 kms from Thessaloniki.

The cemetery was begun in September 1916 for the use of casualty clearing stations on the Doiran front. At the Armistice, it contained about 500 burials, but was greatly increased when graves were brought in from other cemeteries.

KIRECHKOI-HORTAKOI MILITARY CEMETERY

The cemetery is some 15 kms north east of Thessaloniki, on the outskirts of the village of Exochi (formerly Kirechkoi).

XVI Corps Headquarters were at Kirechkoi from January 1916, soon after the opening of the Salonika campaign, until the advance to the Struma in September 1916. The cemetery was begun in March 1916, but it remained a very small one until September 1917, when three General Hospitals came to the neighbourhood. In June, July and September 1918, other hospitals were brought to the high and healthy country beside the Salonika-Hortakoi road, and in September 1918, the influenza epidemic began, which raged for three months and filled three-quarters of the cemetery. The last burial took place in January 1919, but in 1937, twelve graves were brought into the cemetery from Salonika Protestant Cemetery, where their permanent maintenance could not be assured.

KLEIN-VIERSTRAAT BRITISH CEMETERY

KLEIN-VIERSTRAAT BRITISH CEMETERY is located 6 kms south-west of Ieper town centre, on the Molenstraat.

The village of Kemmel and the adjoining hill, Mont Kemmel, were the scene of fierce fighting in the latter half of April 1918, in which both Commonwealth and French forces were engaged. The cemetery was begun in January 1917 by field ambulances and fighting units before the middle of January 1918. After the Armistice, graves were brought in from two smaller cemeteries and from the battlefields of Dikkebus, Loker and Kemmel.

KORTRIJK (ST JAN) COMMUNAL CEMETERY

Kortrijk Communal Cemetery is located 28 kms east of Ieper town centre on the N8 Meenseweg.

Courtrai (now Kortrijk) was in German hands for most of the First World War. In April 1915, its railway junction was severely damaged by Allied airmen, and on 16th October 1918, the town was entered by the 12th Royal Irish Rifles.

St. Jean (now St. Jan) Cemetery was largely used and extended by the Germans, who erected a screen wall bearing the names of the dead by nationalities (the German Extension is in the commune of Heule). In November 1918, No. 44 Casualty Clearing Station was posted at Kortrijk for a week, and it was followed for a period of eight months by No. 62. These two units made a new plot in the southwest part of the cemetery, in which Commonwealth soldiers were buried. This plot was enlarged after the Armistice when graves were brought in from the German plots, the German extension and LA MADELEINE CEMETERY.

LA FERT-SOUS-JOUARRE MEMORIAL

La Ferte-sous-Jouarre is a small town 66 kms to the east of Paris, located on the main road (N3). The LA FERTÉ-SOUS-JOUARRE MEMORIAL commemorates 3,740 officers and men of the British Expeditionary Force who fell at the battles of Mons, Le Cateau, the Marne, and the Aisne between the end of August and early October 1914 and have no known graves.

LA TARGETTE BRITISH CEMETERY, NEUVILLE-ST. VAAST

Neuville-St. Vaast is a village 6.5 kms north of Arras.

LA TARGETTE BRITISH CEMETERY, formerly known as Aux-Rietz Military Cemetery, was begun at the end of April 1917 and used by field ambulances and fighting units until September 1918. Nearly a third of the graves have an artillery connection. Sixteen graves were brought into the cemetery from the immediate neighbourhood after the Armistice.

LAPUGNOY MILITARY CEMETERY

Lapugnoy is a village 6 kms west of Bethune.

The first burials were made in September 1915, but it was most heavily used during the Battle of Arras, which began in April 1917. The dead were brought to the cemetery from casualty clearing stations, chiefly at Lapugnoy and Lozinghem, but between May and August 1918, the cemetery was used by fighting units.

LARCH WOOD (RAILWAY CUTTING) CEMETERY

Larch Wood Cemetery is located 4 kms south-east of Ieper town centre, on the Komenseweg.

The cemetery was begun in April 1915 at the north end of a small plantation of larches. It was used by troops holding this sector until April 1918. It was enlarged after the Armistice when graves were brought in from the battlefields of Ypres and from other smaller cemeteries.

LE TOUQET RAILWAY CROSSING CEMETERY

Le Touquet Railway Crossing Cemetery is located 15 km south of Ieper town centre, on a road leading from the Rijselseweg N365.

The cemetery was used from October 1914 to June 1918, and contains the graves of 28 men of the 1st Rifle Brigade killed in October and November 1914 during fierce German attacks on the 11th Infantry Brigade.

LE TOURET MEMORIAL AND LE TOURET MILITARY CEMETERY

LE TOURET MEMORIAL is located at the east end of LE TOURET MILITARY CEMETERY, on the south side of the Bethune-Armentieres main road. It commemorates over 13,400 British soldiers who were killed in this sector of the Western Front from the beginning of October 1914, to the eve of the Battle of Loos in late September 1915, and who have no known grave. Almost all of the men commemorated on the Memorial served with regular or territorial regiments from across the United Kingdom, and were killed in actions that took place along a section of the front line that stretched from Estaires in the north to Grenay in the south. This part of the Western Front was the scene of some of the heaviest fighting of the first year of the war. Soldiers serving with Indian and Canadian units who were killed in this sector in 1914 and 1915, whose remains were never identified, are commemorated on the NEUVE CHAPELLE and VIMY MEMORIALS, while those who fell during the northern pincer attack at the Battle of Aubers Ridge, are commemorated on the PLOEGSTEERT MEMORIAL.

The Cemetery was begun by the Indian Corps in November 1914, and it was used continuously by Field Ambulances and fighting units until March 1918. It passed into German hands in April 1918, and after its recapture, a few further burials were made in September and October.

LE TREPORT MILITARY CEMETERY

Le Treport is a coastal town approximately 30 kms northeast of Dieppe. During the First World War, it was an important hospital centre. In 1917, a divisional rest camp and a tank training depot were also established in the neighbourhood. The hospitals had been closed by March 1919.

LE VERTANNOY BRITISH CEMETERY, HINGES

Le Vertannoy is a hamlet nearly 1 km west of the village of Hinges, which is a small village 2 kms northwest of the town of Bethune in the Department of the Pas-de-Calais.

The cemetery was begun in April 1918, during the Battles of the Lys, and was used by field ambulances, burial officers and fighting units until the following September.

LEBUCQUIERE COMMUNAL CEMETERY EXTENSION

Lebucquiere is a village 8 kms east of Bapaume.

Lebucquiere village was occupied by Commonwealth forces on 19th March 1917, following the German withdrawal to the Hindenburg Line. It was recaptured by the Germans on 23rd March 1918, and finally reoccupied on 3rd September 1918.

The communal cemetery extension was begun on 24th March 1917 and was used by the 1st Australian Division and other units for almost a year. After the reoccupation of the village in September 1918, it was used again for a fortnight. At the Armistice, the cemetery contained 150 burials, but it was then greatly enlarged when graves were brought in from the surrounding battlefields.

LEEDS (LAWNS WOOD CEMETERY)

During the First World War, the major hospitals in Leeds were the 2nd Northern General with 1,800 beds, and the East Leeds War Hospital with 1,900. The cemetery is located in Otley Road, Leeds.

LEEDS (LAWNS WOOD) CEMETERY contains 138 burial of the First World War, 88 of them forming a war graves plot in Section W. As these graves could not be marked individually, the names of the dead are recorded on a screen wall. The rest of the First World War burials scattered throughout the cemetery. A further screen wall bears the names of 105 casualties of both wars buried in LEEDS GENERAL CEMETERY, where their graves could no longer be maintained.

LIEVIN COMMUNAL CEMETERY EXTENSION

Lievin is a small town in the Department of the Pas-de-Calais, 3.5 kms west of Lens. It was captured by the Canadian Corps on 14th April 1917, and remained in British hands until the end of the War. The Extension was made after the Armistice by the concentration of graves from the battlefields north and south of Lens and from other smaller cemeteries.

LIGNY-ST. FLOCHEL BRITISH CEMETERY, AVERDOINGT

Ligny-St.Flochel is a village about 6.5 kms east of St.Pol. The cemetery was started at the beginning of April 1918 when the 7th Casualty Clearing Station came back from Tincques ahead of the German advance. Two more Casualty Clearing Stations followed in the next four months, but all three had left by November 1918.

LIJSSENTHOEK MILITARY CEMETERY

LIJSSENTHOEK MILITARY CEMETERY is located 12 kms west of Ieper town centre.

During the First World War, the village of Lijssenthoek was situated on the main communication line between the Allied military bases in the rear and the Ypres battlefields. Close to the Front, but out of the extreme range of most German field artillery, it became a natural place to establish casualty clearing stations. The cemetery was first used by the French, and in June 1915, it began to be used by casualty clearing stations of the Commonwealth forces.

From April to August 1918, the casualty clearing stations fell back before the German advance and field ambulances (including a French ambulance) took their places.

LILLERS COMMUNAL CEMETERY AND LILLERS COMMUNAL CEMETERY EXTENSION

Lillers is a small town about 15 kms west-north-west of Bethune.

It was used for billets and headquarter offices from the autumn of 1914 to April 1918. At that time, it was a hospital centre with six Casualty Clearing Stations in the town at one time or another. These units buried their dead on the right of the central path of the communal cemetery. In April 1918, the Germans advanced as far as Robecq; Lillers came under shell-fire, and the units holding this front continued to bury beyond the cemetery boundary, in the extension.

LONDON CEMETERY AND EXTENSION, LONGUEVAL

Longueval is a village 40 kms northeast of Amiens and 12 kms east-north-east of Albert.

High Wood was fiercely fought over during the Battle of the Somme until cleared on 15th September 1916. It was lost during the German advance of April 1918, but retaken the following August. The original LONDON CEMETERY at High Wood was begun when 47 men of the 47th Division were buried in a large shell hole on 18th and 21st September 1916. Other burials were added later, mainly of officers and men of the 47th Division who died on 15th September 1916, and at the Armistice the cemetery contained just over a hundred graves. The cemetery was then greatly enlarged when remains were brought in from the surrounding battlefields, but the original battlefield cemetery is preserved intact within the larger cemetery, now known as the LONDON CEMETERY AND EXTENSION.

LONDON CEMETERY, NEUVILLE-VITASSE

Neuville-Vitasse is a village in the department of the Pas-de-Calais, 5 kms southeast of Arras.

Neuville-Vitasse was captured by the same Division on 9th April, almost entirely lost at the end of March 1918, but regained at the end of the following August. It was later "adopted" by the Metropolitan Borough of Paddington. THE LONDON CEMETERY was made in April 1917, and greatly extended after the Armistice when graves were brought in from other burial grounds and from the battlefields between Arras, Vis-en-Artois and Croisilles.

LONE PINE CEMETERY, ANZAC

LONE PINE CEMETERY, ANZAC is signposted from the road between Eceabat and Bigali in Turkey.

The eight month campaign in Gallipoli was fought by Commonwealth and French forces in an attempt to force Turkey out of the war, to relieve the deadlock of the Western Front in France and Belgium, and to open a supply route to Russia through the Dardanelles and the Black Sea. Lone Pine was a strategically important plateau in the southern part of Anzac which was briefly in the hands of Australian forces, retaken by the Turks and became a strong point, before the Australians recaptured it. The original battle cemetery of around fifty graves was enlarged after the Armistice when scattered graves were brought in from the neighbourhood, and nearby cemeteries.

LONGUEAU BRITISH CEMETERY

The town of Longueau is situated on the southeastern outskirts of Amiens.

LONGUEAU BRITISH CEMETERY was begun in April 1918, when the Allied line was re-established before Amiens; it was used by fighting units and field ambulances until the following August. After the Armistice graves were also brought in from the surrounding battlefields and smaller cemeteries

LONGUENESSE (ST. OMER) SOUVENIR CEMETERY

St. Omer is a large town 45 kms southeast of Calais. Longuenesse is a commune on the southern outskirts of St. Omer.

St. Omer was the General Headquarters of the British Expeditionary Force from October 1914 to March 1916. St. Omer suffered air raids in November 1917 and May 1918, with serious loss of life. The cemetery takes its names from the triangular cemetery of the St. Omer garrison, properly called the Souvenir Cemetery (Cimetiere du Souvenir Francais) which is located next to the War Cemetery.

LOOS BRITISH CEMETERY

Loos (Loos-en-Gohelle) is a village to the north of the road from Lens to Bethune.

The cemetery was begun by the Canadian Corps in July 1917. Further burials were performed after the Armistice by the concentration of graves from the battlefields and smaller cemeteries over a wide area north and east of the village.

LOOS MEMORIAL

The LOOS MEMORIAL forms the sides and back of DUD CORNER CEMETERY. Loos-en-Gohelle is a village 5 kms northwest of Lens, and DUD CORNER CEMETERY is located about 1 kilometre west of the village. It stands almost on the site of a German strong point, the Lens Road Redoubt, captured by the 15th (Scottish) Division on the first day of the battle. The name "Dud Corner" is believed to be due to the large number of unexploded enemy shells found in the neighbourhood after the Armistice. The LOOS MEMORIAL commemorates over 20,000 officers and men who have no known grave, who fell in the area from the River Lys to the old southern boundary of the First Army, east and west of Grenay.

LUTTERWORTH (ST MARY) CHURCHYARD

The market town of Lutterworth is located in Leicestershire, just to the west of the M1, about ten miles south of Leicester.

MADRAS 1914-1918 WAR MEMORIAL, CHENNAI

MADRAS WAR CEMETERY is about 5 kms from the airport and 14 kms from the central railway station. The MADRAS 1914-1918 MEMORIAL is situated at the rear of the cemetery. It bears the names of more than 1,000 servicemen who died during the First World War, who lie in many civil and cantonment cemeteries in various parts of India where it is not possible to maintain their graves in perpetuity.

MARFAUX BRITISH CEMETERY

Marfaux is a commune 18.5 kms from Reims and 16 kms from Epernay.

It was captured by the Germans in May 1918, and retaken, after severe fighting, on 23rd July, by the 51st (Highland) and 62nd (West Riding) Divisions, and the New Zealand Cyclist Battalion.

The cemetery was begun after the Armistice by the concentration of graves from the battlefields and from other Military Cemeteries in the Marne.

MAROEUIL BRITISH CEMETERY

Maroeuil is a village in the Department of the Pas-de-Calais, 6 kms northwest of Arras.

The cemetery was begun by the 51st (Highland) Division when Commonwealth forces took over the Arras front in March 1916, and it retained its association with that division until the summer of 1918. Almost half of the graves are those of Highland territorials, and many of those remaining are of London territorials who were at Maroeuil from July to December 1916. The cemetery also contains the graves of 25 officers and men of tunnelling companies of the Royal Engineers who died in mine explosions. The cemetery was protected from observation by the crest of the hill behind it and whenever possible, bodies were brought back to it from the front line by tramway.

MAROILLES COMMUNAL CEMETERY

Maroilles is a village in the Department of the Nord, some 30 kms southeast of Valenciennes,

Maroilles was the scene of fighting on 25th August 1914, but then remained in German hands until it was captured on 5th November 1918. The cemetery contains just twenty War Graves.

MARTEVILLE COMMUNAL CEMETERY, ATTILLY

Marteville is situated 8 kms west of St Quentin; the British Plot is on the northern side of the Communal Cemetery. The village of Attilly was occupied in April 1917, and British burials were made in the Communal Cemetery by fighting units in April and May 1917, and January, March, September and October 1918, and by the enemy in March 1918.

MEAULTE MILITARY CEMETERY

Meaulte is a village in the Department of the Somme, immediately south of Albert.

It was held by Commonwealth forces (and inhabited by three-quarters of its civilian population) from 1915 to 26th March 1918, when it was evacuated after a rearguard fight by the 9th (Scottish) Division. It was recaptured on 22nd August 1918.

The military cemetery was begun in December 1915, and used until February 1917. A few further burials were made after the recapture of the village and after the Armistice, graves (mainly of 1918) being brought in from the neighbouring battlefields and other burial grounds.

MENIN ROAD NORTH MILITARY CEMETERY AND MENIN ROAD SOUTH MILITARY CEMETERY

Menin Road South Military Cemetery is located 2 kms east of Ieper town centre.

The Menin Road ran east and a little south from Ypres (now Ieper) to a front line which varied only a few kilometres during the greater part of the war. The position of this cemetery was always within the Allied lines. It was first used in January 1916, and continued to be used by units and Field Ambulances until the summer of 1918. The cemetery was increased after the Armistice when graves were brought in from isolated positions on the battlefields to the east and other cemeteries.

MENIN ROAD NORTH MILITARY CEMETERY was on the north side of the road at almost the same point. It was used by the units and Field Ambulances of another Corps from May 1915, until August 1916, and again to a small extent in 1917 and 1918.

MERVILLE COMMUNAL CEMETERY

Merville is a town 15 kms north of Bethune and about 20 kms southwest of Armentieres.

Merville was the scene of fighting between the Germans and French and British cavalry early in October 1914, but from the 9th of that month until 11th April 1918, it remained in Allied hands. In October 1914, and in the autumn of 1915, the town was the headquarters of the Indian Corps. It was a railhead until May 1915, and a billeting and hospital centre from 1915-1918; several Casualty Clearing Stations also were there.

On the evening of 11th April 1918, in the Battles of the Lys, the Germans forced their way into Merville, and the town was not retaken until 19th August. The cemeteries were not used again until the concentration of battlefield burials into the Extension began, after the Armistice.

MERVILLE COMMUNAL CEMETERY was used by French troops (chiefly cavalry) in October 1914, and for Commonwealth burials from that date until August 1916 (in the case of officers, to March 1918).

MERVILLE COMMUNAL CEMETERY EXTENSION was opened in August 1916, and used by Commonwealth and Portuguese hospitals until April 1918. It was enlarged after the Armistice when graves were brought in from the battlefields immediately north and east of Merville.

METZ-EN-COUTURE COMMUNAL CEMETERY BRITISH EXTENSION

Metz-en-Couture is a village situated in the extreme southeastern corner of the Department of the Pas-de-Calais.

The village was captured on the 4th and 5th April 1917, evacuated on 23rd March 1918, and retaken the following 6th September. It was noted for its extensive system of underground cellars. It was later "adopted" by the County Borough of Halifax.

The Communal Cemetery was used by the enemy for the burial of German soldiers and also of three R.F.C. Officers, whose graves have now been removed to the British Extension. On the east side of it, a German Extension was made containing the graves of 252 German soldiers, and one man of the Chinese Labour Corps; the German graves have now been removed to other cemeteries and the Chinese grave to the British Extension.

The British Extension was begun in April 1917, and used until March 1918, and two graves were added in the following September. Further burials from METZ-EN-COUTURE BRITISH CEMETERY No. 2, were moved after the Armistice.

MIKRA BRITISH CEMETERY, KALAMARIA

Mikra British Cemetery is situated approximately 8 kms south of Thessaloniki, in the municipality of Kalamaria (behind the army camp of Ntalipi).

At the invitation of the Greek Prime Minister, M. Venizelos, Salonika (now Thessalonika) was occupied by three French Divisions and the 10th (Irish) Division from Gallipoli in October 1915. Other French and Commonwealth forces landed during the year, and in the summer of 1916, they were joined by Russian and Italian troops. In August 1916, a Greek revolution broke out at Salonika, with the result that the Greek national army came into the war on the Allied side. The town was the base of the British Salonika Force and it contained, from time to time, eighteen general and stationary hospitals. Three of these hospitals were Canadian, although there were no other Canadian units in the force. The earliest Commonwealth burials took place in the local Protestant and Roman Catholic cemeteries, and the Anglo-French (now Lembet Road) Military Cemetery was used from November 1915 to October 1918. The British cemetery at Mikra was opened in April 1917, remaining in use until 1920. The cemetery was greatly enlarged after the Armistice when graves were brought in from a number of burial grounds in the area.

MOEUVRES COMMUNAL CEMETERY EXTENSION

Moeuvres is a village 10 kms west of Cambrai. It remained in German hands during the Battle of Cambrai, 1917, in spite of three days of desperate attack. It was partly taken by on 11th September 1918, and cleared on the 19th. The communal cemetery was extended to the west by the Germans between November 1917 and March 1918. The British Extension was made between September and October 1918, and was enlarged after the Armistice when graves were brought in from the battlefields on the Cambrai-Bapaume road.

MONT HUON MILITARY CEMETERY, LE TREPORT

Le Treport is a small seaport 25 kms northeast of Dieppe.

During the war, Le Treport was an important hospital centre and by July 1916, the town contained three general hospitals, a Convalescent Depot and Lady Murray's British Red Cross

Society Hospital. Canadian and USA General Hospitals arrived later, but all of the hospitals had closed by March 1919.

MONTECCHIO PRECALCINO COMMUNAL CEMETERY EXTENSION

Montecchio Precalcino is a town in the Province of Vicenza, 4 kms north of Dueville and 17 kms north of the town of Vicenza.

The Italians entered the war on the Allied side, declaring war on Austria in May 1915. Commonwealth forces were at the Italian front between November 1917 and November 1918, and rest camps and medical units were established at various locations in northern Italy behind the front, some of them remaining until 1919.

Between April 1918 and February 1919, those who died from wounds or disease in three Clearing Stations were buried either here or at Dueville. Certain graves were brought in after the Armistice from other burial grounds in the area.

MOREUIL COMMUNAL CEMETERY ALLIED EXTENSION

Moreuil is a village in the Department of the Somme, 18 kms southeast of Amiens.

The village and Moreuil Wood were the scene of desperate fighting in March and April 1918, in which Commonwealth and French infantry, and the Canadian Cavalry Brigade, took part. The village was lost to the Germans, but was retaken on 8th August. The extension was made after the Armistice when graves were brought in from the neighbouring battlefields

NETLEY MILITARY CEMETERY

The cemetery lies within a park maintained by Hampshire County Council on the site of the former hospital.

NETLEY MILITARY CEMETERY is a permanent military cemetery, the property of the Ministry of Defence. The cemetery was at the back of the Royal Victoria Military Hospital and was used during both wars for burials from the hospital.

NETTLETON (ST MARY) CHURCHYARD

The village of Nettleton is in Wiltshire. The graveyard contains just one War Grave.

NEUVE-CHAPELLE BRITISH CEMETERY AND NEUVE-CHAPELLE MEMORIAL

The village of Neuve Chapelle is some 5 kms north of La Bassee and 20 kms west-south-west of Lille.

NEUVE-CHAPELLE BRITISH CEMETERY was begun during the Battle of Neuve-Chapelle, which began on 10th March, 1915, and used until the following November. The Cemetery was known at one time as Moggs Hole Cemetery.

The Indian Memorial at Neuve Chapelle commemorates over 4,700 Indian soldiers and labourers who lost their lives on the Western Front during the First World War and have no known graves. The location of the memorial was specially chosen as it was at Neuve Chapelle in March 1915 that the Indian Corps fought its first major action as a single unit.

NEW MUNICH TRENCH BRITISH CEMETERY, BEAUMONT-HAMEL

Beaumont-Hamel is a village about 24 kms southwest of Arras.

It was attacked and taken on the 13th November 1916. Munich Trench was occupied by the 51st (Highland) Division on the 15th November 1916; New Munich Trench being dug on the previous night by the 2/2nd Highland Field Company and a company of the 8th Royal Scots, and lengthened by the 8th Devons in December.

The cemetery was made in the spring of 1917, when units cleared the battlefield.

NIEDERZWEHREN CEMETERY

The city of Kassel lies in the centre of Germany, approx 165 kms south of Hannover.

The cemetery was begun by the Germans in 1915 for the burial of prisoners of war who died at the local camp. During the war, almost 3,000 Allied soldiers and civilians, including French, Russian and Commonwealth, were buried there. In 1922-23, it was decided that the graves of Commonwealth servicemen who had died all over Germany should be brought together into four permanent cemeteries. Niederzwehren was one of those chosen and in the following four years, more than 1,500 graves were brought into the cemetery from 190 burial grounds in Baden, Bavaria, Hanover, Hesse and Saxony.

NORFOLK CEMETERY, BECORDEL-BECOURT

Becordel-Becourt is a village just east of Albert. The cemetery was begun in August 1915 and used until August 1916. After the Armistice it was nearly doubled in size when graves were brought in from the battlefields nearby.

NOYON NEW BRITISH CEMETERY AND NOYON OLD BRITISH CEMETERY

Noyon is a town 32 kms northwest of Soissons, on the road to Roye (D6/D934)

Noyon was the British G.H.Q. on 26th to 28th August 1914. It was entered by the Germans on 1st September 1914, by the French on 18th March 1917, and by the Germans again in March 1918. The French finally retook it on 29th and 30th August 1918. It was twice bombarded by the enemy, and in 1918 practically destroyed.

NOYON OLD BRITISH CEMETERY was made by the 46th Casualty Clearing Station and the 44th Field Ambulance in March 1918, in a woodyard near the railway station. It contained the graves of 144 soldiers from the United Kingdom, one American medical officer, two Italian and three French soldiers. All these graves except the French were removed after the Armistice, to the New British Cemetery.

Noyon French National and New British Cemeteries are side by side, on the hill north of the town. The former was made in 1919, and contains the graves of 1,721 French soldiers, of whom 693 are unidentified.

NOYON NEW BRITISH CEMETERY was made after the Armistice by the concentration of graves from other burial grounds and from the battlefields.

OOSTTAVERNE WOOD CEMETERY

Oosttaverne Wood Cemetery is located 6 kms south of Ieper town centre on the Rijselseweg N336.

The "Oosttaverne Line" was a German work running northward from the river Lys to the Comines Canal, passing just east of Oosttaverne. It was captured on 7th June 1917, the first day of the Battle of Messines. There were two cemeteries, No. 1 and No. 2, used until September 1917. The present cemetery was completed after the Armistice when graves were brought in from the surrounding battlefields (including many from Hill 60) and from smaller cemeteries.

OVILLERS MILITARY CEMETERY

Ovillers is a village about 5 kms northeast of the town of Albert.

On 1st July 1916, the first day of the Battle of the Somme, the two villages of Ovillers and La Boisselle were attacked, but not captured until 17th July. They were lost during the German advance in March 1918, but they were retaken on the following 24th August.

OVILLERS MILITARY CEMETERY was begun before the capture of Ovillers, as a battle cemetery behind a dressing station. It was used until March 1917, by which time it contained 143 graves. The cemetery was increased after the Armistice when Commonwealth and French graves where brought in, mainly from the battlefields of Pozieres, Ovillers, La Boisselle and Contalmaison.

OXFORD ROAD CEMETERY

The cemetery is located to the northeast of the town of Ieper. Oxford Road was the name given to a road running behind the support trenches, from a point west of the village of Wieltje, southeastwards to the Potijze-Zonnebeke road. The original OXFORD ROAD CEMETERY was used by the units fighting on this front from August 1917 to April 1918. In October 1917, another cemetery, known as OXFORD ROAD CEMETERY NO. 2, was started close by, and now forms part of the cemetery as it appears today. After the Armistice, scattered graves from the battlefields east and southeast of Ypres (now Ieper) were brought into the cemetery.

PEAKE WOOD CEMETERY, FRICOURT

Fricourt is a village about 5 kms east of Albert.

Peake Wood was the name given by the army to a copse on the southeast side of the road to Contalmaison. The wood fell into Allied hands on 5th July 1916, but the cemetery was not begun until later in the month. It was used as a front line cemetery until February 1917, but was in German hands from the end of March 1918, until nearly the end of the following August.

PERNES BRITISH CEMETERY

Pernes-en-Artois is a small town on the main road from Lillers to St. Pol.

The cemetery was not begun until April 1918, when the 1st and 4th Canadian Casualty Clearing Stations came to Pernes, driven back by the German advance. In May, two further Clearing Stations arrived, and in August, they were joined by another. Almost all the burials were made by these units, but a few of the graves were brought into the cemetery after the Armistice.

PICQUIGNY BRITISH CEMETERY

Picquigny is a small town in the Department of the Somme, about 13 kms northwest of Amiens.

During the first four years of the First World War, Picquigny was on the lines of communication for French and Commonwealth forces, and there are ten burials from these years in the communal cemetery, opposite the church.

At the end of March 1918, two Clearing Stations were brought to Picquigny to deal with casualties of the German advance on Amiens, and the British Cemetery was opened a little west of the town.

PIETA MILITARY CEMETERY

The Cemetery is located in Triq id-Duluri (Our Lady of Sorrows Street), 2 kms southwest of Valletta on the road to Sliema.

From the spring of 1915, the hospitals and convalescent depots established on the islands of Malta and Gozo dealt with over 135,000 sick and wounded, chiefly from the campaigns in Gallipoli and Salonika, although increased submarine activity in the Mediterranean meant that fewer hospital ships were sent to the island from May 1917.

PLOEGSTEERT MEMORIAL

The PLOEGSTEERT MEMORIAL stands in BERKS CEMETERY EXTENSION, which is located 12.5 kms south of Ieper town centre. It commemorates more than 11,000 servicemen of the United Kingdom and South African forces who died in this sector during the First World War and have no known grave. The memorial serves the area from the line Caestre-Dranoutre-Warneton to the north, to Haverskerque-Estaires-Fournes to the south, including the towns of Hazebrouck, Merville, Bailleul and Armentieres, the Forest of Nieppe, and Ploegsteert Wood. The original intention had been to erect the memorial in Lille. Most of those commemorated by the memorial did not die in major offensives, but were killed in the course of the day-to-day trench warfare which characterised this part of the line, or in small scale set engagements, usually carried out in support of the major attacks taking place elsewhere. It does not include the names of officers and men of Canadian or Indian regiments (they are found on the Memorials at VIMY and NEUVE-CHAPELLE), nor those lost at the Battle of Aubers Ridge on 9th May 1915, who are commemorated on the LE TOURET MEMORIAL.

BERKS CEMETERY EXTENSION, in which the memorial stands, was begun in June 1916, and used continuously until September 1917. In 1930, graves were brought in from ROSENBERG CHATEAU MILITARY CEMETERY AND EXTENSION, about 1 km to the northwest, when it was established that these sites could not be acquired in perpetuity. This had been used by fighting units from November 1914 to August 1916. The extension was begun in May 1916 and used until March 1918. Together, the ROSENBERG CHATEAU CEMETERY AND EXTENSION were sometimes referred to as 'Red Lodge'.

HYDE PARK CORNER (ROYAL BERKS) CEMETERY is separated from BERKS CEMETERY EXTENSION by a road. It was begun in April 1915, and used at intervals until November 1917. Hyde Park Corner was a road junction to the north of Ploegsteert Wood. Hill 63 was to the northwest, and nearby were the 'Catacombs', deep shelters capable of holding two battalions, which were used from November 1916 onwards.

POELCAPELLE BRITISH CEMETERY

POELCAPELLE BRITISH CEMETERY is located 10 kms north-east of Ieper town centre on the Brugseweg (N313).

Poelcapelle (now Poelkapelle) was taken by the Germans from the French on 20th October 1914, entered by the 11th Division on 4th October 1917, evacuated by Commonwealth forces in April 1918, and retaken by the Belgians on 28th September 1918. POELCAPELLE BRITISH CEMETERY was made after the Armistice when graves were brought in from the surrounding battlefields and smaller cemeteries.

POPERINGHE OLD MILITARY CEMETERY AND POPERINGHE NEW MILITARY CEMETERY

POPERINGHE OLD MILITARY CEMETERY is located some 10 kms west of Ieper town centre, in the town of Poperinge itself. The town of Poperinghe (now Poperinge) was of great importance during the First World War because, although occasionally bombed or bombarded at long range, it was the nearest place to Ypres which was both considerable in size and reasonably safe. It was at first a centre for Casualty Clearing Stations, but by 1916 it became necessary to move these units further back, and field ambulances took their places. The earliest Commonwealth graves in the town are in the communal cemetery, which was used from October 1914 to March 1915. The Old Military Cemetery was made in the course of the First Battle of Ypres and was closed, so far as Commonwealth burials are concerned, at the beginning of May 1915. The New Military Cemetery was established in June 1915.

PORTSDOWN (CHRIST CHURCH) MILITARY CEMETERY

The cemetery is to the rear of the church in Portsdown, Hampshire

PORTSMOUTH NAVAL MEMORIAL

The Memorial is situated on Southsea Common overlooking the promenade.

After the First World War, an appropriate way had to be found of commemorating those members of the Royal Navy who had no known grave, the majority of deaths having occurred at sea where no permanent memorial could be provided.

An Admiralty committee recommended that the three manning ports in Great Britain - Chatham, Plymouth and Portsmouth - should each have an identical memorial of unmistakable naval form, an obelisk, which would serve as a leading mark for shipping. The Portsmouth Naval Memorial was unveiled by the Duke of York (the future George VI) on 15th October 1924.

POTIJZE CHATEAU WOOD CEMETERY

The cemetery is located to the northeast of Ypres.

The old chateau grounds contain three Commonwealth War Graves Commission cemeteries, all formed in the spring of 1915, and used for the burial of Commonwealth soldiers until 1918.

POZIERES BRITISH CEMETERY, OVILLERS-LA-BOISSELLE AND POZIERES MEMORIAL

Pozieres is a village 6 kms northeast of the town of Albert.

The POZIERES MEMORIAL relates to the period of crisis in March and April 1918, when the Allied Fifth Army was driven back by overwhelming numbers across the former Somme battlefields, and the months that followed before the Advance to Victory, which began on 8th August 1918.

The Memorial commemorates over 14,000 casualties of the United Kingdom, and 300 of the South African Forces, who have no known grave, and who died on the Somme from 21st March to 7th August 1918. The memorial encloses POZIERES BRITISH CEMETERY, the original burials of 1916, 1917 and 1918, carried out by fighting units and field ambulances. The remaining plots were made after the Armistice, when graves were brought in from the battlefields immediately surrounding the cemetery, the majority of them of soldiers who died in the autumn of 1916 during the latter stages of the Battle of the Somme, but a few represent the fighting in August 1918.

PROSPECT HILL CEMETERY, GOUY

Gouy is a village to the east of the road between Cambrai and St. Quentin.

On 3rd October 1918, the 1st King's Own Yorkshire Light Infantry captured Prospect Hill. The cemetery was made by the 50th Division and the 18th Field Ambulance immediately after. After the Armistice graves were brought in, mainly from the battlefields north of Gouy, and almost exclusively of men who died in October 1918.

PROWSE POINT MILITARY CEMETERY

Prowse Point Military Cemetery is located 11.5 kms south of Ieper town centre.

This cemetery is unique on the Salient for being named after an individual. It is the site of a stand which featured the heroism of a Major Charles Prowse - later as Brigadier-General C.B. Prowse, D.S.O. (Somerset Light Infantry); he would be killed on the first day of the Battle of the Somme, and is buried in Louvencourt Military Cemetery. The cemetery was used from November 1914 to April 1918.

PUCHEVILLERS BRITISH CEMETERY

Puchevillers is a village on the D11 about 19 kms northeast of Amiens.

In June 1916, just before the opening of the Battles of the Somme, the 3rd and 44th Casualty Clearing Stations came to Puchevillers; later, the South Midland Casualty Clearing Station also used the cemetery. There are also graves of men who died in the German advance in 1918, many of whom were buried by the 49th Clearing Station in March 1918, or by the 48th Labour Group in August.

QUEANT ROAD CEMETERY, BUISSY

Buissy is a village about 2 kms south of the main Arras to Cambrai road (D939) and about 25 kms from Arras.

The village was reached by the Third Army on 2nd September 1918, after the storming of the Drocourt-Queant line, and it was evacuated by the Germans on the following day. Queant Cemetery was made by the 2nd and 57th Casualty Clearing Stations in October and November 1918. It then consisted of 71 graves, but was greatly enlarged after the Armistice when 2,200 graves were brought in from the battlefields of 1917-1918 between Arras and Bapaume, and from other smaller burial grounds in the area

RAILLENCOURT COMMUNAL CEMETERY EXTENSION

Raillencourt is a village in the Department of the Nord, about 5 kms west of Cambrai on the main road to Arras.

The village was captured by the Canadian Corps on 28th September 1918, in the Battle of the Canal du Nord. The extension to the communal cemetery was made by the Canadian Corps after the capture of the village. It was enlarged in 1923 when graves were brought in from NORTH CEMETERY, RAILLENCOURT.

REDOUBT CEMETERY, HELLES

From Helles, continue on the road to Alciptepe, and the cemetery will be found on your left.

The eight month campaign in Gallipoli was fought by Commonwealth and French forces in an attempt to force Turkey out of the war, to relieve the deadlock of the Western Front in France and Belgium, and to open a supply route to Russia through the Dardanelles and the Black Sea.

The Allies landed on the peninsula on 25-26th April 1915; the 29th Division at Cape Helles in the south, and the Australian and New Zealand Corps north of Gaba Tepe on the west coast, an area soon known as Anzac. REDOUBT CEMETERY takes its name from the chain of forts made by the Turks across the southern end of the peninsula in the fighting for Krithia and the Redoubt Line on which the advance halted in May.

The cemetery was begun by the 2nd Australian Infantry Brigade in May 1915, and continued in use until the evacuation. It was greatly increased after the Armistice when the battlefields were cleared and graves were brought in from other smaller cemeteries.

RED CROSS CORNER CEMETERY, BEUGNY

Beugny is a village 5 kms northeast of Bapaume.

The cemetery was started between April 1917 and March 1918 by field ambulances and fighting units. When the cemetery fell into German hands in March 1918, they added the 25 Commonwealth burials (all from 21st March 1918), and began another cemetery alongside (BEUGNY MILITARY CEMETERY NO. 3). Commonwealth forces retook the cemetery in September 1918. The German graves were removed after the Armistice, and the Commonwealth burials among them were transferred, partly to DELSAUX FARM CEMETERY, and partly to FAVREUIL BRITISH CEMETERY.

ROCLINCOURT MILITARY CEMETERY

Roclincourt is a village a little to the east of the road from Arras to Lens.

The French troops, who held this front before March 1916, made a military cemetery (now removed), on the southwest side of which the present Commonwealth cemetery was made. It was begun in April 1917, and contains many graves of 9th April, the first day of the Battles of Arras. It continued in use, as a front-line cemetery, until October 1918, and after the Armistice graves, mostly from the battlefield north of Roclincourt, were brought in.

ROCQUIGNY-EQUANCOURT ROAD BRITISH CEMETERY, MANANCOURT

Rocquigny and Equancourt are two villages in the Department of the Somme, some 13 kms north of Peronne and 12 kms southeast of Bapaume.

Etricourt was occupied by Commonwealth troops at the beginning of April 1917 during the German withdrawal to the Hindenburg Line. It was lost on the 23rd March 1918 when the Germans advanced, but regained at the beginning of September.

The cemetery was begun in 1917 and used until March 1918, mainly by the 21st and 48th Casualty Clearing Stations posted at Ytres, and to a small extent by the Germans, who knew it as "Etricourt Old English Cemetery". Burials were resumed by Commonwealth troops in September 1918, and the 3rd Canadian and 18th Casualty Clearing Stations buried in it in October and November 1918.

ROISEL COMMUNAL CEMETERY EXTENSION

Roisel is a small town 11 kms east of Peronne.

The town was occupied by British troops in April 1917, and evacuated after a strong defence by the 66th (East Lancashire) Division in the evening of 22nd March 1918. It was retaken in the following September.

ROISEL COMMUNAL CEMETERY EXTENSION was begun by German troops, who buried immediately to the north of the Communal Cemetery. It was developed in October and November 1918, by four Casualty Clearing Stations, and it was completed after the Armistice by the concentration of British and German graves from the country north, east and south of Roisel.

ROMERIES COMMUNAL CEMETERY EXTENSION

Romeries is a village approximately 16 kms south of Valenciennes and 4 kms northeast of Solemes.

Part of the II Corps retired through this area during the Retreat from Mons in August 1914, and in October 1918, Commonwealth forces returned during the Advance to Victory. Briastre was captured on 10th October 1918, Belle Vue Farm on 20th October, Romeries itself and Beaudignies on 23rd October, and Englefontaine on 26th October. The Battle of the Sambre, the last great action of the war, carried the front forward into Belgium and ended with the Armistice. ROMERIES COMMUNAL CEMETERY EXTENSION is one of the burial grounds of those who died between these dates. After the Armistice, graves were brought in from isolated positions on the battlefield and other small cemeteries.

ROYAL IRISH RIFLES GRAVEYARD, LAVENTIE

Laventie is a village and commune, in the Department of the Pas-de-Calais, about 11 kms southwest of Armentieres.

The Rue-du-Bacquerot runs southeast of Laventie, towards Fleurbaix; and the position of the road behind the British front line, during the greater part of the war, made it the natural line of a number of small British cemeteries. One of these was begun in November 1914, and used, at first, particularly by the 1st Royal Irish Rifles.

The ROYAL IRISH RIFLES GRAVEYARD was carried on by fighting units until July 1916. It was increased after the Armistice by the concentration of graves (chiefly of 1914-15 and 1918), from the battlefields east of Estaires and Bethune, and from other smaller cemeteries.

RUE-PETILLON MILITARY CEMETERY, FLEURBAIX

Fleurbaix is a village 5 kms southwest of Armentieres on the D22.

British soldiers began burying their fallen comrades at Rue Pétillon in December 1914, and the cemetery was used by fighting units until it fell into German hands during the Spring

Offensive of 1918. The Allies recaptured this sector of the front in September 1918, and when the war ended in November, the cemetery was the site of twelve Battalion burial grounds. Many of those laid to rest here had died of wounds in a dressing station that was located in the buildings adjoining the cemetery, which were known as 'Eaton Hall' during the war. The cemetery was enlarged in the years after the Armistice when graves were concentrated here from the battlefields around Fleurbaix and a number of smaller burial grounds.

STE. MARIE CEMETERY, LE HAVRE

STE. MARIE CEMETERY is one of the town cemeteries, but it is actually situated in the commune of Graville-St. Honorine, overlooking Le Havre from the north. During the First World War, Le Havre was one of the ports at which the British Expeditionary Force disembarked in August 1914. Except for a short interval during the German advance in 1914, it remained No. 1 Base throughout the war, and by the end of May 1917 it contained three general and two stationary hospitals, and four convalescent depots. The first Commonwealth burials took place in mid August 1914. A memorial marks the graves of 24 casualties from the hospital ship 'Salta' and her patrol boat, sunk by a mine on 10th April 1917. The memorial also commemorates by name the soldiers, nurses and merchant seamen lost from the 'Salta' whose bodies were not recovered, and those lost in the sinking of the hospital ship 'Galeka' (mined on 28th October 1916), and the transport ship 'Normandy' (torpedoed on 25th January 1918), whose graves are not known.

ST PATRICK'S CEMETERY, LOOS

The cemetery is near Loos-en-Gohelle, Pas de Calais.

St. Patrick's Cemetery was begun during the Battle of Loos by French and British troops, and used in 1916. It was closed in June 1918, but a small number of graves were brought into it after the Armistice from the battlefields between Loos and Hulluch.

ST SEVER CEMETERY EXTENSION, ROUEN

ST SEVER CEMETERY and ST. SEVER CEMETERY EXTENSION are located within a large communal cemetery, situated on the eastern edge of the southern Rouen suburbs of Le Grand Quevilly and Le Petit Quevilly. During the First World War, Commonwealth camps and hospitals were stationed on the southern outskirts of the city. Almost all of the hospitals at Rouen remained there for practically the whole of the war. They included eight general, five stationary, one British Red Cross and one labour hospital, and No. 2 Convalescent Depot. A number of the dead from these hospitals were buried in other cemeteries, but the great majority were taken to the city cemetery of St. Sever. In September 1916, it was found necessary to begin an extension, where the last burial took place in April 1920.

SAILLY-SAILLISEL BRITISH CEMETERY

Sailly-Saillisel British Cemetery is 16 kms east of Albert and 10 kms south of Bapaume.

Sailly-Saillisel, standing at the north end of a ridge, was the objective of French attacks in September and October 1916, and was captured on 18th October. The village remained in Allied hands until 24th March 1918 when it was lost during the German advance, but was recaptured on 1st September 1918. The cemetery was made after the Armistice when graves were brought in from isolated positions, chiefly south and east of the village, and from small burial grounds.

SALONIKA (LEMBET ROAD) MILITARY CEMETERY

The Cemetery is on the northern outskirts of Thessalonika.

At the invitation of the Greek Prime Minister, M. Venizelos, Salonika (now Thessalonika) was occupied by three French Divisions and the 10th (Irish) Division from Gallipoli in October 1915. Other French and Commonwealth forces landed during the year and in the summer of 1916, they were joined by Russian and Italian troops. In August 1916, a Greek revolution broke out at Salonika, with the result that the Greek national army came into the war on the Allied side. The town was the base of the British Salonika Force and it contained, from time to time, eighteen general and stationary hospitals. Three of these hospitals were Canadian, although there were no other Canadian units in the force. The earliest Commonwealth burials took place in the local Protestant and Roman Catholic cemeteries. SALONIKA (LEMBET ROAD) MILITARY CEMETERY (formerly known as the Anglo-French Military Cemetery) was begun in November 1915, and Commonwealth, French, Serbian, Italian and Russian sections were formed. The Commonwealth section remained in use until October 1918, although from the beginning of 1917, burials were also made in MIKRA BRITISH CEMETERY. After the Armistice, some graves were brought in from other cemeteries in Macedonia, Albania and from Scala Cemetery, near Cassivita, on the island of Thasos.

SANCTUARY WOOD CEMETERY

Sanctuary Wood Cemetery is located 5 kms east of Ieper town centre.

Sanctuary Wood is one of the larger woods in the commune of Zillebeke. It was named in November 1914, when it was used to screen troops behind the front line. There were three Commonwealth cemeteries at Sanctuary Wood before June 1916, all made in May-August 1915. The first two were on the western end of the wood, the third in a clearing further east. All were practically obliterated in the Battle of Mount Sorrel, but traces of the second were found and it became the nucleus of the present Sanctuary Wood Cemetery.

At the Armistice, the cemetery contained 137 graves. From 1927 to 1932, the cemetery was extended as far as 'Maple Avenue', when graves were brought in from the surrounding battlefields. They came mainly from the communes immediately surrounding Ypres, but a few were taken from Nieuport (on the coast) and other smaller cemeteries.

SANDHURST (ST MICHAEL) CHURCHYARD

There are two WWI graves in the graveyard surrounding the church, located in Lower Church Road.

SAVY BRITISH CEMETERY

Savy is a village 6.5 kms west of St Quentin. After hard fighting, it was taken on the 1st April 1917, with Savy Wood captured the following day. On 21st March 1918, Savy and Roupy were successfully defended, but the line was withdrawn after nightfall. The village and the wood were retaken on 17th September 1918. SAVY BRITISH CEMETERY was made in 1919, and the graves from the battlefields and from small cemeteries in the neighbourhood were brought in.

SERRE ROAD CEMETERY NO. 1

The village of Serre is 11 kms north-north-east of Albert.

In June 1916, the road out of Mailly-Maillet to Serre and Puisieux entered No Man's Land about 1,300 metres south-west of Serre. On 1st July 1916, attacks north and south of this road were made, and although parties reached Serre, the attack failed; a further attack on 13th November also failed. Early in 1917, the Germans fell back to the Hindenburg Line, and on 25th February, Serre was occupied. The village changed hands once more in March 1918, and remained under German occupation until they withdrew in August.

In the spring of 1917, the battlefields of the Somme and Ancre were cleared, and a number of new cemeteries were made, three of which are now named from the Serre Road. SERRE ROAD CEMETERY NO. 1 was begun in May 1917. The rest of the cemetery was added after the Armistice, when graves were brought in from the nearby battlefields and from nearby smaller cemeteries.

SERY-LES-MEZIERES COMMUNAL CEMETERY

Sery-les-Mezieres is a commune 38 kms west of Laon.

There are 4 First World War Commonwealth burials in the Military Section of the southeast part of the cemetery.

SHINFIELD (ST MARY) CHURCH CEMETERY

The cemetery is to the south of the church, hidden in a housing estate. It is best reached by taking the small path to the right of the house opposite the church.

SHREWSBURY GENERAL CEMETERY

Burials from the Military Hospitals in Shrewsbury were made in this cemetery. It is located off Roman Road, to the southwest of the city centre.

SKOPJE BRITISH CEMETERY

The war cemetery is northeast of the town, one kilometre north of the railway station in Bulevar Jugoslavija.

Skopje was captured by the Bugarians in October 1915, and re-entered by French cavalry at the end of September 1918. SKOPJE BRITISH CEMETERY was created after the Armistice when burials were gathered together from Kumanovo British Cemetery, Prilep French Military Cemetery, Veles British and French Military Cemteries and other burial grounds. The great majority of those who died were men of the Royal Amy Service Corps who died of influenza after the Armistice with Bulgaria.

SOISSONS MEMORIAL

The town of Soissons stands on the left bank of the River Aisne, approximately 100 kms northeast of Paris.

The original British Expeditionary Force crossed the Aisne in August 1914, a few kilometres west of Soissons, and re-crossed it in September a few kilometres east. For the next three and a half years, this part of the front was held by French forces and the city remained within the range of German artillery. At the end of April 1918, five divisions of Commonwealth forces (IX Corps) were posted to the French 6th Army in this sector to rest and refit following the German offensives on the Somme and Lys. Here, at the end of May, they found themselves facing the overwhelming German attack which, despite fierce opposition, pushed the Allies back across the Aisne to the Marne. Having suffered 15,000 fatal casualties, IX Corps was withdrawn from this front in early July, but was replaced by XXII Corps, who took part in the Allied counter attack that had driven back the Germans by early August and recovered the lost ground.

THE SOISSONS MEMORIAL commemorates almost 4,000 officers and men of the United Kingdom forces who died during the Battles of the Aisne and the Marne in 1918, and who have no known grave.

SOFIA WAR CEMETRY

SOFIA WAR CEMETERY is part of the Sofia Protestant Cemetery, a section of the main town cemetery. It contains the graves of Commonwealth servicemen who died as prisoners of war, or with the occupying forces, following the Bulgarian capitulation in September 1918.

STAGLIENO CEMETERY, GENOA

The Italians entered the war on the Allied side, declaring war on Austria, in May 1915. Commonwealth forces were at the Italian front between November 1917 and November 1918, and rest camps and medical units were established at various locations in northern Italy behind the front, some of them remaining until 1919.

From November 1917 to the end of the war, Genoa was a base for Commonwealth forces, and the three Stationary Hospitals were posted in the city.

TALANA FARM CEMETERY

From Ieper, the Cemetery is located on the Diksmuidseweg road (N369) in the direction of Boezinge. The commune of Boesinghe (now Boezinge) lies on both sides of the Yser Canal. The village itself is on the west side of the canal, and was, during the greater part of the War, directly faced by the German front line on the east side; but to the south of it the German line sloped away from the canal, and Talana Farm was just one kilometre from the edge of the Salient. Dragoon Camp was across the canal, due east of the village, and within the German lines until 31st July, 1917. Talana Farm was one of a group of farm houses named by the army from episodes of the South African war. The cemetery was begun by French troops in April 1915, taken over by the British in June 1915, and was used by fighting units until March 1918.

TEHRAN WAR CEMETERY AND TEHRAN MEMORIAL

TEHRAN WAR CEMETERY is situated within the British Embassy residential compound at Gulhek, which is approximately 13 kms from Tehran. Within the cemetery is the TEHRAN MEMORIAL commemorating casualties from both World Wars.

The War Cemetery was built in 1962. There are now 412 Commonwealth burials of the 1914-1918 war, thirteen of which are unidentified, commemorated in this site.

TERLINCTHUN BRITISH CEMETERY, WIMILLE

TERLINCTHUN BRITISH CEMETERY is situated on the northern outskirts of Boulogne.

The first rest camps for Commonwealth forces were established near Terlincthun in August 1914, and during the whole of the First World War, Boulogne and Wimereux housed numerous hospitals and other medical establishments. The cemetery at Terlincthun was begun in June 1918 when the space available for service burials in the civil cemeteries of Boulogne and Wimereux was exhausted. It was used chiefly for burials from the base hospitals, but also contains the graves of 46 RAF personnel killed at Marquise in September 1918 in a bombing raid by German aircraft. In July 1920, the cemetery contained more than 3,300 burials, but for many years, Terlincthun remained an 'open' cemetery and graves continued to be brought into it from isolated sites and other burials grounds throughout France, where their maintenance could not be assured.

THIEPVAL MEMORIAL

The Thiepval Memorial will be found on the D73, next to the village of Thiepval, off the main Bapaume to Albert road (D929).

On 1st July 1916, supported by a French attack to the south, thirteen divisions of Commonwealth forces launched an offensive on a line from north of Gommecourt to Maricourt. Despite a preliminary bombardment lasting seven days, the German defences were barely touched, and the attack met unexpectedly fierce resistance. Losses were catastrophic and with only minimal advances on the southern flank, the initial attack was a failure. In the following weeks, huge resources of manpower and equipment were deployed in an attempt to exploit the modest successes of the first day. However, the German Army resisted tenaciously, and repeated attacks and counter-attacks meant a major battle for every village, copse and farmhouse gained. At the end of September, Thiepval was finally captured. The village had been an original objective of 1st July. Attacks north and east continued throughout October and into November in increasingly difficult weather conditions. The Battle of the Somme finally ended on 18th November with the onset of winter.

In the spring of 1917, the German forces fell back to their newly prepared defences, the Hindenburg Line, and there were no further significant engagements in the Somme sector until the Germans mounted their major offensive in March 1918.

The THIEPVAL MEMORIAL, the Memorial to the Missing of the Somme, bears the names of more than 72,000 officers and men of the United Kingdom and South African forces who died in the Somme sector before 20th March 1918, and who have no known grave. Over 90% of those commemorated died between July and November 1916. The memorial also serves as an Anglo-French Battle Memorial in recognition of the joint nature of the 1916 offensive, and a small cemetery containing equal numbers of Commonwealth and French graves lies at the foot of the memorial.

TILLOY BRITISH CEMETERY, TILLOY-LES-MOFFLAINES

Tilloy-les-Mofflaines is a village 3 kms southeast of Arras, on the south side of the main road to Cambrai. It was taken by Commonwealth troops on 9th April 1917, but it was partly in German hands again from March to August 1918.

The cemetery was begun in April 1917 by fighting units and burial officers, and includes casualties from later fighting in 1917 and the first three months of 1918, and the clearing of the village in August 1918. These 390 original burials were increased after the Armistice when graves were brought in from a wide area east of Arras and from smaller burial grounds.

TINCOURT NEW BRITISH CEMETERY

Tincourt is a village about 7 kms east of Peronne and Tincourt.

The villages of Tincourt and Boucly were occupied by British troops in March 1917, during the German Retreat to the Hindenburg Line. From the following May until March 1918, Tincourt became a centre for Casualty Clearing Stations. On 23rd March 1918, the villages were evacuated, and they were recovered, in a ruined condition, about 6th September. From that month until December 1918, Casualty Clearing Stations were again posted to Tincourt.

The cemetery was begun in June 1917, and used until September 1919. After the Armistice it was used for the reburial of soldiers found on the battlefield, or buried in small French or German cemeteries.

TORQUAY CEMETERY AND EXTENSION

The cemetery is located on the outskirts of the town.

TROIS ARBRES CEMETERY, STEENWERCK

Steenwerck is a village on the D77, about 6 kms southeast of Bailleul, and to the east of the road from Bailleul to Estaires. It remained untouched for much of the First World War, but on 10th April 1918, it was captured by the Germans and remained in their possession until the beginning of October. The site for TROIS ARBRES CEMETERY was chosen for the 2nd Australian Casualty Clearing Station in July 1916, and used by that hospital until April 1918. A few further burials were made in the cemetery after the German withdrawal at the end of 1918, and after the Armistice, over 700 graves were brought into it from the battlefields of Steenwerck, Nieppe, Bailleul and Neuve-Eglise.

TYNE COT CEMETERY AND TYNE COT MEMORIAL

TYNE COT CEMETERY is located 9 kms northeast of Ieper town centre, on the Tynecotstraat, a road leading from the Zonnebeekseweg (N332).

'Tyne Cot' or 'Tyne Cottage' was the name given by the Northumberland Fusiliers to a barn which stood near the level crossing on the Passchendaele-Broodseinde road. The barn, which had become the centre of five or six German blockhouses, or pill-boxes, was captured by the 3rd Australian Division on 4th October 1917, in the advance on Passchendaele. One of these pill-boxes was unusually large, and was used as an advanced dressing station after its capture. From 6th October to the end of March 1918, 343 graves were made, on two sides of it. The cemetery was in German hands again from 13th April to 28th September, when it was finally recaptured, with Passchendaele, by the Belgian Army. TYNE COT CEMETERY was greatly enlarged after the Armistice when remains were brought in from the battlefields of Passchendaele and Langemarck, and from a few small burial grounds. It is now the largest Commonwealth war cemetery in the world in terms of burials. At the suggestion of King George V, who visited the cemetery in 1922, the Cross of Sacrifice was placed on the original large pill-box. There are three other pill-boxes in the cemetery.

The TYNE COT MEMORIAL forms the north-eastern boundary of TYNE COT CEMETERY and commemorates nearly 35,000 servicemen from the United Kingdom and New Zealand who died in the Ypres Salient after 16th August 1917, and whose graves are not known. The memorial stands close to the farthest point in Belgium reached by Commonwealth forces in the First World War until the final advance to victory.

VAILLY BRITISH CEMETERY

Vailly-sur-Aisne is a small town within the Department of the Aisne, on the north bank of the Aisne River. It is 13 kms east of Soissons and 18 kms south of Laon.

The village was the point at which the 3rd Division crossed the river Aisne on 13th and 14th September 1914 during the Allied advance from the Marne. It fell to the German forces in 1915, was retaken by the French during the Chemin des Dames Offensive in April 1917, lost again to the Germans in June 1918, and finally captured by the French on 15th September 1918. VAILLY BRITISH CEMETERY was established after the Armistice when the remains of Commonwealth soldiers were brought here from other burial grounds and battlefields throughout the region. Most of those buried here were killed during the Battle of the Aisne in September 1914, but the cemetery is also the final resting place of over sixty Commonwealth soldiers who were killed or mortally wounded in the summer of 1918.

VALENCIENNES (ST ROCH) COMMUNAL CEMETERY

VALENCIENNES (ST ROCH) COMMUNAL CEMETERY is situated on the northeast side of Valenciennes, about 1.5 kms from the centre.

Valenciennes remained in German hands from the early days of the First World War until the beginning of November 1918, when it was entered and cleared by the Canadian Corps; 5,000 civilians were found in the town. In November and December 1918, four Casualty Clearing Stations were posted at Valenciennes, and the last of them did not leave until October 1919.

The Communal Cemetery of St. Roch was initially used by the Germans in August and September 1914, but Commonwealth plots were made adjoining the German, containing the graves of October 1918 to December 1919; and bodies brought from other cemeteries or from the battlefields.

VALLEY CEMETERY, VIS-EN-ARTOIS

Valley Cemetery lies south of Vis-en-Artois, some 12 kms southeast of Arras.

The cemetery was begun on 31st August 1918 with the burial of 31 officers and men of the 3rd Canadian Infantry Battalion, who had died the previous day in the capture of Orix Trench; ten further burials were made during the early part of September. In 1924-25, remains were brought in from the battlefields and from Thilloy German Cemetery. This was just to the north of the voillage of Ligny-Thilloy, and was a Dressing Station cemetery containing the graves of four Australian soldiers, three from the United Kingdom, and about three hundred Germans.

VERMAND COMMUNAL CEMETERY

Vermand is a village 12 kms east of St Quentin, in the Department of the Aisne.

Vermand was later "adopted" by the Borough of Cambridge. The Communal Cemetery was used in April and May 1917, and March and September 1918, for British burials.

VERMELLES BRITISH CEMETERY

Vermelles is a village 10 kms northwest of Lens.

Vermelles was in German hands from the middle of October 1914 to the beginning of December 1914, when it was recaptured by the French. The cemetery was begun in August 1915 (though a few graves are slightly earlier), and during the Battle of Loos, when the Chateau was used as a dressing station, From April 1917 to the Armistice, the cemetery was closed; but after the Armistice some graves were re-grouped and others were brought in from the battlefields to the East.

VIEILLE-CHAPELLE OLD MILITARY CEMETERY AND VIEILLE-CHAPELLE NEW MILITARY CEMETERY, LACOUTURE

Vieille-Chapelle is a village northeast of Bethune.

The Old Military Cemetery (now removed) was closed in November 1915, as being too near the school; and the New Military Cemetery was begun in that month and used by fighting units and Field Ambulances until March 1918. The village and the cemetery fell into German hands in the following month during the Battles of the Lys; but in September 1918, on the German retirement, some further burials took place. The remainder of the cemetery was made after the Armistice, by the concentration of British, Indian and Portuguese graves from the neighbouring battlefields and from other cemeteries, but the Portuguese graves were removed to RICHEBOURG-L'AVOUE PORTUGUESE NATIONAL CEMETERY in 1925; three German prisoners' graves have also been removed.

VILLERS-PLOUICH COMMUNAL CEMETERY

Villers-Plouich is a village in the Department of the Nord, 24 kms north of Gouzeaucourt.

Villers-Plouich was captured in April 1917, lost in March 1918; and regained at the end of the following September, when the 1st East Surreys were the first troops to enter the village. It was later "adopted" by the Borough of Wandsworth.

VIMY MEMORIAL

The Vimy Memorial overlooks the Douai Plain from the highest point of Vimy Ridge, about eight kms northeast of Arras on the N17 towards Lens.

On the opening day of the Battle of Arras, 9 April 1917, the four divisions of the Canadian Corps, fighting side by side for the first time, scored a huge tactical victory in the capture of the 60 metre high Vimy Ridge. After the war, the highest point of the ridge was chosen as the site of the great memorial to all Canadians who served their country in battle during the First World War, and particularly to the 60,000 who gave their lives in France. It also bears the names of 11,000 Canadian servicemen who died in France - many of them in the fight for Vimy Ridge - who have no known grave.

VIS-EN-ARTOIS MEMORIAL

Vis-en-Artois and Haucourt are villages on the straight main road from Arras to Cambrai about 10 kms southeast of Arras. This Memorial bears the names of over 9,000 men who fell in the period from 8th August 1918 to the date of the Armistice in the Advance to Victory in Picardy and Artois, between the Somme and Loos, and who have no known grave. They belonged to the forces of Great Britain and Ireland and South Africa; the Canadian, Australian and New Zealand forces being commemorated on other memorials to the missing.

VLAMERTINGHE MILITARY CEMETERY AND VLAMERTINGHE NEW MILITARY CEMETERY

VLAMERTINGHE is located 5 kms west of Ieper town centre (Vlamertinge is the modern spelling of Vlamertinghe).

For much of the First World War, Vlamertinghe was just outside the normal range of German shell fire, and the village was used both by artillery units and field ambulances. VLAMERTINGHE MILITARY CEMETERY was started by French troops in 1914, and was taken over by Commonwealth forces in April 1915. It was used by fighting units and field ambulances until June 1917, when the land adjoining the cemetery was claimed for a military railway, preventing further extension.

From June 1917, the VLAMERTINGHE NEW MILITARY CEMETERY was begun in anticipation of the Allied offensive launched on this part of the front in July. Although the cemetery continued in use until October 1918, most of the burials are from July to December 1917.

VOORMEMZEELE ENCLOSURES NOS 1, 2 AND 3

The VOORMEZEELE ENCLOSURES are located 4 kms southwest of Ieper town centre, on the Voormezeele Dorp.

Origianlly four, but now reduced to three, the Voormizeele Enclosures were originally regimental groups of graves, begun very early in the First World War, and gradually increased until the village and the cemeteries were captured by the Germans after very heavy fighting on 29th April 1918. No.1 and No.2 are now treated as a single cemetery.

WANQUETIN COMMUNAL CEMETERY EXTENSION

Wanquetin is a village approximately 12 kms west of Arras and approximately 6 kms north of Beaumetz. A few burials were made in the communal cemetery from March to November 1916, but in October 1916, the 41st Casualty Clearing Station came to the village, and by the end of November it had become necessary to begin the extension. The last graves made in the cemetery were 23 men of the 3rd Canadian Machine Gun Battalion, killed on 24th September 1918 in a German daylight air raid over Warlus.

WARFIELD (ST MICHAEL THE ARCHANGEL) CHURCHYARD EXTENSION

The Churchyard Extension is on the opposite side of Church Lane from the church. It contains two graves from WWI.

WARLENCOURT BRITISH CEMETERY

Warlencourt British Cemetery lies on the east side of the D929, to the southeast of Warlencourt village and 5 kms southwest of Bapaume.

Warlencourt, the Butte de Warlencourt, and Eaucourt-L'Abbaye, were the scene of very fierce fighting in 1916. Eaucourt was taken early in October, but the Butte (a Roman mound of excavated chalk, about seventeen metres high, once covered with pines) was attacked by that and other divisions, but not relinquished by the Germans until the following 26th February, when they withdrew to the Hindenburg Line. The cemetery was made late in 1919, when graves were brought in from small cemeteries and the battlefields of Warlencourt and Le Sars.

WARLOY-BAILLON COMMUNAL CEMETERY EXTENSION

Warloy-Baillon is a village about 21 kms northeast of Amiens along the D919 to Arras.

The first Commonwealth burial took place in the communal cemetery in October 1915, and the last on 1st July 1916. By that date, field ambulances had come to the village in readiness for the attack on the German front line eight kilometres away, and the extension was begun on the eastern side of the cemetery. The fighting from July to November 1916, on the northern part of the Somme front, accounts for the majority of the burials in the extension, but some are from the German attack in the spring of 1918.

WASSIGNY COMMUNAL CEMETERY

Wassigny is a commune 32 kms northeast of St Quentin and 11 kms south of Le Cateau, just off the D27.

Wassigny was captured on 18th-19th October, 1918. The French and German War Graves have been removed from the Communal Cemetery.

WAVANS BRITISH CEMETERY

Wavans is a village 14 kms northwest of Doullens and 32 kms northeast of Abbeville.

Wavans British Cemetery was made by the 21st Casualty Clearing Station bewteen May and September 1918.

WESTOUTRE BRITISH CEMETERY

WESTOUTRE BRITISH CEMETERY is located 11.5 kms southwest of Ieper town centre on a road leading from the N375 Dikkebusseweg.

The village of Westoutre (now Westouter) remained in Allied hands from the early months of the First World War to the Armistice, but in the summer of 1918, after the Battles of the Lys, it was less than two and a half kilometres from the front line.

WESTOUTRE BRITISH CEMETERY was begun in October 1917. It was used until the following April, and again in August-October 1918. A further fifty graves were brought into it from the battlefields of the Ypres salient, from BIXSCHOTE GERMAN CEMETERY and KEMMEL FRENCH CEMETERY after the Armistice. French units used the cemetery in April-August 1918, but these graves were later removed.

WIMEREUX COMMUNAL CEMETERY

Wimereux is a small town situated approximately 5 kms north of Boulogne.

It was the headquarters of the Queen Mary's Army Auxilliary Corps during the First World War, and in 1919 became the General Headquarters of the British Army. From October 1914 onwards, Boulogne and Wimereux formed an important hospital centre, and until June 1918, the medical units at Wimereux used the communal cemetery for burials, the southeastern half having been set aside for Commonwealth graves, although a few burials were also made among the civilian graves. By June 1918, this half of the cemetery was filled, and subsequent burials from the hospitals at Wimereux were made in the new military cemetery at Terlincthun.

WOKINGHAM (ALL SAINTS) CHURCHYARD

Travelling from Bracknell, All Saints Church is on the right side of the London Road, just before the one-way system is reached. There are seven graves from WWI in the churchyard.

WOKINGHAM (ST SEBASTIAN) CHURCHYARD

The graveyard is situated around the church on Nine Mile Road, just west of the traffic lights outside Ravenswood Village. Most of the graves, from patients who died at nearby Pinewood Hospital, are to the west of the church, but one is on the north side.

WORTHING (BROADWATER) CEMETERY

Located on South Farm Road, Worthing, north of the railway station.

The entrance to the cemetery is just south of Broadwater Green.

YPRES (MENIN GATE) MEMORIAL

Ypres (now Ieper) is a town in the Province of West Flanders. The Memorial is situated at the eastern side of the town on the road to Menin (Menen) and Courtrai (Kortrijk). Each night at 8pm, the traffic is stopped at the MENIN GATE while members of the local Fire Brigade sound the 'Last Post' in the roadway under the Memorial's arches.

The MENIN GATE is one of four memorials to the missing in Belgian Flanders, which covers the area known as the Ypres Salient. Broadly speaking, the Salient stretched from Langemarck in the north to the northern edge in Ploegsteert Wood in the south, but it varied in area and shape throughout the war. The Salient was formed during the First Battle of Ypres in October and November 1914, when a small British Expeditionary Force succeeded in securing the town before the onset of winter, pushing the German forces back to the Passchendaele Ridge. The Second Battle of Ypres began in April 1915, when the Germans released poison gas into the Allied lines north of Ypres. This was the first time gas had been used by either side, and the violence of the attack forced an Allied withdrawal and a shortening of the line of defence. There was little more significant activity on this front until 1917, when in the Third Battle of Ypres, an offensive was mounted by Commonwealth forces, to divert German attention from a weakened French front further south. The initial attempt in June to dislodge the Germans from the Messines Ridge was a complete success, but the main assault northeastward, which began at the end of July, quickly became a dogged struggle against determined opposition and the rapidly deteriorating weather. The campaign finally came to a close in November with the capture of Passchendaele. The German offensive of March 1918 met with some initial success, but was eventually checked and repulsed in a combined effort by the Allies in September. The battles of the Ypres Salient claimed many lives on both sides, and it quickly became clear that the commemoration of members of the Commonwealth forces with no known grave would have to be divided between several different sites.

The site of the MENIN GATE was chosen because of the hundreds of thousands of men who passed through it on their way to the battlefields. It commemorates casualties from the forces of Australia, Canada, India, South Africa, and the United Kingdom, who died in the Salient. In the case of United Kingdom casualties, only those prior to 16th August 1917, with a few exceptions, are listed. United Kingdom and New Zealand servicemen who died after that date are named on the memorial at TYNE COT, a site which marks the furthest point reached by Commonwealth forces in Belgium until nearly the end of the war. New Zealand casualties that died prior to 16th August 1917 are commemorated on memorials at BUTTES NEW BRITISH CEMETERY and MESSINES RIDGE BRITISH CEMETERY.

ZANTVOORDE BRITISH CEMETERY

ZANDVOORDE BRITISH Cemetery is located 8 kms southeast of Ieper town centre, on the Kruisekestraat a road leading from the Meenseweg (N8), connecting Ieper to Menen.

On 30th October 1914, the village of Zantvoorde (now Zandvoorde) was held by the 1st and 2nd Life Guards, numbering between three and four hundred men. It was bombarded for over an hour with heavy guns and then taken by the 39th German Division and three attached battalions. The whole front of the 3rd Cavalry Division was driven back to the Klein-Zillebeke ridge. The village could not be retaken, and remained in German hands until 28th September 1918. The Household Cavalry Memorial, unveiled by Lord Haig in May 1924, stands on the south side of the village at the place where part of the Brigade was annihilated in 1914. ZANTVOORDE BRITISH CEMETERY was made after the Armistice, when remains were brought in from the battlefields and nearby German cemeteries. Many were those of soldiers who died in the desperate fighting round Zantvoorde, Zillebeke and Gheluvelt in the latter part of October 1914.

For further information on all cemeteries and memorials, see the Commonwealth War Graves Commission website www.cwgc.org

APPENDIX III

OTHER NATIVES

According to SDGW, the following men were born or grew up in what is now the borough of Bracknell Forest, but their name does not appear on any of the local war memorials. In some cases, they had moved away, in some cases there was no family to put their name forward, but there may be other reasons why their name was not included

BRACKNELL

Henry Birch

Regiment	$2/5^{th}$ Battalion, Durham Light Infantry
Date of death	14th October 1918
Cemetery	Kirechkoi-Hortakoi Military Cemetery

Frederick Leslie Maurice Caudwell

Regiment	17th Battalion, Lancashire Fusiliers
Date of death	9th September 1918
Cemetery	Tyne Cot Memorial

Frederick William Cole

Regiment	11th Battalion, Royal West Kent Regiment
Date of death	7th October 1916
Cemetery	Thiepval Memorial

Birth registration and census returns suggest this man may have been born in Windsor

Edwin Collins

Regiment	2nd Battalion, Royal West Surrey Regiment
Date of death	1st October 1918
Cemetery	Thiepval Memorial

Henry John Dallimore

Regiment	18th Division Ammunition Column H.Q., Royal Garrison Artillery
Date of death	6th November 1918
Cemetery	Busigny Communal Cemetery Extension

Albert Charles Death

Regiment	12th Battalion, London Regiment
Date of death	7th October 1916
Cemetery	Thiepval Memorial

Birth registration suggests this man may have been born in Wokingham; census returns lists his birth place as Wokingham, Binfield and Arborfield

John Victor Eacott

Regiment	154th Heavy Battery, Royal Garrison Artillery
Date of death	15th June 1917
Cemetery	Vlamertinghe New Military Cemetery

Birth registration and census returns suggest this man may have been born in Hurley

William John Fowler

Regiment	1st Battalion, Royal West Kent Regiment
Date of death	26th October 1914
Cemetery	Le Touret Memorial

Charles James Harris

Regiment	9th Battalion, Royal Fusiliers
Date of death	30th November 1917
Cemetery	Cambrai Memorial, Louverval

Richard George Hartridge

Regiment	7th Battalion, Royal West Surrey Regiment
Date of death	1st July 1916
Cemetery	Dantzig Alley British Cemetery, Mametz

John Henry Mayhew

Regiment	1st Battalion, Middlesex Regiment
Date of death	24th October 1918
Cemetery	Romeries Communal Cemetery Extension

Harry Charles Paice

Regiment	2nd Battalion, Royal Berkshire Regiment
Date of death	1st April 1918
Cemetery	Moreuil Communal Cemetery Allied Extension

Philip Shrimpton

Regiment	3rd Brigade, New Zealand Field Artillery
Date of death	8th September 1916
Cemetery	Heilly Station Cemetery, Mericourt L'Abbe

George Stevenson

Regiment	1st Battalion, Bedfordshire Regiment
Date of death	5th May 1915
Cemetery	Ypres (Menin Gate) Memorial

Charles Reginald Jack West

Regiment	11th Battalion, Royal West Kent Regiment
Date of death	7th October 1916
Cemetery	Warlencourt British Cemetery

Thomas Whiteman

Regiment	15th Battalion, Royal Warwickshire Regiment
Date of death	3rd September 1916
Cemetery	Thiepval Memorial

EASTHAMPSTEAD

Harry George Bowyer

Regiment	$2/4^{th}$ Battalion, Oxfordshire and Buckinghamshire Light Infantry
Date of death	21st March 1918
Cemetery	Pozieres Memorial

Census returns suggest this man may have been born in Winkfield

Charles Henry Clements

Regiment	8th Battalion, Royal Berkshire Regiment
Date of death	18th August 1916
Cemetery	Thiepval Memorial

Walter Neale

Regiment	17th Battalion, Nottinghamshire and Derbyshire Regiment
Date of death	6th November 1916
Cemetery	Thiepval Memorial

Ernest Norris

Regiment	8th Battalion, Royal Berkshire Regiment
Date of death	27th August 1918
Cemetery	Bernafay Wood British Cemetery, Montauban

Birth registration and census entries show this man born at Huntspill, Somerset. It may be that he was working in Easthampstead when he attested (at Reading), but not born here

APPENDIX IV

OTHER RESIDENTS

The following men listed their place of residence as one of the parishes with the borough of Bracknell Forest when they attested, or had next of kin living in the parish when they lost their lives.

BRACKNELL

Charles Richard Brockwell

Regiment	2nd Battalion, Royal West Kent Regiment
Date of death	29th September 1916
Cemetery	Basra Memorial

Sidney Thomas Brogden

Regiment	8th Battalion, Royal Berkshire Regiment
Date of death	25th September 1915
Cemetery	Loos Memorial

John Davis

Regiment	16th Battalion, Middlesex Regiment
Date of death	22nd October 1916
Cemetery	Thiepval Memorial

William Day

Regiment	2nd Battalion, Royal Berkshire Regiment
Date of death	9th May 1915
Cemetery	Ploegsteert Memorial

Records may indicate a surviving relative living in Bracknell; there is no evidence the deceased man ever did

John Harley

Regiment	13th Battalion, Worcestershire Regiment
Date of death	4th June 1915
Cemetery	Helles Memorial

Harry Knight

Regiment	1st Battalion, Royal Berkshire Regiment
Date of death	22nd April 1916
Cemetery	Lievin Communal Cemetery Extension

Records may indicate a surviving relative living in Bracknell; there is no evidence the deceased man ever did

Edward Walter Matthews

Regiment	1st Battalion, Royal Berkshire Regiment
Date of death	29th April 1917
Cemetery	Arras Memorial

Ernest William May

Regiment	9th Battalion, Royal Sussex Regiment
Date of death	18th August 1916
Cemetery	Thiepval Memorial

John Norris

Regiment	2/1st Battalion, Oxfordshire and Buckinghamshire Light Infantry
Date of death	22nd August 1917
Cemetery	Tyne Cot Memorial

William Park

Regiment	12th (West Somerset Yeomanry) Battalion, Somerset Light Infantry
Date of death	8th November 1917
Cemetery	Beersheba War Cemetery

Herbert Lucraft Purser

Regiment	12th Battalion, Royal Fusiliers
Data of death	31st July 1917
Cemetery	Ypres (Menin Gate) Memorial

James Richardson

Regiment	1st Battalion, Royal Berkshire Regiment
Date of death	28th September 1915
Cemetery	Loos Memorial

Adam Walter Scott

Regiment	3rd Battalion, Grenadier Guards
Date of death	4th March 1917
Cemetery	Combles Communal Cemetery Extension

Thomas Thompson

Regiment	10th Battalion, Lincolnshire Regiment
Date of death	5th November 1916
Cemetery	Trois Arbres Cemetery, Steenwerck

John Thomas Wells

Ship	Royal Navy, H.M.S. 'India'
Date of death	20th October 1917
Cemetery	Vestre Toten Churchyard, Norway Died of pneumonia while interned in Norway, his ship having been sunk by a German U-boat on 8th August 1915

Ernest George Wooff

Regiment	7th Battalion, Royal Sussex Regiment
Date of death	9th April 1917
Cemetery	Arras Memorial

EASTHAMPSTEAD

Alfred William Brooker

Ship	Royal Navy, HMS 'Tornado'
Date of death	23rd December 1917
Cemetery	Plymouth Naval Memorial

Charles George Denyer

Regiment	7th Battalion, Royal Sussex Regiment
Date of death	25th July 1917
Cemetery	Arras Memorial

William Walter Lambden

Regiment	3rd/6th Battalion, Devonshire Regiment
Date of death	2nd April 1916
Cemetery	Greenwich Cemetery, London

Howard Leonard Such

Regiment	7th Battalion, Essex Regiment
Date of death	18th March 1916
Cemetery	Tottenham Cemetery, London

John Caradini Wilson

Regiment	3rd Battalion, Australian Infantry
Date of death	21st May 1915
Cemetery	Alexandria (Chatby) Military and War Memorial Cemetery

William Wynn

Regiment	Base Depot, Army Service Corps
Date of death	2nd June 1917
Cemetery	Chatby Memorial
	Died on board a hospital ship and buried at sea

Lightning Source UK Ltd.
Milton Keynes UK
UKOW02n0724190614

233611UK00002BA/3/P